# To Conquer
# Death

*Seeing Beyond the Darkness*

# TO CONQUER DEATH

## Seeing Beyond the Darkness

COREY PIPER

Published in Hygiene, Colorado, by Horatio Press.

First Printing: September 2015

Ordering Information:
Special discounts are available on quantity purchases by corporations, associations, churches, educators, and others. For speaking engagements, please contact Corey Piper at the below listed address.

Unless otherwise indicated, Scripture quotations are taken from the Holy Bible, New King James Version.

U.S. trade bookstores and wholesalers: Please contact Corey Piper at c3piper@me.com

Horatio Press
PO Box 374
Hygiene, CO 80533

ISBN: 978-1-5151-0544-2
Library of Congress Control Number: 2015908532

*To all of those dear friends who helped me raise Faye; all of those magnificent family members who supported me; all of those doctors, nurses, social workers, and students whom I have had the privilege of getting to know—I thank all of you. What we do matters. We are not alone: God waters us with the abundance of people He has poured into our lives.*

*And this is to my wife Beth, and my daughters Faye and Avery. Without their love, my life would be so dim.*

# TABLE OF CONTENTS

# ABOUT THIS BOOK

This is a life-journey book which I have been working on for over two decades, and it is comprised of a unique combination of personal reflections, short stories, and poetry written during times of grief and gladness; mayhem and harmony. But, fair warning: even though you may sometimes wonder why I am talking about *that*, stick with it. I firmly believe that if you read this book from beginning to end you will be blessed by the journey.

However, it is important to keep in mind several things that this book is *not*. For one, *it is not a book about grief.* I do talk about my experiences with grief, but it is not primarily about those experiences. I am placing grief within the larger context of my life rather than as a singular event.

Secondly, *it is not a book about abortion as a political issue.* My wife and I had to deal with that issue and I will explain why we chose to do what we did, but my focus is not on the politics of it, but on the heart of it.

Thirdly, *it is not a theological treatise.* I do discuss some deep theology, but please keep in mind that it comes from a layman's perspective. I am just a human being trying to make sense of the world around me and I hope that some of my musings will help you, too.

And that brings me to what the book is about: *how to conquer death in the midst of a dying world.* If I were to write a pop-psychology success book, I might call it *How to Live Forever in One Easy Step*, but that's just too cheesy even for me. When Jesus died on the cross and rose from the dead, He didn't just conquer our fear of death—He conquered death itself. And He conquered it for us. That one event should cause all of us to stop and think deeply about why we are here and where we are going. Death is not just an event, it is a wake up call.

I hope that you will walk with me through the last twenty-three years of my life, and I hope you will weep with me and rejoice with me. God is so much more than our idols will allow us to believe, and I love smashing idols.

On a more technical note, *To Conquer Death* is a unique book in that it is structured like a symphony, and it is intended to elicit a full range of emotions, just like a symphony. I have tried to take the idea of "book" and modify it just enough to accommodate the feelings and thoughts I have experienced in my life. I want the structure to help communicate the meaning. I don't want to just tell you my ideas; I want you to feel them.

There may be moments when you will be overwhelmed by sorrow, and moments when you will rejoice. There will be opportunities to think deeply about the universe, and reminders to just relish every moment. Life is all of these things—profundities and fun—and we must remember to live every day.

*To Conquer Death* is divided into four movements:

Movement One, *The Heart of Eternity*, focuses on broad themes and is intended to be an expansive overview of humanity's various responses to death and God's plan of redemption.

Movement Two, *Eden*, slows down and focuses on defending the historical reality of God's word, which is worthy of our full trust. God gave us life, death entered the world, and the Gospel is our only hope.

Movement Three, *The Heart of Darkness*, is more thoughtful and philosophical in tone. It explores the emotional questions people have about life and death, good and evil.

Movement Four, *Gethsemane*, is the Finale. It ties together all the topics which have been discussed, and it culminates with a crescendo to God's solution to the most serious problem we have: death.

I will also use musical terms throughout the book:

**Section**: Each movement is subdivided into thematic forms. This will be the equivalent of "Chapter."

**Overture**: Normally musical, in this case I will use poetry.

**Introduction**: The opening section for a piece of music.

**Exposition**: The first section of a movement, introducing the melodies and themes unique to that movement.

**Interlude**: A short work interposed between the parts of a longer composition.

**Coda**: The concluding passage of a composition.

**Development**: The elaboration of a particular theme or idea. I use it as the equivalent of an appendix.

# FOREWORD

By Matt Boswell
*Pastor of Redemption Church in Duvall, Washington.*

Death.

Most of the time when I'm having a discussion on this topic, people inevitably say they do not fear it. Usually, I don't believe them. I think this is something people say because that is what you are supposed to say. I get it! It appears far nobler to hold a stiff upper lip in the face of certain doom than to suffer with a quivering one. But if I am to be candid here, we should see death as something to be feared. You're foolish not to. It's unnatural. It's unsettling. More to the point, it's a punishment. The last time I checked punishments were meant to produce a level of fear. In our story, death is the brutal consequence of an ancient arrogance that assumed God doesn't mean what he says. Had our first ancestors actually feared death we would not have to pretend like we don't. But they didn't and we do (or we should if we don't). Well, that is until One came into our story of death to reintroduce our original story.

Life.

In the story of Life only One

- has conquered death to produce aliveness in those who are under the sway of death;
- has the authority to overcome the consequences of our curse and produce a status of eternally living;
- has the power to take the pains and sorrows of this world and conform every single one of those to good for those who love Him;

- can make sense out of all the senselessness and turn the dust of our suffering into eternal nuggets of eternal reward; and
- can make all things beautiful in their time.

This Book.

My friend Corey has not written a book about death. He has not even written a book about Life. He's written a book about Jesus.

The Jesus who descended into the ugly, cold, hopeless pit of death to ignite a blaze of life that makes people fully alive. The Jesus who rescues us even while we are dead in our trespasses and sins. The Jesus who makes all things new in their time. The Jesus who will one day return us not simply to Eden, but a Garden City built by God.

It is this same Jesus who binds souls together in this life, which is why I have the privilege to pen this foreword. Throughout these pages you will go on a journey with my personal friends Corey, Tierre and Peter; all of us friends bound through Jesus.

Tierre is the initial catalyst to this journey. Tierre and I had been friends since 7th grade, though I'm not sure she would say we started out as friends. She was the pale blond with a feisty spirit and I was the class clown who made it his mission to drive her crazy. However, in time we became sincere friends in youth group and eventually she married my dear friend Corey. Tragically their marriage was cut short through Tierre's death, but it was in loving exchange for the life of their precious baby Faye. I still remember the moment I received the news that Tierre had passed away. I was at work, stepped behind some file cabinets and just wept. I wept for Corey, for baby Faye, and honestly I wept over death. Tierre was the first friend I had lost. Death was no longer "out there," no longer a theoretical discussion among pastoral interns at 1:00 a.m., but a real in-your-face, shot-to-the-gut reality. Yet Tierre would not be the first dear friend I would loose.

I met Peter the same year as Corey. In retrospect I find the relationship kinda funny. Corey and I were both married men who had managed to become friends with a punkish—though profoundly sincere—high school kid named Pete. Pete was a strange mesh of reckless and wise, brash and sensitive. In time, Pete grew into his own, as you will see, but Pete and I always remained close. Pete was perhaps the primary agent that Jesus used to move Corey along through the years of healing after Tierre's death. Every adventure was Corey, baby Faye, and Pete. Ecclesiastes says that a three-strand cord is not easily broken, and these three were unbreakable. Sadly, cancer is a formidable foe and it claimed our friend Peter in the summer of 2011. While I was devastated for Peter's family, I was equally devastated for my friend Corey. This was the second time Corey had lost a pillar friendship out of due season.

My friend Corey has lost much in the last twenty-three years (including his father just this year). Yet loss is opportunity when seen in light of Christ. Throughout these pages Corey will take us on a journey of life, death, and life anew as he reflects on loss in light of the eternity that is set in our hearts. Yes, death is devastating. Yes, death marks dark times for the living. Yet through Corey's story I have seen light burst forth out of the darkness. And by God's good grace some of those rays now cast their light on the pages before us.

Pastor Matt Boswell

# Overture

We are unique in history, for we sit atop time and can look back at the ancient horizon—the sunrise of existence—the beginning of all things. We can listen to God's song that binds all things together; the Song of Ages that resonates throughout creation—

> The Stars proclaim
> His limitless glory;
>
> Wildflowers whisper
> Aromas sweet;
>
> The Mountains resound
> With anthems array;
>
> The Oceans demand
> Their sirens be heard;
>
> The Rivers churn
> Their ceaseless praise;
>
> The Forests chant
> Their ancient, solemn hymn;
>
> The Valleys' mists
> Murmur a Lullaby;
>
> The Lakes intone
> The flowing love sonnet;
>
> The Robin-breasted moon
> Inspires language above words.

We can see the valleys and peaks between now and then, monuments to God's greatness, observing what He has done. And we can perceive a steep cliff falling away in the distance—a frightening descent, the bottom of which we cannot properly see. Many folds and hills, troughs and forests lie between here and there, and time plods through the catastrophic scars which were made. But in the midst, on a peak, a wooden cross can be seen, standing tall, immovable, undaunted; a shining beacon whose beams reach back to the beginning, and forward to the future.

**Mists of Time**

On either side of this cross stretches the vast world, extending to the left and to the right, but between the beginning and now the song fills the air. It stirs the soul with its melody and penetrates one's heart with its strength. In it we can hear Eve's grief and Noah's courage; Abraham's faith and Joseph's endurance; the sorrow of God's people and the song of Moses; Joshua's war cry and David's psalms; Jeremiah's laments and Nehemiah's penance. And this Song of Ages reaches our hearts, sometimes as a sigh lilting with tears; sometimes as a shout rejoicing with praise. But it remains.

And the cross. It was necessary, but God's voice faltered on that day and the song became a dark refrain. God's death.

Silence.

The soil of the earth stained red with Christ's blood, and the rocks drank every living drop, but a low tone, a rumbling tremor, began to vibrate in the hearts of mankind. It was felt not heard, and the song took on a new melody. It started softly, but soon it was heard again when the Song of Ages rose up out of the grave and invaded hearts everywhere. God's voice and His mighty symphony reverberated across all time, more clearly than ever, back to the beginning and forward to the end, and nothing that had gone before was ever the same. It was as if this moment had always been, and the strings and winds of the song celebrated in unison, and the percussion and the brass heaved a final blast which shook the very foundations of the earth, and every soul reverberated with His song.

Lies try to say the song isn't real, but the song is and will ever be. It is the symphony of our redemption, and the music is eternal.

# Introduction

I have learned from firsthand experience that the question "If God is good, why is there death and suffering?" is far from merely an intriguing intellectual curiosity. It is, in fact, an emotional cry of the heart that desperately hopes there is an answer. When my wife died from a heart defect that she had had since birth, but which had gone undetected until she was pregnant, it completely altered my perception of reality. It gutted me and lay open my beliefs to the raw uncertainty of doubt, and thus began my quest to resolve this cry of my heart—of all of our hearts.

I had grown up a Christian, my dad being a reverend for the Disciples of Christ, and I had been baptized when I was ten. However, it wasn't until after high school that I at last took it all seriously—that is personally—and I really started to live for Christ. I went on an overseas mission trip, got involved with youth ministry, discipled teens, interned, organized mission trips to Mexico, and wrote follow-up materials. It was a rich, growing, exciting, visionary time in my life, and although a man once told me I was wasting my time, I know God was guiding me.

It was during this time that Tierre and I got married and we moved from Sedona, AZ to Spokane, WA so I could continue my pastoral training. Within a year she became pregnant. At this point I lost my internship because I needed to support my new family. Then we found out about my wife's heart defect, called Eisenmenger's Syndrome, and the pregnancy seemed like a defeat, a mistake, because my visions were fading away. Everything seemed to be falling apart.

After spending five months at the University of Washington Medical Center in Seattle, WA, getting the best care we could have ever hoped for, Tierre gave birth to our daughter Faye. Tierre's blood oxygen levels had been low because of her condition. She faithfully followed doctor's orders and didn't exert herself; as a result, Faye was born perfectly healthy (Eisenmenger's is not genetic). She is a gem and every doubt about whether we had done the right thing, in spite of all our challenges, vanished.

But when Tierre died four days later from residual complications, my heart also stopped beating. The only thing that kept me from completely dissipating away was the compassion of our friends at church, our families, and Faye herself. I had a little girl now to take care of and no amount of despair, grief, or challenge was going to override her need for me to love her.

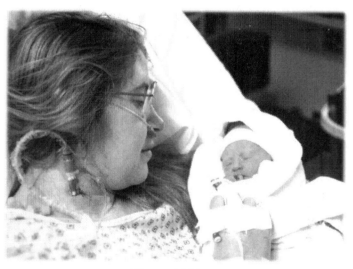

**Tierre with Faye**

But as the initial shock and intense pain gradually wore off, I started to reassess what I believed and the question "If God is good, why is there death and suffering?" took on an entirely new tone. Could I trust the Bible's account of our origins? Was there really a God? Did the fall of mankind in the Garden of Eden actually happen, or was it just a nice story to keep me blinded from the truth: we evolved and death is just a natural feature of the universe?

I suppose, in a way, I never really did lose my faith in God's word, but it certainly was challenged and I'm thankful for that. Some of my cartoonish images had to be corrected and brought into the realm of what's real; and I had to realize that if God's answer to the question "Why is there death?" is to be trusted, then it had to match the evidence. If what I experienced wasn't consistent with what I believed, then what good was the Bible?

These same criteria hold true for every other religion and philosophy. If atheism is to be trusted, then what it says must match the evidence. If naturalism, Buddhism, or Islam are to be trusted, then their explanation of why there is suffering and death must be consistent with our experience, and if none of them provide a viable solution, then what good are they? We are all trying to make sense of the universe in which we dwell, and we want to find not only the answer which satisfies us, but also the right answer: the one which will sufficiently account for the existence of death and suffering *and solve it*. We all need an answer to that question.

Sadly, though, it is usually only when we are personally confronted with death that our placid acceptance of the way things are really begins to get churned up. For most of our lives we can live as if we were passive observers of the hardships of humanity, casting a pitying eye on those who suffer, dispassionately watching them swirl down into dark-throated Charybdis, thinking that we have all the answers. But then we find ourselves swirling down, and the sting of our imminent death instigates tumultuous, inescapable contemplations. We would be so comfortable without death.

Death, then, is a subpoena being delivered to everyone's doorstep: it orders us to account for what we believe.

Maybe you are facing impending death right now and are in the midst of asking these hard questions. Maybe you fear asking these questions. Maybe you fear the answers. Maybe you fear the loss of your faith, or maybe you fear you will actually start believing in God and His word—that the Bible actually has answers. Whatever your current opinion, death obligates every single one of us—the philosopher, the professor, the theologian, and the farmer— to reevaluate everything that we have ever believed. We must either refine our theology or forever abandon it, for when death knocks on our door it will influence everything we believe ever thereafter.

**Faye - 5 Days Old**

# MOVEMENT ONE

# THE HEART OF ETERNITY

"He has made everything beautiful in its time. Also He has put eternity in their hearts, except that no one can find out the work that God does from beginning to end."

Ecclesiastes 3:11

# TIERRE

I first became aware of my desire for eternity on the day my wife died. For the first time I was introduced to death and life, hope and despair, fear and joy. I had been safe and secure from such problematic challenges for my entire life, but now I knew (and there is no comfortable way to say this) that God was no longer just the God of Life—He was also the God of Death. He planted and uprooted; He healed and killed; He built and tore down. He was no longer only the cool God at the exciting concert— He was now the hooded God at the morgue.

And I wept.

But my lessons weren't over, yet. Indeed, they were just beginning. A few days later—on the day I took my daughter home from the hospital—I was driving our green "Mystery Machine" van when Faye started screaming for attention. I pulled over, changed her poopy diaper, nestled her back into her car seat (she was very tiny and blankets were stuffed all around her), and we resumed our journey to Spokane.

And I began to realize how very different my life had become.

Intellectually and emotionally I was dealing with a lot, but I could never allow those fears, doubts, and debates to interfere with raising Faye. Her needs trumped my own. But still, when the lights went off and she was peacefully asleep, I would weep uncontrollably. Shadows haunted me and prayers rescued me, and those first few months exist in my memory now as dimly hazed, half-lit moments. Yes, I smiled and joked and played and walked amongst the living, but I was a vapor. A wind could have wafted me away above the trees and I would have been lost forever. But, somehow, my desire for eternity kept me sane even though I was confused about what God was doing.

When my feet finally started touching the ground again and my soul became stronger, I resumed my education and pursued—with a lot of help—my teaching degree. Families took care of Faye on a rotating schedule while I attended classes, but after I picked her up in the afternoon we went home, played, ate, and read together. It was a beautiful time and became what I believe parenting is all about. But once she was in bed I would resume my studies, write, make calls, and watch baseball.

While I was at school, though, I discovered how lonely social interaction could be. Time and again I would be withering inside with a smile on my face while I walked across campus or took notes in class. I did not want to burden the world with my grief, but, still, didn't everyone know? I knew I had no right to darken their days, to blight their joy. It wouldn't have been fair to all those acquaintances—or productive—and I never wanted pity for myself, but I felt alone. Grief, I discovered, is something that I had to carry alone. Not that people didn't care, it's just that the world of darkness I was living in was a terrifying place to enter. Those who had been there didn't want to return, and those who had never been there couldn't imagine it.

After two years of struggling with whether I wanted new friends to know about my grief or not, I finally had to take off my wedding ring because it had become a token of pain and I couldn't take the inadvertent questions anymore. So, I hung it on a chain around my neck close to my heart where eternity dwelt.

It was then that I was finally free to explore what had happened to my wife—and what had happened to me—and I began to explore eternity.

# MAN'S QUEST FOR ETERNAL YOUTH

"Let me hope," thought I, "or my heart will be as icy as the fountain, and the whole world as desolate as this snowy hill."

Hawthorne, "The Vision of the Fountain"

Doubts and fears assail me. My soul is a ship loaded with the cargo of turmoil: abandonment, frustration, inadequacy, foolishness.

At every moment disaster is imminent.
I can hope for the best, believe the best,
   but too often I walk blindly into the worst.

I'm not denying
That, maybe, there is something
To making things happen
   by positive thinking.
But my experience is that fate happens,
   even though my will is opposed to it.
I can believe in a good future for me,
   just as I know that the sun will rise tomorrow,
But I can believe it that surely and still it doesn't happen.
   -Yet?

I held my wife in my arms as the light left her eyes.
I know she went to paradise,
   but I so hoped she would stay.
I have heard many people say
That it is just the natural course of life,
   but
    why does it seem so—unnatural?
Poe-like?

Why do I feel in my heart that death is rank?
And if positive thinking allows me to believe a lie,
What advantage is that to me?
Therefore, I'm going to allow myself to hate death.
Hate everything about it.
Hate the suffering.
Hate the slow decline.
Hate the acceptance.
I don't like it when people give up.
It makes me feel as though someday I might not care either.
I cannot imagine that.

But at times I have tried to imagine my death:
What it would feel like,
What my gravestone would say, ("Good luck up there!")
And I try to believe that in the final moment
I would yet cry out, 'Life!'

Life—always...
I hope...
God help me....
Please.

For the first few years after my wife passed away, I wrestled with particularly intense emotions: grief, anger, fear, shame, loneliness, depression, and even with why I had been so incapable of preventing her death. Hadn't I thought positively? Hadn't I envisioned a good outcome? Hadn't I prayed for God's intervention? And so a harsh reality slapped me upside the head: even though I could want the best, desire it, and even take action to accomplish it, still it may not work out the way I thought it should. Death had stolen my wife from me in spite of all my pleas to the contrary, and it made me feel weak.

However, I wasn't depressed only because I had just lost my wife against my will. Another truth was pressing on my heart like a pile of stones: death would come inevitably for me and there was nothing I could do about it. As a result of these powerful emotions, I began to crave life more. It wasn't like the sensation that some feel when they realize how precious and fleeting life really is and so they cherish every moment as if it is their last. It was more like I never wanted a last moment. It became clear to me that I don't want to die. Ever. I want to live for eternity. I don't want to just cherish life while I have it and then let it go. I want life. I want the strength of life. I want its vibrancy, its hopefulness, its dreams, and its energy to continue in me without end, without ever failing. I never want to grow weary; I don't want to be forgotten; I don't want to be beaten down; I don't want to live in pain or despair or with shattered dreams. I want life. Forever.

I had never felt such a powerful desire for life more than in those first few years, which is, ironically, why I was also so depressed. Death was apparently unconquerable. Even though I wanted life, I knew death was awaiting me. I'm thankful for that realization now, because it was then that I began to explore what possibilities life held out for me, to see the Gospel in an entirely new light, and to see how many misunderstandings I had accepted about death.

Naturalism teaches that death is inevitable and necessary. Why do some Christians believe that, too? Some religions even ridicule our instinct for survival and teach us to resign ourselves to death's invincibility. Is this also what a Christian should believe? Others say death doesn't exist at all, and, after I die, I'll realize that.... Hmmm.

The Gospel, however, promises us immortality. In fact, it guarantees us eternal life. I have become confident that our desire for immortality exists for a reason, and that it isn't foolish to believe we will live forever. God put eternity in our hearts and it is fomenting, waiting for the day it will be fulfilled without a flaw. It is the single most important quest of all mankind. Life is our future and we need to get used to it.

> Sometimes I hope
> As I stand here—
>     and cry,
> That my sorrow will
> Turn
>     to joy
> In that twinkling of an eye.

# I Want Life!

Wouldn't it be cool to know you would never die? That is, of course, if sin, regret, and shame were not a part of the picture, and if certain parameters were met such as health, success, and freedom. If those things were true, wouldn't all of us choose life over death? Think of all the things you could achieve! All the places you could go to and enjoy! And what if you were given an eternity to see, to understand, to grow, to learn, to experience joy, to pursue your dreams, to be with the people you love, to explore, and to do whatever your greatest (non-sinful) desire would be? Would you intentionally turn it down? Doesn't 80 or so years seem so short?

As much as we may struggle in this life, we must never forget that life is beautiful and there are moments when we experience what immortality could be like:

When we win the championship game;

When we are playing in the backyard with our children;

When we hold our newborn baby for the first time;

When the mists clear in the morning;

When the stars pierce the blackness;

When the morning light breaks above the trees.

These are glimpses—tastes—of how magnificent God's gift of life can be. These are moments when immortality seems possible and even desirable, and life is all we have ever hoped it would be.

And life is all around us, everywhere thriving. Even those places where life should never be able to succeed: on the polar ice caps; on the arctic tundra; in the deepest recesses of the ocean; on the tallest peaks; in the fiercest deserts.

Life is strong.

I remember staring in awe and wonder at a tree growing healthy and upright out of the side of a cliff. It could have been a perfect Christmas tree, but there it clung, miraculously. I have also seen twisted and mangled trees perpetually harangued by the wind, seemingly sucking their life force from the rocks. Ugly and deformed, I marveled at their strength. Anything can grow in tended fields and nutrient rich hillsides, but only the truly tough can survive in those conditions.

Life permeates everything. Can't you feel life?

Can't you remember the energy of youth?

Can't you remember the passion to succeed?

Can't you remember the unassailable tenacity to exist, free?

Life! Not oppression.

Life! Not Conflict and stress.

Life! Not disease, weakness, and decay.

Life! Not fear.
Life! In spite of the presence of death.
Don't you want to see an eternity of sunrises?
Life is, after all, what God designed us for.


## *At World's End*

Unlike many people, I personally loved *Pirates of the Caribbean: At World's End*. Some critics saw it as disorienting, convoluted, and a "rigid, bow-breaking downer" (Villarreal), but I got the sense that the writers were trying to go beyond mere action and they wanted to explore some deeper human themes.

First and foremost of those themes was the nature of the afterlife, hence the title, *At World's End*. Close to the beginning of the movie Jack Sparrow is working off his sins in a sort of purgatory, and the final scene is of Jack Sparrow sailing off in a dinghy on a quest to find the Fountain of Youth. Jack doesn't want to die (again) and so he lives his life searching, plotting, and hoping to solve the problem of death.

The truth is we are all Jack Sparrow. We want to be the person who sails away, free and full of life; we want to be the person who finds that elusive fountain. What greater adventure could anyone ever embark on? His quest is symbolic of our quest: we don't want to die and we'll do almost anything to avert death.

Think about it. Everything we invent, establish or want to achieve is directed toward the goal of circumventing death. Refrigerators so food won't spoil, water purifiers so water won't poison us, clothing so we don't die of exposure, shelter so the weather won't snuff us out, farming so we can eat and not starve, nutritional supplements so we can stave off disease, pharmaceuticals so we can mitigate disease, hospitals so we can maybe cure our maladies. The list is practically endless. Even the Buddhist monk in the most remote cave, eats.

Also, isn't procreation partly due to the fact that we want our immortal genes to live on through our children after we die? We want to pass on our values and our achievements to the next generation because it gives us a sense of undying significance. Some authors and poets are motivated to write because they want to be immortalized in their words, their minds and hearts unveiled to millions for generations to come. Massive monuments are built in order to commemorate great men (and not so great). Actors act, singers sing, architects build, governments are established, and artists sculpt all to, perhaps, be remembered after they die. We even make little plaques with people's names on them and brief summaries of their lives and place them on graves to remember the fact that someone was once alive and did things. The following is on a real gravestone:

> Jedediah Goodwin
> Auctioneer
> Born 1828
> Going!
> Going!!
> Gone!!!
> 1876
> (Shaputis)

A pretty good summary of life itself, don't you think? So let's deal with the honest, no-cards-hidden truth: no one wants to die. And yet, as universal as this feeling is, there is an active campaign to convince us that we are supposed to accept death as an inevitable certainty; that even though everyone wants to continue the adventure and no one really wants to be forgotten or to fade away into the sunset, we are supposed to let that notion go. Not me, and I bet not you.

We are the thirsty, wandering in a desert, searching for water to keep us alive; we are the homeless, looking for the security and safety of a loving home; we are the hungry, longing for an endless feast where neither need nor fear will ever haunt us again. From the aborigine to the farmer; from the shaman to the scientist, our fundamental desire is human: we want to live forever.

And once my mind tuned into this truth as a radio tunes into a frequency, I saw that it completely pervades the human experience. Our desire to live saturates our literature, our sciences, our history, our religious practices, our modern media and our marketing strategies. We humans have demonstrated time and again that we would take on any challenge, chance any danger—and commit any atrocity—if the reward were an eternal existence. We may die, but the dream of life can't. Tune in with me and listen to the heartbeat of humanity.

# Ancient Quests

## *Qin Shi Huang*

At first, Qin Shi Huang had been content with preparing a suitable home for his eternal soul in the afterlife. He ordered a magnificent tomb to be built, complete with a scale model of his precious China. It was a secure abode and his body would never be disturbed; it was a glorious home, suitable for such an imperial spirit as his.

However, he feared how he might be treated in the afterlife by those souls who had gone before. He had been unimaginably cruel to tens of thousands of people and if they were populating the world beyond they would want to exact revenge—eternal revenge. Therefore, he commissioned the building of an army of terra-cotta warriors who would protect him from the vengeful spirits of his dead enemies and subjugated peasants. But, even these effigies weren't enough to assuage his fear of death and he realized that he really wanted nothing less than physical immortality.

One means he experimented with was promoted by a rising political and social philosophy called Taoism. Founded as an alternative to legalistic Confucianism in the 4th century BC, Taoism believes that humans can become immortals, called *Hsien*, through the pursuit of various breathing techniques, dietary restrictions, and a lifestyle of balanced moderation. It is extremely difficult to achieve, but it is supposed to be possible.

He was also introduced to alchemy, which pursued immortality by chemical means and was practiced in the ancient world by every major culture: the Egyptians, the Sumerians, and the Harappans. His alchemists concocted potions with the hope of putting together the right combination which would make their Emperor immortal. Ironically, the most promising elixir that they thought would uncloak the Tree of Life was made of a highly toxic substance, Mercury, which he ingested with his food for years. He began hallucinating, became paranoid, and slowly descended into the abyss of a diseased mind. The flaming sword guarding the Tree of Life was not so easily by-passed.

Qin Shi Huang—the once great warrior who had united all the warring states of China in the 3rd century BC, who had become the First Emperor of the Qin Dynasty, who had expended a hundred-thousand lives extending the Great Wall, and who had committed endless resources and commissioned countless men to discover the secret of immortality—convulsed in a final passion of life and died at age forty-five.

## Gilgamesh

Gilgamesh is the legendary king who reigned in ancient Sumeria around 2700 BC, long before Qin Shi Huang was born. He, too, was a cruel despot known for enslaving his people to meaningless building projects. The city he ruled was the magnificent city of Uruk—the largest of his age—but in spite of his many victories what he is best remembered for is not his success, but his extraordinary failure: he couldn't conquer death.

According to the legend, the gods chose his closest companion, Enkidu, to die. However, Gilgamesh was not willing to let him remain in the clutches of death so he made the desperate journey to the land of the dead to demand of Utnapishtim (who had survived the Great Flood) the secret of how the gods had made him immortal.

Utnapishtim reluctantly reveals the secret—a plant that grows at the bottom of the sea—and Gilgamesh's long quest to raise his friend from the dead comes to a seemingly successful end. However, finally content, he falls asleep and when he awakens he discovers a serpent has eaten the plant. His quest has been an utter failure, but from that moment onward he simply lives a good life as a good king and he gives up his foolish need to raise his friend from the grave. Such is the lesson we should all learn, right?

## Legends of the Garden

I particularly enjoy hearing stories of magical places where, if you were lucky enough to find them, you could become immortal. In Chinese legend there is a place called *Penglai* Mountain where the Eight Immortals live, and on this mountain grows fruit that will give you eternal youth. In Irish mythology there is an island named *Magh Meall* (the Pleasant Plain), later known as *Tir Tairngire* (The Land of Promise), and it is described as an island that stands upon 'four legs of white silver' and has a unique tree upon which grows "wonderful apples." On this island there is no sickness or death, and it is a place of eternal youth, splendor, music, energy, life, and bliss (ÓhÓgáin). In Japanese mythology, there is the legend of a dragon-palace under the sea called *Ryūgū-jō* where one day at the palace is like a hundred years on earth. Hollywood came up with their own variation in the movie *Brigadoon*, where a town wakes up for one day every hundred years.

What makes these places unique is the possibility of finding them while still alive. These places are not an underworld, but rather an otherworld that allows for people to discover them either through the gracious reward of a god or by an accident. If you help the right god, or stumble across the right cave beneath a rock, or get blown off course on the sea, you'll find the land of immortality. They are ancient precursors to *The Twilight Zone* in that they are realms of another dimension. They are Faeryland, Narnia, or *Lost*, an island just out of phase with the rest of the world. They are places just beyond our normal ken and normal time, and the key to their grip upon our imagination is that it is possible to get there without having to die. If you do find it, though, the reward is immortality and everlasting health. Worth the effort, don't you think? What would you give to find such a secret? What would you do to protect such a secret?

## The Water of Life

This is for all you girls about forty-two
Tossing pennies into the Fountain of Youth.
—Martina McBride

The Fountain of Youth is another fascinating legend that has been around for millennia. The image of water as a source of life crosses all cultural and literary boundaries, and water seems to be a universal metaphor for life. This should not be surprising to us since where does life thrive? Next to water. Think of the most lush, green jungle you can think of. What do we call them? Rain forests. Where does life struggle? In deserts. How long can we survive without food? Upwards of Forty days. How long can we survive without water? Three.

And water is everywhere. Clouds are water vapor, and the earth is like a huge sponge. It is estimated that there are 326 million trillion gallons of water on earth and 70% of the surface of the planet is covered by oceans which contain 98% of all water. The remaining 2% is drinkable, and 1.6% of that is in the polar ice caps (*How Stuff Works*). And don't forget that our bodies are composed of about 70% water, and our brains of about 85%. Every cell is bathed with water inside and out and it is the key to all metabolic reactions. Basically, without water no life could exist.

It seems obvious, then, that water is the elixir of life, but, unfortunately, it can also be the elixir of death. The Roman military recognized that foul or stagnant water was a source of disease: "...the army should never continue in the neighborhood of unwholesome marshes any length of time.... Bad water is a kind of poison and the cause of epidemic distempers" (Flavius). Today we know that water-borne bacteria, parasites, and viruses are the specific cause of many maladies. Even in the U. S. where our water sources are meticulously managed, "From 1971 to 1988 there were 564 water-borne infectious outbreaks involving 140,000 people" (Barzilay).

More recently, however, our industrialized world has introduced entirely new carcinogenic water-borne agents such as arsenic, asbestos, radium, uranium, radon, nitrates, and a myriad of organic chemicals into our water. One man, Dr. Masaru Emoto, in order to counteract bad water, has allegedly "imprinted [water] with frequencies to support creativity, balance and conscious awareness" (Emoto). He doesn't claim it will bestow immortality, but he does claim it could cure every malady we have and it will even restore a childlike joy for living. A modern Fountain of Youth.

Scientists and medical practitioners at least agree that we should drink about eight glasses of water a day because "stress, chronic pain, and degenerative diseases" can be attributed to dehydration (Batmanghelidj). And who hasn't felt good after a nice cool drink of high quality $H^2O$? Go Waterboy! So, buy Dr. Emoto's super hydrating hexagonal Indigo water if you want, or go searching for the Fountain of Youth with Captain Jack and all the rest. Humanity has been searching for that elusive fountain for millennia.

A story was told that Alexander the Great had a cook who accidentally discovered life-regenerating waters when a dried fish he was cleaning came back to life. He refused to tell Alexander where the pond was and so he was thrown into the sea and became an everlasting demon.

A Hindu legend speaks of a princess who was led to a pool of water by two Asvins, demigods, where she gained eternal life. Ponce de Leon supposedly heard rumors of such a fountain that could be found on an island named Bimini, and as he sought for it—and gold—he accidentally discovered Florida. Most likely, the legend he had heard originated from the ancient story of Quetzalcoatl, the god of learning who taught the Tollans (citizens of Mexico long before the Aztecs) how to grow magnificent crops. Quetzalcoatl taught them how to live peacefully but he didn't teach them the art of war, so when his evil brother Tezcatlipoca showed up, Quetzalcoatl said to the Tollans, "My brother has arrived and will drive me from the city. It is best that I go to the Land of the Sun in the west and drink from the fountains there. Thus I can return with my power rejuvenated, young and strong, to become once again the friend and protector of Tollan" (*The Evil of Tezcatlipoca*). From this it seems that Quetzalcoatl was not an immortal god, just a knowledgeable man, and he never found the fountain either for he never returned and the Tollans were wiped out.

The modern novel *Tuck Everlasting* is about a family who drinks from a spring beside a tree, unwittingly conferring on themselves eternal life. It explores whether an eternal physical existence would be a blessing or a curse. If given the choice, would you choose the sorrow of leaving behind everyone you knew in order to gain eternal life for yourself? And, what would people pay to drink from such a water source if it were discovered and entered the marketplace? (A lot, considering what we will pay for mere bottled water.)

In a Japanese fairy tale, an old woodcutter finds a spring far out in the woods, and after he drinks a little from it he discovers he is youthful again. He returns to tell his wife and at first she doesn't believe he is her husband because he looks so young, but once he convinces her, she decides to drink from the spring alone while her husband guards the house. Her husband gets worried when she doesn't return that evening, so he goes to the spring and discovers his wife has become an infant. She drank too much.

When Fangorn gave Merry and Pippin a bowl of water:

> The drink was like water, indeed very like the taste of the draughts they had drunk from the Entwash near the borders of the forest, and yet there was some scent or savour in it which they could not describe: it was faint, but it reminded them of the smell of a distant wood borne from afar by a cool breeze at night. The effect of the draught began at the toes, and rose steadily through every limb, bringing refreshment and vigour as it coursed upwards, right to the tips of the hair. Indeed the hobbits felt that the hair on their heads was actually standing up, waving and curling and growing.

And who can forget when Indiana Jones poured the healing waters from the cup of Christ onto his dying dad?

Closely associated with the idea of life-extending water, is the belief in a magical elixir. The Greek gods had Ambrosia, the drink of the immortals. The Hindu gods could give you Amrita. Medieval alchemists wanted to produce the Philosopher's Stone, a potion by some accounts, and across the ancient world Harmal seeds, derived from a small, bushy desert shrub named Syrian Rue, were considered the base for the drink of the immortals. As we have already seen, gold and mercury were believed to extend one's life if ingested, but other substances such as jade, hematite, sulfur, pearl, coral and arsenic (and many more) were experimented with over the centuries as well. Today, Green Tea, Aloe Vera, and Beta-carotene top the list of the innumerable number of elixirs all developed to improve the quality and the length of your life. And everyone hopes that the Amazonian rainforest grows something that will cure all cancers.

From all these quests to find a magical island or a magical elixir—historical and imaginary—we can see that mankind's ancient longing has bridged all cultures and infatuated every era. But the quests so far have been tame compared to what some people were willing to do.

# Dark Quests

The sad truth is that the desire for physical immortality can become so powerful, so overwhelmingly seductive, that some people will commit the most horrible atrocities imaginable in order to attain that ultimate goal. The allure of this life and the fear of dying have justified such gruesome activities as drinking blood, cannibalism, and one particularly appalling pagan practice: sacrificing children en masse so the king could bathe in their blood.

## *Vampires*

Considering the fascination with vampires in today's culture, I think it is important to understand the historical origins of this concept. John Michael Greer explains that:

> In the traditions and phenomena of vampirism…we are dealing with the last survivals of *an ancient technique aimed at personal immortality* [emphasis added]. That technique once had a deeper and more spiritual meaning, according to magical tradition; those who took part in it did so as an act of sacrifice, removing themselves from the cycle of reincarnation for a time in order to serve some purpose that required more than a single lifetime…. It was only much later, when the original purpose of the system had been lost, that it fell into the hands of the selfish and greedy, and turned into an attempt to cheat death altogether. (Greer)

The roots of vampirism are actually best understood by studying the ancient Egyptian religion. According to the Egyptians, the body and the spirit are permanently linked. After death, while the spirit would try to reach the Fields of Yalu, the embalmed body would remain in its coffin (not rise up Bela Lugosi-style), and the longer the body lasted, the better the spirit's chances of achieving happiness. But since the mummified body was just a dry husk, the spirit needed some other life force to sustain itself and so family members, or paid priests, would leave food for the spirit in the tomb. But, if someone stopped delivering food regularly, then the spirit would have to wander the earth on its own trying to find the sustenance it needed, which could involve feeding off the life force of the living. Think, *The Mummy*.

And, as Greer noted, this concept is what developed into the parasitic exploitation of the living for the sake of the dead we now call vampirism, where the body wanders the earth, not the spirit. In Bram Stoker's *Dracula* he explains that "When they [the undead] become such, there comes with the change the curse of immortality. They cannot die, but must go on age after age adding new victims and multiplying the evils of the world." Vampirism, therefore, is a particularly selfish existence requiring the intentional harm of living individuals. Vampires want to avoid the second death; they want to remain connected to the flesh of this life and continue to live in this world. Theirs is the quest for physical immortality at any cost.

## Frankenstein

In Mary Percy Shelley's classic novel, Frankenstein, (which is much different than the 1931 movie) Dr. Frankenstein (Fronkensteen!) experiments on corpses to see if he can reanimate their tissue. He describes himself as having been "embued with a fervent longing to penetrate the secrets of nature" and at the age of thirteen, with exposure to some ancient writers, he "entered with the greatest diligence into the search of the philosopher's stone and the elixir of life...." (Shelley, 36-37). He devoted his life to this quest, sacrificing love and family, and after years of studying philosophy and mathematics, and, most horrible of all, the dead tissue of humans in various stages of decomposition, he finally discovers the secret to life.

Immediately after animating his new creation he is ecstatic, but soon he is horrified by it and he abandons it to fend for itself, trying to forget what he has done. The creature, though, wanders the countryside, hiding, and gradually learns how to speak and read. After several years, completely disillusioned by his experiences with humanity, he wants to find his creator and exact vengeance for creating him.

The monster begins by killing a close friend of Dr. Frankenstein's and threatens to kill more if he doesn't build him a bride whom he can love and who will love him in return. Refusing, Dr. Frankenstein then makes it his life's quest to destroy the abomination he has made. So, his original desire to circumvent death and to achieve immortality instead results in an apparently immortal monster that kills everyone he has ever loved.

But I wonder if we have learned his lesson? If you think we have outgrown the need for this quest, or that it is only the stuff of fiction, think again. Probably the most notorious and evil monster of the 20th century, Hitler, believed that he could achieve immortality. In one of the more famous psychological studies of Hitler, written while he was still alive, Walter C. Langer points out that Hitler believed:

> ...he was of divine origin and was under its protection.... The experience he [Hitler] reports at the front, when a voice told him to pick up his plate and move to another section of the trench just in time to escape a shell which killed all his comrades, must certainly have strengthened this belief to a marked degree and paved the way for his vision later on. (Langer, 173)

Langer hypothesizes "that a fear of death is one of the powerful unconscious streams which drives Hitler on in his mad career.... With him, as with many others of his type, it may well be a case of *immortality of any kind at any price* [emphasis added]" (Langer, 179).

Hitler, apparently, was so afraid of dying that he justified his inhuman slaughter of millions of people based upon his delusion that he was fated to live for the next thousand years as the leader of his beloved Germany. What a scary world if that had been true. I also suspect that the cruel medical experiments he conducted were a satanically inspired, Frankensteinian search for immortality gone wild.

And yet Dr. Frankenstein only experimented on corpses; Hitler experimented on the living.

But that was Hitler and way back in the 30's and 40's. And vampires aren't real and isn't it true that we, modern man, have grown up? Haven't we evolved to the point that such a primitive desire for immortality is ridiculous, delusional? Modern science has removed our ignorance and proven that death is normal and merely a part of the natural cycle of life. The ancients' dream of immortality was based upon superstition; we are scientifically educated. A fountain of water that will make you young again? Ha! A fairy tale.

But the truth is that the desire for immortality is alive and well today. In fact, it may be more popular than ever because the modern biomedical version has given our ancient quest a shot of Botox (hey, if you don't look old, you're not), and since atheism teaches there is nothing after our body dies, why not try to live forever? Therefore, no longer relegated to the realm of fantasy and snake oil practitioners who grind up dog's testicles to give you that youthful glow, the genetic fountain of youth is as chic today as the most elegant evening gown.

# Modern Quests

Years ago I remember listening to a geneticist being interviewed on the radio. I am paraphrasing, but his core message was that he believed that unlocking the genetic code would allow us to eventually cure all disease. Cancer? Gone. Heart disease? Cured. He also implied that with such therapies we could potentially extend life indefinitely—immortality. Of course we would still have to fear traumas like car accidents and falling off cliffs, but disease? No more.

I am even today reading books by distinguished scientists who are still hoping for the same outcome. If we can just get enough funding, or if George W. Bush wouldn't have limited our ability to experiment on human embryos, then maybe we could advance our understanding of what makes us age. (By the way, is killing embryos in the hope of curing all disease really any different than the ancient practice of slaughtering innocent children to bathe in their blood for the benefit of an elite few?) Discovering the genetic reasons for why we age and how we age, therefore, has become the latest manifestation of the quest for the Fountain of Youth:

> …the high priests of our secular age, the
> molecular biologists, have begun to address
> mortality in a way no group, no generation, and
> no society has ever dreamed of before…. nothing
> less is at stake than a partial or nearly total repeal
> of mortality; from another perspective, we might
> be witnessing a postmodern, molecular version of
> the Fountain of Youth tale…. (Hall, 3)

Hall acknowledges that the heart behind this quest is ancient; he also warns that success is not possible. Most geneticists accept the fact that humans have a limited life span and they are skeptical of any claims that immortality is possible. Some cellular biologists have demonstrated that we have a biological warranty, called the Hayflick Limit, and to them it's ridiculous to believe we could ever physically live forever because life has a cutoff point and indefinite survival is not possible.

Therefore, since we have a mortality time bomb ticking away in us, they are focusing their efforts on trying to stretch out our lifespan while improving our quality of life. Their quest is to stave off the effects of aging until eighty or ninety years old. If on average we now enjoy optimal health from ages twenty to sixty, in the future we will enjoy that same quality of life from twenty to ninety. We'll die, but we will have lived healthier, longer lives.

One line of modern research theorizes that by limiting caloric intake by up to 40%, life spans can be significantly lengthened while still enjoying optimal health. Scientists hypothesize that our insulin signaling system is repressed when we eat less, thereby reducing the amount of insulin in our blood. As a result, "…calorie-restricted animals age more slowly and maintain their tissue integrity well into old age;…" (Arking, 191).

It must be noted that they have only demonstrated that this is possible in worms, fruit flies, mice and rats, and that to accomplish the same thing in humans is still under experimentation.

However, Taoism—as noted earlier—has been practicing a calorie-restricted diet for over 2,000 years for the same purpose: to extend life spans while enjoying optimal health benefits. Science seems to be a Johnny-come-lately on this bandwagon, but, on the other hand, if they could produce a drug that could extend your life by cutting out almost half of your calories, wouldn't you take that pill? Thinner and a longer life without all that spiritual discipline stuff and self-denial? Sounds good to me.

But, in spite of some scientists' restraint in their hope to solve death, others refuse to bow down to our "Darwinian Warranty." They see scientific proof as a mere obstacle, not an immutable law. For them, coming up with some way to outwit and outlast our genetic limitations would make them the ultimate survivor. How about this for a mission statement: "The mission of the Immortality Institute is to conquer the blight of involuntary death" (Immortality Institute). They're serious, folks. In spite of all the overwhelming evidence to the contrary, the hope remains that if we were to unlock the cell's secrets and figure out which gene caused aging, we could at last succeed at what everyone before us has failed. In fact, it could be argued that our desire for immortality is better funded and more popular than it has ever been in history. Sex may sell by appealing to our lusts, but life-extension technology sells because it brings hope. "The marriage of hard-core molecular genetics, our most precise and vaunted life science, with perhaps our oldest and most alluring human fantasy—eternal youth in a bottle—is one of the most intriguing (not to say amusing) aspects of recent gerontological research" (Hall, 191).

And Sonia Arrison points out in her article "Done with Death":

> …it is an entirely human response to try to fix problems that are harming people — including death. Some 150,000 people die globally every day. In the U.S., it's about 200,000 a month (6,500 a day). Given these numbers, it does seem rather odd that we aren't demanding a solution now. Perhaps one reason is that we live in a culture of death — a culture that has convinced us that death is natural, good, and impossible to fight against, so we shouldn't even try. But we should try…. (Arrison)

So, even after all these millennia it seems that modern man still hopes to extend life indefinitely. We don't seem to want to settle for anything less. Sure we've been trying for thousands of years without success (as far as we know??? Just kidding), but the potential is alluring; devilishly alluring.

And no modern line of research exploits this innate hope more than Cryonics. This is the process of freezing one's body immediately after death in liquid nitrogen with the hope that someday it will be able to be revived and healed. On the Cryonics Institute's webpage they say,

> When and if future medical technology allows, our member patients hope to be healed, rejuvenated, revived, and awakened to a greatly

extended life in youthful good health, free from disease or the aging process. (Cryonics)

Sounds pretty cool to me.

As a comical example of the influence of this idea, I live close to Nederland, Colorado where they celebrate The Frozen Dead Guy with a weeklong festival every year. It includes festivities such as coffin races, a polar plunge and a hearse parade. Morstoel was frozen after he died in 1989 in Norway, and through a series of events ended up in this rustic mountain town where he has become a town icon and a tourist attraction. Immortality doesn't always come in the form we thought.

Another nifty idea on how to live forever is by downloading one's consciousness into a supercomputer, or into a cyborg. A guy named Ian Pearson predicts this will be possible by the year 2050—at least for the rich. Forget about the body, be your computer, and connect with all of your other virtual buddies. We could call it The Virtual Heaven. (I just hope there won't be any massive solar flares.)

Nanotechnology is also on the horizon of some farsighted visionaries. From an MSNBC review of Ray Kurzweil's book, *Fantastic Voyage: Live Long Enough to Live Forever*, "Kurzweil writes of millions of blood cell-sized robots, which he calls 'nanobots,' that will keep us forever young by swarming through the body, repairing bones, muscles, arteries and brain cells. Improvements to our genetic coding will be downloaded via the Internet. We won't even need a heart" (Lindsay). Hasn't he read Michael Crichton's *Prey* or seen *Stargate*? Nanotechnology may be anything but benevolent to mankind.

Ironically, these quests are promoted as cutting edge science, but what, really, is the difference between drinking a potion and being injected with nanobots? Both promises are equally alluring and are equally failures (or will be). In spite of how much we want to succeed, immortality seems to hover always on the horizon of discovery.

### *Death is swallowed up in victory.*

So why do we still believe eternal life is possible? Why is our desire for eternity so tenacious in the face of such overwhelming odds? In spite of all the educational efforts of naturalistic scientists and their frustration with why more people don't believe them, why don't we just give up the quest? Why don't we believe this is all there is?

I believe it's because we instinctively know that we are supposed to live forever. In and of itself, this desire in no way proves that we once did live forever, or that we will, but it at least can be considered an indicator light that death and suffering is an affront to everything we hold dear. The desire for eternity is in us, and like a homing pigeon, we keep trying to find our way back home.

I also believe that only the Bible promises us the sure-fire, proven cure to disease, aging, and death. No longer do we have to hope to stumble across an otherworld or a lost fountain, or for science to make nanobots. No longer do we need to believe in unconfirmed theories and false promises. No longer do we need to be told to give up on the hope for immortality. The Bible records that death has been conquered and the way to physical immortality has been opened. Jesus, the true Messiah, is the living actualization of all our quests. He is the Fountain of Youth we have been searching for; He is the Living Water (John 4:10); Christ's blood gives us immortality (John 6:54); and He alone is at world's end (1 Corinthians 15:51-57).

And He isn't a fairy tale, a legend, or a false promise.
He is Life.

*Jesus, the true Messiah, is the living actualization of all our quests.*

# DEATH

"On this home by Horror haunted—tell me truly, I implore—
Is there—*is* there balm in Gilead?—tell me—tell me, I implore!"
Quoth the raven, "Nevermore."

Edgar Allen Poe, *"The Raven"*

Why is there death? Where did it come from? Did it rise with us out of a miry goo to perfect us and weed out the weak? Did it arrive to punish us and snuff out sin?

When did it begin?

Is life really just a fatal disease?

Will death ever end? Does death only mean "The End"? "Nevermore?"

Dwell on it. Think about it all night long. Nightmares. Eerie images. Mortal thoughts. Unanswerable questions. What is the meaning of life?

Death: a mystery shrouded in riddles; an unpleasant thought on a sunny day; a glance over your shoulder; a shadow always following. It can attack without warning, but sometimes it likes to see you suffer. See you scream.

Some have gone insane because they thought about death too much and they couldn't escape their fears. It gnaws, scratches, shrieks, haunts, hinders and howls in our face at every move we make. We insure against it; we make laws to help avoid it; we go to the doctor, exercise, pray, eat right, and carry mace with us. We even make fun of it.

All to merely postpone the inevitable, or make it not seem so bad.

Even Lazarus died—again.

And death is creative: quick death, slow death, painful death, painless death, fall asleep, blow up. However it may happen, it will! But on an every day basis I don't ever really believe that death will happen to me. But if, for a moment, in the darkest moments of the night when emotion controls reason and I realize that I actually will die—the sting is paralyzing; the actuality is terrifying.

We don't want it. We wish we could solve it. And yet we can't escape it. We want to know what is beyond it, but we just can't quite prove what we think.

Where did death come from? Why is it here?

Why does it scare me to death?

## Death Encounters

The first time I ever encountered death within my family was when my grandfather died. He had been a dairy farmer for practically his entire life, and he was cut from the mold of men who could build anything they needed. He built his house, barn, shop, garage, silo, dike, gravel digger, whatever. My grandmother told me she remembers not really thinking all that much of what her husband was able to do. She thought everyone could do these things.

My grandfather was a unique man whose structures still stand to this day, but now he's dead and the world has lost an interesting and creative person. I wish even now, almost 30 years later, that when I visit the farm I could sit down, talk with him, and learn from him. I only knew him when I was an immature child—what would it be like to converse with him now that I'm an adult? I wish his great granddaughter could meet him, glean from him wisdom and insight. I really wish he hadn't died. I hate the fact that he is dead. It bothers me deeply.

Years before my grandfather's death, though, I went to my first funeral. I was in the seventh grade and a fellow student, an eighth grader, someone I kind of knew, died in a three-wheeler accident. I'm ashamed to this day that I went to his funeral just to take the day off school, but what was death to me then? I didn't understand loss, sorrow, fear, confusion. To this day, I can picture his accident as it was described to me as if I had been present.

He was riding along on a three-wheeler having fun, and he drove down a brown, barren embankment too fast. Tree roots protruded from the ground like old, craggy arms and his three-wheeler bounced, threw him off, then flipped and crushed his head. I sometimes wonder what he would be doing now if he had lived beyond the ripe old age of thirteen.

Even if you haven't faced the death of someone close to you—yet—at some point we all lose someone we love to that dreaded tyrant, death, and then you will understand the pain and horror involved.

And along with that enlightenment inevitably will come feelings of sadness, loss, and remorse; of reflection and anger; and oh, unpleasant thought—the realization that someday you will succumb to its dreaded embrace as well, and others will grieve for you.

Dreadful.

Am I being too honest? Are you depressed yet?

But we still haven't answered the question "What is death?" It may terrify us, but what is it? Please notice that for now the question isn't "What happens to us after we die?" The question is, "What is death?" This is simply a logical inquiry into the essence and nature of the thing we are exploring.

Close your eyes. What do you see? What images come to mind?

Blackness? Loneliness? Light? Reunions? The Grim Reaper? Fear?

I know this may be a painful exercise, but it's time to face this issue. We need to meet it head-on like Lou Piniella confronts an umpire: in your face, kicking dirt, and throwing bases. Yes, it's a topic we don't like to talk directly about because it is so easy to gloss over its harsh reality and skip to the punch line. "Ignore death," we say in our hearts. "Let's talk about how we all go to heaven. Death is bad, yes, and unpleasant, but let's not talk about that." Sorry.

# Defining Death

Surprisingly, in my research I have discovered that defining death is not as easy as one might think. There are so many opinions out there about what death is, and mostly they are expressed in the form of euphemisms. For example, in the movie "Patch Adams" there is a humorous interchange between a terminal patient who isn't taking the news of his demise very well, and Dr. Adams (Robin Williams) breaks the ice by getting him to lighten up a little:

> PATCH ADAMS. Death. To die. To expire. To pass on. To perish. To peg out. To push up daisies. To push up posies. To become extinct. Curtains, deceased, demised, departed and defunct. Dead as a doornail. Dead as a herring. Dead as a mutton. Dead as nits. The last breath. Paying a debt to nature. The big sleep. God's way of saying, "Slow down."

> BILL DAVIS. To check out.

> PATCH ADAMS. To shuffle off this mortal coil.

BILL DAVIS. To head for the happy hunting ground.

PATCH ADAMS. To blink for an exceptionally long period of time.

BILL DAVIS. To find oneself without breath.

PATCH ADAMS. To be the incredible decaying man.

BILL DAVIS. Worm buffet.

PATCH ADAMS. Kick the bucket.

BILL DAVIS. Buy the farm.

PATCH ADAMS. Take the cab.

BILL DAVIS. Cash in your chips.

As you can see, we have a lot of creative ways of indirectly referring to an event which is quite frightening, and that's okay, I guess, to a certain degree. But when we say things like, "Death is just a part of the cycle of life," or "It's just the beginning of a new journey," I get a little queasy. Those make it sound so trivial. If you're a nihilist, you might say death is just the end of our existence. When we die, we die. Epicurus taught, "Accustom yourself to believing that death is nothing to us, for good and evil imply the capacity for sensation, and death is the privation of all sentience; therefore a correct understanding that death is nothing to us makes the mortality of life enjoyable, not by adding to life a limitless time, but by taking away the yearning after immortality" (Epicurus). Or we could take the Buddha's advice and listen to the wise men of old who said, "Grieve not…That which is subject to death has died, that which is subject to destruction is destroyed" (*Dhammapada Commentary*, 20). Or we could come on board with the naturalist Baron D'Holbach: "Death is nothing more than a passage into a new mode of existence:

it is the eternal, the invariable, the unconquerable law of Nature, to which the individuals of his order, each in his turn, is obliged to submit" (D'Holbach, chap. 5).

Even others contend that the concept of the afterlife is just a psychological gimmick made up by religions in order to make us feel better in spite of the fact that we all know we're just going to end up in a grave, unconscious forever. But if death is that easy to dismiss, why do we spend our lives trying to avoid it? If it's so ordinary, why don't we just accept it in the same way we accept drinking water? Why does it bug us so much?

It's because of what it is.

## *The Medical Definition*

In Webster's II, death is defined as

> The act of dying: cessation of life. 2. The state of being dead. (I love that one. Death is being dead. Really helpful.) 3. A personification of the destroyer of life, usually represented as a skeleton holding a scythe.

Hmmm. Not very illuminating. I also went online to wikipedia.com. It was a little more beneficial and made some interesting observations about key features of biological death which I have summarized:

> It is irreversible; a person is considered dead when the electrical activity in their brain ceases; the most common cause of death is Anoxia, or, the pathological state in which tissues do not get enough oxygen. There are, of course, other determiners such as rigor mortis, or dependent lividity.

It is interesting to note that historically it has always been difficult to determine exactly when death occurs if there weren't any obvious physical signs. It used to be that when the heart stopped and breathing ceased, death had occurred, but then CPR came along and suddenly "death" became reversible.

It also used to be important to wait three days just to make sure the person had actually died. The Irish Wake originated as a strategy to ensure the deceased was deceased. The body would rest in the main room and everybody would tell stories, play games, and get drunk. The level of debauchery involved varied, but the basic principal was: "Just in case he's not dead we should wait a few days before burial." It is a recorded fact that some coffins would be reused and when the lids were opened scratch marks were found inside. For the wealthy, a string could be run down into a coffin, whereby its occupant, if he awoke, could ring a bell above ground. Saved by the bell! People would also be employed in order to sit all night in the graveyards and listen for those bells. Hence, the graveyard shift.

But, still, the medical definition of death is not quite sufficient for me. It's practical but not illuminating. It's so clinical. It doesn't really capture what I feel. When my grandfather died there was so much more to it than merely a "cessation of life."

## *The Emotional Definition*

Shakespeare actually gets closer to a satisfactory definition:

> Death, death: O, amiable lovely death!
> Thou odoriferous stench! sound rottenness!
> (The Death of King John III.iv.25-26)

Now that is getting closer to the mark. The smell and the image of rottenness emphasize the sarcasm in the first line, "amiable lovely death!" Death is not friendly and it is not lovely. Death stinks. That begins to make sense to me because that's how I feel when I see death.

In the larger context of this quote, the character Constance is filled with overwhelming grief and anger because of the death of her son, Arthur. Later in this same scene she says:

> If I were mad, I should forget my son,…
> I am not mad: too well, too well I feel
> The different plague of each calamity.

It makes me cry to read the entire passage, and to hear the passion in her grief. I can relate; maybe you can, too.

When my wife passed away (an interesting euphemism in and of itself), I became a dark pit of despair and emptiness. That, unfortunately, is the typical reaction when someone we love dies. Other reactions are to hate God, to become suicidal, to hide from the world in a cavernous depression, or to just pretend it isn't all that bad, as if we just closed a book and ended a story. The effects of the death of someone we love are unpredictable, life changing, and impossible to prepare for. Sallie White, the wife of the great editorialist William Allen White of Emporia, Kansas, went into an emotionally dark place after the tragic death of their sixteen-year-old daughter, Mary White. It is said that before her daughter's death, she was vivacious and outgoing, but after, she was evermore morose.

And so, if we are to define death adequately, we must include the emotional effects because someone's death most powerfully influences our hearts. Merely a sterile, biological definition without the emotional features will always fall short of capturing the true meaning of death. None of us are purely Vulcan.

But, on the other hand, we can get too sappy and emotionally sickly-sweet when it comes to death. On a grief-oriented website, I found several poems which were designed to comfort the grieving, but which went too far, in my opinion, in trying to give death a positive spin:

> Death is a beginning
> Revealing truth.
>
> Death is a necessity
> A journey should not last forever.
>
> Death is an adventure
> Shared by all.
>
> Death is a friend
> Carrying you home.
>
> Death is a mourning veil
> Falling lightly on grief.
>
> Death is a velvet cloak
> Not to resist.
>
> Death is a relief
> An end of pain.
>
> Death is an end
> A letting go. (Cobb)

That's beautiful, unless you remember what death is going to do to you. The poem reminds me of my childhood set of Charles Schultz's "Happiness is..." bed sheets. Charlie Brown, Snoopy, Lucy, and Linus all had their own definition of what "Happiness is" and I remember feeling so good reading those just before going to sleep. However, can you imagine Charlie Brown and friends quoting the above poem "Death is…"? Even on sky blue bed sheets, I doubt it would have the same effect.

In fact, I believe that reading a poem like the one above is more like taking morphine—it numbs your emotions to the reality of what's happening. It tries to make you feel good about something you shouldn't feel good about. Take for example, the line "Death is a beginning." How can the loss of my ability to move, breathe, and enjoy the company of others be a beginning? It's the end. The poem, of course, is implying that our eternal spirit will live on in a glorious afterlife with our loved ones. And yet, even though I believe that our spirit—our essential energy—will live on, that doesn't necessarily mean that this new beginning will be pleasant for everyone. Is Hitler thinking, "Hey, Death is a beginning"?

"Death is a necessity/A journey should not last forever." Who made up that rule? Why can't a journey last forever? True, we all will die, but who says that's the way things ought to be? I believe we were originally intended to live forever and to enjoy life to its fullest forever.

"Death is an Adventure." Exciting!

"Death is a Friend." Would you call up death to hang out with you at the mall? "Hey Sally. This is my new friend, Death."

Is Death really any of these things? Is it a "Velvet Cloak"; a "Mourning Veil"?

Gag me with a scythe!

Chalk it up to my stubbornness, but I believe that confronting the truth of what something is, is more constructive than hiding from it. For example, would that poem bring comfort to a child standing at the edge of a mass grave looking for his mother?

"Don't worry, death is an adventure!"

Or to a bloated, starving child?

"It's okay, Johnny. Death is your friend."

When I see death, I feel hatred; I want justice; I want restoration; and I want a solution. We've just been so conditioned to put on a happy face that we try to soothe the pain with platitudes, and, as a result, too many people have been locked up in a prison of despair simply because they have been taught not to hate death. They have been told that they should see it as a "doorway," but when they can't they get even more depressed because they think their feelings are unspiritual.

So, why don't we just admit death terrifies us? Why don't we just call it what it is: "Death is awful and I hate everything about it"?

Here's my version of the poem:

> Death is the end
> And then comes judgment.
>
> Death is a punishment,
> Sin should not last forever.
>
> Death is a shipwreck
> Shared by all.
>
> Death is our enemy
> Dragging us away from home.
>
> Death is a mourning veil
> Of pain and grief.
>
> Death is a shroud
> To be resisted to the bitter end.
>
> Death is the culmination
> Of all our pain.

Death is a thief
Stealing everyone we love.

Not exactly uplifting, but oh so true. Unfortunately.

I lost my grandfather. I lost my wife. My best friend died three years ago. I just recently lost my father. I miss them. They are no longer a part of my life except in the context of my memories. Their presence; their smiles, their laughter, their hopes, dreams, tears, and passions are all lost to me.

They died. It's time to weep. And it would be wrong to *not* grieve their loss. *I am supposed to feel sorrow*.

Now we are getting closer to a working definition of death: Death is not only the biological cessation of life, it is also the relational cessation of interaction. A dead person no longer functions biologically or relationally. And that is the reason we feel such grief—a person we love is now gone. Death is so sad.

Enkidu's last words to Gilgamesh were:

Why am I to die,
You to wander on alone?
Is that the way it is with friends?
(Tablet II)

Enkidu's motion through this life was going to cease. No longer would he run and fight alongside his friend; no longer would he make a difference in the lives of others. His ability to relate to others, show love, and enjoy life, would all be gone.

Dreadful. No doubt.

---

*It would be wrong to not grieve their loss. I am supposed to feel sorrow.*

---

## *The Spiritual Definition*

And yet, even that definition seems incomplete. Death has to be more significant than just merely turning off a switch like the android Data can do on Star Trek. (For you non-nerds, Data has a hidden button on his back and only a few people know how to find it.) Wouldn't that be convenient and even, if our lives were miserable, attractive? I'm done. Turn me off.

The burning question remains, though: Aren't we more than merely biological machines? Aren't we more than a bag of chemicals? Don't we have a spirit? A soul? An eternal consciousness? If we're only machines, then the first two definitions are more than adequate. Life just stops so enjoy it while you have it. Make a difference and then die. The message of atheism is that simple so go ahead, shut this book and move on if that's what you believe. But the message of Christianity is far more complex and requires a bit more explanation. And a bit more courage.

If we do have a spirit, death takes on an added significance. For the sake of argument, let's agree for the moment that we do have an eternal spirit and that at the point of death it ceases to animate our physical bodies and lives on in an independent state of existence, whatever condition that may be. So, then, we should add to our definition of death the concept of separation: Death causes our body to cease functioning and it ends our relationships, but it also separates our life force from our body. The Bible uses a phrase that describes this event as "giving up the ghost." Genesis 25:8 records: "Then Abraham gave up the ghost, and died in a good old age, an old man, and full of years; and was gathered to his people."

Biblically, however, there is one more definition associated with death: separation from God. When God told Adam that "on the day you eat of it, you shall surely die," God did not necessarily mean that Adam's body would keel over and cease functioning right on the spot. However, we mustn't consider it an empty threat because what if their immediate death was supposed to have happened? I believe they *were* supposed to have died immediately, but that God's mercy held back His hand of wrath. Nevertheless, something did die that day: Adam and Eve's relationship with God. It was shattered beyond all recognition.

Just as our bodies cease to relate to the people we know and love when we die, even so our spirits can no longer relate to God because of sin. Physical death, therefore, becomes an analogy—a symbol—of something far more important: our spiritual separation from God. God grieves for us in the same way we grieve for those who have died. It causes Him that much pain. When we experience the pain and sorrow from the death of someone we love, we are supposed to become aware that God feels that way about us. Let me put it bluntly: death is supposed to terrify us so that we will wake up to the more terrifying reality that we are separated from God. If we try to convince ourselves that death is just normal, we won't pursue a cure.

Our spirit is like a hermit living alone in the mountains and we are withering in isolation. God designed us to be so intimately connected with Him that when Adam and Eve sinned, it not only separated us from Him, it began a process of biological death that was inherited by their descendants: us. And that is why, instead of death being analogous to an electrical switch being turned off, it is more like we are a cell phone with a battery which wears down slowly over time until our body finally fails. Adam and Eve disconnected themselves from the constant power source of God's presence when they sinned, and now all of us—their children—are independent, alone.

---

*If we try to convince ourselves that death is just normal, we won't pursue a cure.*

Physical death, therefore, is a by-product of our spiritual death. Our spirit needs His spirit, but sin separates us. It was Adam and Eve's close, cherished, perfect relationship with the immortal God of the universe that died that day, and when God called out in the Garden, "Adam, where are you?" no more wretched words have ever been spoken.

> He [Adam] came, and with him Eve...
> Love was not in their looks, either to God
> Or to each other, but apparent guilt,
> And shame, and perturbation, and despair,
> Anger, and obstinacy, and hate, and guile.
> (*Paradise Lost*, IX, 109 — 114)

Death, far from being natural, is the single most hideous plague that will ever haunt mankind. And we hide from that truth to our despair.

# TRUE FAITH IS NEVER BLIND

That which was from the beginning, which we have heard, which we have seen with our eyes, which we have looked at and our hands have touched—this we proclaim concerning the Word of life. The life appeared; we have seen it and testify to it, and we proclaim to you the eternal life, which was with the Father and has appeared to us. We proclaim to you what we have seen and heard, so that you also may have fellowship with us. And our fellowship is with the Father and with his Son, Jesus Christ.

1 John 1:1-3

The above passage contains a special rebuke for me because for years I never noticed its empirical emphasis. I missed John's primary point that he and the other disciples had had a sensory experience of Jesus and that John was trying to convince us that Jesus is real, not just a story. Life had become flesh; the Creator had become the created; the Eternal had become mortal.

Jesus isn't just the figurehead of a philosophical or religious movement because of His really cool, insightful teaching: God revealed Himself as a man and He conquered death. There's something to be said for that achievement! He actually lived, died, and then bodily rose from the grave. Match that! What Jesus did had been anticipated by the prophets—He was expected—and when He arrived, He proved that God—the Word of Life, the ever-existing creator—does exist. Pay attention!

However, early in my Christian walk I didn't fully understand how important the historical foundation of Christianity was. For example, when I worked in Marina del Rey just after high school, I had many conversations about Christianity with my boss' father, but he always had that pitying "What a stupid, naive kid" attitude toward me as he blew smoke in my face. He made it clear he didn't believe in a God—in any spiritual thing whatsoever. He told me that he would only believe what he could touch. He wasn't going to be fooled by silly superstitions and unconfirmed ideas. He was empirical, a man of science, a man of practicality and of the here and now.

I wish I had understood the above passage better then, because what I said to him at the time was that God is spirit and He can't be touched, but nevertheless He is real. True, but not the complete answer.

What I've come to realize and accept since then is that we humans do have a need to verify what we have been told. My boss's dad wanted proof and that is fine with God. Yes, God is spirit and nobody has seen God (John 1:18), but He doesn't expect us to believe in Him without any corroborating evidence. Jesus is the evidence.

For example, when the angels appeared to the shepherds, they were at first afraid. But after listening they followed directions and as a result, "The shepherds returned, glorifying and praising God for all the things they had heard and seen, which were *just as they had been told"* (Luke 2:20) [emphasis added]. The empirical evidence matched the angelic revelation and that is how it should be, because God doesn't make claims He is unwilling to back up, and we shouldn't believe claims that are not backed up. They believed and then it was proven. In fact, God eagerly wants to confirm His existence to us, and He supports all of

His claims. If our attitude is to go where the evidence leads, then our only direction can be toward God.

## *Jesus is the evidence*

As another example, in Luke 24:36-39 Jesus appears to His disciples for the first time after his resurrection, and their reaction is forgivable: "they were startled and frightened and thought they saw a spirit. And he said to them, 'Why are you troubled, and why do doubts arise in your hearts? See my hands and my feet, that it is I myself. Touch me, and see. For a spirit does not have flesh and bones as you see that I have.'" Jesus recognized their need for evidence. He knew they were having trouble believing (who wouldn't?), and He showed them the proof they needed.

Now, some may object that I am promoting an attitude similar to that of doubting Thomas, so I want to make sure that I am not misunderstood: faith is definitely the confidence in things not seen (Heb. 11). I have never seen God, and yet I believe He exists. That is faith.

Thomas' sin, however, wasn't that he needed proof, it was that he doubted the proof. In spite of all the evidence that had been stacked up in front of him, he wouldn't believe it. He had heard the testimony of his friends; he had heard Jesus teach on it; he had walked with Jesus and seen all the miracles; and he knew Scripture and what the Promised Messiah would do. And yet he wanted more. That was the sin of Thomas: he didn't believe the evidence.

Jesus' rebuke to him tells us a lot: "Blessed are they who did not see, and yet believed" (John 20:29). Thomas had seen and still doubted. He knew the truth and still doubted the truth. We, however, do not have the luxury of having walked and talked with Jesus ourselves, and that is what makes us "blind" in one sense. However, we have the scriptures and the testimony of those who did see. We have as much information as we need to make a decision.

God is concerned for our subjective need for truth and our objective need for proof, and He doesn't expect us to trust Him without cause. Faith, far from being blind, is the courage to believe the evidence. God may Himself be unseen, but He has made Himself known through creation, the nation of Israel, and Jesus.

> Psalm 19:1: "The Heavens declare the glory of God."

> Deut. 4:34-35: "…did God ever try to go and take for Himself a nation from the midst of another nation, by trials, by signs, by wonders, by war, by a mighty hand and an outstretched arm, and by great terrors, according to all that the Lord your God did for you in Egypt before your eyes? To you it was shown, that you might know that the Lord Himself is God; there is none other besides Him."

> Psalm 77:14 "You are the God who does wonders; You have declared Your strength among the peoples."

> Acts 2:22-24: "Men of Israel, hear these words: Jesus of Nazareth, a Man attested by God to you by miracles, wonders, and signs which God did through Him in your midst, as you yourselves also know— Him, being delivered by the determined purpose and foreknowledge of God, you have taken by lawless hands, have crucified, and put to death; whom God raised up, having loosed the pains of death, because it was not possible that He should be held by it."

Indeed, I have come to fully accept that faith grows best when planted in the soil of proof. I have faith—complete confidence—that my parents love me because they have proven it. Likewise, God has given us every reason to trust Him and to be confident that He exists and that He loves us, and yet some people still don't trust Him. I'm not promoting a "faith because…" mentality, but rather the idea that the kind of faith the Bible is talking about isn't the same as believing in fairies or in Santa Claus. God isn't real because I believe in Him, nor does He obscure Himself just to test me. God is real. He has expressed Himself in creation, and the evidence is overwhelming. Some people refuse to believe the evidence and they live their lives in darkness. They have blinded themselves. But the light is all around us, overwhelming us, infusing us with His glory. We need to believe what actually is instead of running away. Believe in God—there is no doubt that He exists. And when you believe, the universe opens up: you see the universe for what it really means—it points to God.

And that is why what I should have said to my boss' dad all those years ago was "God became flesh in order to prove that the invisible God exists and to show us what He is like." As Jesus put it, "He who has seen Me, has seen the Father" (John 14:9b). God wants people to have confidence that He is not a fantasy. He wants us to know beyond a shadow of a doubt that He loves us and that His word is true.

I should have told him, "Jesus is the empirical evidence you are looking for."

The historical record of Scripture, therefore, is vitally important to our understanding of the universe as well as why death exists. It records God's activity and that is why, in my opinion, its claims are constantly under attack. If its history is true, then its claims about God, life and death are true; if it isn't true, then any other belief system could possibly be true. Some say that if one wants to believe in a god, that's fine, but don't try to define that god. And if we don't want to believe in a god, that's fine, too. Who can really know?

But if Scripture is an accurate record of history, those kind of open-ended belief systems must be closed. No longer can people say, "I'll just wait and see who is right and then decide which side I'm on." God has informed us and has demonstrated His credibility, and that is the aggravating thing about Scripture: it forces a decision.

The Red Sea crossing? Bogus, or much less than the exaggerated version in the Bible.

Manna from heaven? Just lucky coincidence.

The sun standing still?

A great fish swallowing a man? Sounds like Pinocchio.

A man rising from the dead? A nice story, but lots of myths have utilized that theme without requiring it to have actually happened.

A good God? An all powerful God? We wish He were, but just look around at this planet and tell me again that God is good when He won't even stop a disaster. Just try and tell me He's all powerful when He can't even stop an earthquake from killing thousands of people.

A creator God who made all things rapidly and functionally complete? Seriously, who believes that anymore?

These appear to be pretty powerful counter-claims. They create a gulping sensation and a stuttering response from most of us, even me as I'm sitting here writing this. But, like I said in the introduction, these questions are not merely intellectual curiosities. They are, at their root, questions which arise from an emotional need for a sensible answer; something that will explain this world around us. We need answers, and although I'm not going to address all of the above attacks in this book (although I will in my blog), I want to lay out what Scripture actually says about death. We will get to the proofs later, but, for now, I would like to bring the Bible's message into focus, even if you don't believe that message. Let's sit down in the optometrist's chair and click through all the lenses until God's message becomes clear.

# The Ballad of Salvation

Flow into me sacred muse,
My soul thirsts—
Holy Spirit—
My cry, do not refuse.
Awaken me!
Open my eyes,
Reveal the truth
Behind my sightless lies.

Sing to me!
I need to understand
The song of ages,
The ballad of salvation.

Recite to me
Our shattered ~
   Rhyme.

We need to know
   why
Our hearts engulfed with countless fears;
   why
Our world engorged with sin's repast,
Flesh's carnal feast?

Why is Death consuming us?

The mystery of the grave haunts our days,
   But we perfume our corpses,

And we layer gore upon the face of death,
   As rouge.

Why?

Arise now Holy Spirit:
   Speak.
The expanse of time is known only to thee—
   All of our crimes,
   All of our disease,
   All of our bloody, endless violence.

We are not god enough to be free of your voice,
We need your answer,
   —desperately—
Why this companionship of death?

_____

*Threats will not avail,*
*But even so,*
*I will choose to disclose*
*The source of all your sorrow.*

*Upon you water will I pour,*
   *though it drown;*
*On you a light will I shine,*
   *though it blind;*
*To you a song will I sing,*
*Though you may sigh in grief.*

*Indeed, you stand upon a treacherous ledge,*
      *Terrifying,*
*High above a misty chasm.*
*And to you the bottom is as hidden*
*As your minds are shrouded.*

*You clutch desperately to cracks and protrusions,*
*Hoping not to fall,*
*The height staggering,*
*The edge—alluring.*

*The edge.*
*It tempts your soul though you resist;*
*You glance, and then you step—*

*And from the first agonizing knowledge of freedom*
*   you enslave yourself to passion;*
*   you smell the perfume of a thousand breathless*
*nights,*
*Always hoping for more,*
*   Undaunted*
*Even as your moans turn to screams of horror.*
*The steam of destruction rises*
*above the cone of the volcano,*
*But you step*
*   Anyway.*
*      Gladly.*

*Are you sure you want to know?*
*About the pulse and throb and longings*
*   Of the human heart?*

———————

Speak, though my soul may come to grief. I must know.


## In the Beginning

God is our Creator. He created all things with the precision of an architect, the common sense of a welder, and the heart of an artist. Everything that exists is designed to be intricately interrelated, a web of such slender filaments and delicate structure that a whisper can make it sing; a symphony of light and sound so infinitely small and immeasurably large, that it always defies what we think we know; a vast cosmos of discovery with a horizon that never ends. The greatest minds can explore it and wonder; but even the simplest can see its wonder.

The creator God always exists and will always exist, and He exists independent of the laws that govern our universe. He was before the laws because He is the Creator of those laws, but He is also the source of those laws for they are contained in Him and when He created, those laws became external to Him. He will forever be even after those laws will someday cease to be expressed in creation, but He will never cease. His substance is beyond our ability to define, for He is not confined to the laws He created. But He is not beyond our ability to know, because His creation is an expression of His character: He is order and compassion; justice and love; above us but among us. Our Maker. Our Friend.

In a searing appearance of light that brought order to the chaos, God spoke and the fundamental symmetry of our universe was born: light balancing darkness, day and night, light matter and dark matter. Light was at first a superheated, unified substance in which a nanosecond seemed an eternity. Then this indiscrete ocean of light that was everywhere, quickly cooled into discrete structures of photons, electrons, and protons; a vast invisible sea of radiation. There has never been a "beyond" because only that which is can be and chaos was vanquished when light invaded the darkness and became evening and morning, the first day.

From this original unified, symmetrical, alternating sea of light and dark, He then began separating off the first elements into above and below. Some elements would become terrestrial bodies; others would become celestial. But in between He knit the fabric of the cosmos, space itself—the heavens—weaving together the laws which would sustain and guide the future planets and stars through their paths.

Evening and morning, the second day.

Then He spun the lower, heavier elements into planets, including earth. The original, invisible elements—those infinitesimally small energy particles created on day two—rapidly coalesced into visible matter; structures of metal, rock, soil, air, and water. The lighter elements He trapped in the atmosphere, organizing, spinning, meshing, integrating them all into a stable ecosystem, setting the stage so that life could thrive.

And at this time, God formed the first man from the dust who beheld the arrival of life: fresh, wondrous, alive with musical sounds, ambrosial smells, and vibrant, fertile colors (see Development A "Irreconcilable Differences?" for a full defense of the idea that Adam was created on day three).

All things were formed to work individually but with unity; independently but with interdependence; and all things were necessary for all other things to function. And God had written into these original forms the instructions which told them what they would become and would remain: the trees, the flowers and all plant life were set in place, fully formed, and fully functional. Time could not exist without light and dark; the plants could not survive without air; air could not remain without plants. And a river ran through the midst of the garden, the earth being watered with a mist that ascended from out of the earth, setting the stage for what was yet to come—something even more wondrous.

Evening and morning, the third day.

Out of this underlying structure of the universe, the stars and galaxies were being rapidly fashioned and became visible in various stages, complete and operational, and the heavens became the measure of the elaborate waltz we call time: motion, distance, speed, days and years. Sirius and Orion; the Pleiades, the Mazzaroth; the Bear, the sun, the moon.

Evening and morning, the fourth day.

On earth, though, the garden bower framed the Divine Glory as Jehovah Elohim walked with Adam and showed him the beauty all around, explaining that all was his except for one tree, at which point, perhaps, a tear of pure light fell from Jehovah's eyes, knowing what would come. But what was a tear to Adam? He had awakened alone in the garden made for him and he was content; not aware yet of what he did not have.

Jehovah Elohim knew, though, that Adam was incomplete and that he needed a crown upon his head, a sustainer, his equal. So, He formed the birds which harmonized with the song of creation, exulting in concentus the joy of life. With wings they soared aloft—the Sparrow, the Finch, the Robin, and others more fair and wild—and they danced to their own melody. And yet they weren't suitable companions for Man. He also formed the creatures of the deep, but Adam knew them not.

Evening and morning, the fifth day.

On the sixth day, though, God put on display the unlimited extent of His creativity, and formed the behemoth, the lion, the wolf—and so many more—designing them with the mechanism for the potential varieties that they would become. Adam named each one according to their unique characteristics, but God knew that none of them were a suitable fit for him, and at the end of the day God knew what He had to do; what He had intended to do all along. He caused a deep sleep to fall upon Adam, and took from his rib a cell, added information to half, and completed from this new configuration the pinnacle of His creation: man and woman. Perfection. (For more on this, see Development B: "Adam's Rib")

Delighted with what He had done, He set man and woman over His creation, not as slaves, but as caretakers, beloved stewards, wise gardeners who enjoyed the simplicity of living. Unaware of death, without knowledge of evil, sinless in heart, mind, and body, conversant with animals and angels, friends of God walking freely throughout His creation, the beloved expression of His love and vision. They were one in heart and mind, this first man and first woman, and when God beheld them, He proclaimed that He was finished and said of all He saw, "It is very good."

## *The Fall*

Who knows how long Adam and Eve enjoyed this blissful existence. Some people have assumed that the fall happened immediately following the week of creation in spite of the fact that there is nothing in the text that implies that. Personally, I believe that it was years before Satan finally succeeded in deceiving Adam and Eve. Maybe it was a year, maybe fifty, but it certainly wasn't on day eight that the fall of mankind happened.

And yet, no matter how long it was, it was not long enough. Adam and Eve were walking in the midst of the garden when they came upon a serpent, which then pointed out to Eve that the forbidden tree was nearby and convinced her to taste its fruit. After she ate, death immediately began to course through her veins and the new sensation gave her intoxicating power, inspiring her to convince Adam to also taste and eat. After he did, they together knew evil and became ashamed—and fascinated. Good, by its loss, had become more clear, and now it had also become unattainable. Never could they have envisioned what the price of that knowledge would cost, what their crime would spawn, what misery the world would endure, what sorrow a man on a cross thousands of years hence would suffer in order to right the wrong they had chosen on that day.

Oh, they grieved, too, and they knew everything had changed for them—as when the adulterer gets caught—but they were now blind, defensive, naked. They tried to justify their actions, but only in their own eyes were they innocent. They couldn't see what they had done, or if they could, they could only suppress the guilt. But have pity on them. Who could have born the raw weight of such pain?

God, though, already had a plan in place in order to correct their crime. Freely they had chosen to enslave themselves to rebellion, but in due time He would pay for their crime Himself, and restore to them what they had given up so readily. To the serpent, God diminished his capacities; to Adam, He said work would constantly have challenges and to dust he would return; to Eve, He promised pain in childbirth, but He also foretold that a child of hers would make all things right. He would be the One who would conquer the serpent and reveal his lies. He would be the One to conquer death.

In anticipation of the fulfillment of that promise, they named their first son Cain, the Possessor (or redeemer), but he was not at all as they had expected him to be. After he murdered his younger brother, they exiled him to the wide world—as they had been from Eden—and they could only watch grimly as his descendants became increasingly defiant and ravaged the earth, the same earth they had been commissioned to care for.

But then another child was born to Eve, and they named him Compensation, Seth, and they thought he might become the promised son. I wonder when they realized it wasn't to be Seth, either. And I wonder what Eve thought as she grew older and the world became increasingly wicked and the reality of the fabulous enlightenment she had been promised by the serpent wasn't at all as it had been sold to her. It was as if she thought she was moving into a mansion, but it turned out to be a prison. And I wonder what they thought just before their spirits left their bodies, which, now vacated, decayed into the dust as God had said they would. Did they despair in that final twinkling of an eye? Or were they confident that God would yet keep His promise and send the One who would vanquish the suffering they themselves had so carelessly unleashed upon the world?

# The Flood

So close to perfection, humankind once lived much longer lives than we do today, and the world was much different than we see, now. But, as a result, wickedness had a longer time to ferment in men's hearts and accountability seemed further away. Cruelty, murder, rape, depravity, injustice, insanity, corruption, war, tearing the flesh of brothers: all reigned on the earth in grim abundance—the same earth which God had made to be so different than what it had become. None of this was as it should be, and the further away men's hearts strayed from God, the more grief they caused. And the most bitter heartache of all came when men began to believe that God Himself was the One who had created the violence; that He had made us to be brutal; that He actually wanted it to be this way.

For any of us, watching the hardening of a person's heart is a difficult thing to witness because there comes a time when nothing can soften that heart: it can only be broken. God became grieved at our sin and He knew that mankind would soon become permanently lost if He didn't do anything. We would become completely unredeemable and when that moment came, His creation would forever be adrift and His enemy would have won. He saw that what He had originally created—intricate functionality and moral purity—was now awash in blood, violence, and corruption. He did not design or desire this agony, but He bore it patiently and pleaded with us to return. He watched and waited for our hearts to remember Eden, but we didn't—or wouldn't. He withheld His wrath for nearly two thousand years, but when there was only one man left in all the earth who would yet believe, He finally had to act.

Noah found favor in the eyes of the Lord, and God chose him to preserve the human race and the animals which would come aboard the Ark. Noah could have disobeyed and the world would have been lost, but he did obey and the seed of God's promise was saved from destruction. It is a grievous reality, the Flood, but God had to end the unrestrained injustice on earth, didn't He? If God is love, then sin must be dealt with, doesn't it? Wouldn't He be an evil God if He allowed the world to be governed by murderers and slave-owners? Wouldn't He be evil if He didn't punish such barbarity?

His heart is crushed by the atrocities of mankind. Aren't you appalled by the slaughter of innocent children? Aren't you enraged when you see images of the emaciated corpses of the holocaust? Aren't you bitter because of racial injustice? Aren't you infuriated at the rape and exploitation of women to sate the lust of monstrous men? If you are, then you understand the heart of God. Do you want these things to end? Do you want God to do something about them? Well, then, you can't complain when God does do something about them. God saw that these bestial behaviors had completely saturated mankind and we were only evil continually. How could He allow such horrors to continue and still be good?

We want justice, and He stopped a reign of terror. Shall we blame Him? He stood in the gap; He vanquished the decaying, rank deeds of the once divine image. In no way were mankind's actions His actions, and the only way to keep alive the promise to restore us to our former glory was for God to restrain the tide of evil that was then overwhelming the earth.

And so, when the destruction began and the windows of heaven were shattered and the fountains of the deep were broken open, God's wrath was poured out upon the unrighteousness of mankind, and His justice was shown to be inescapable—who could stop His hand?—and it was only His mercy that saved Noah and his family.

And one might think that Noah's descendants would remember God's wrath and listen to Him. Right?

## The Tower

Even after a year spent on the Ark; after the sacrifice; after the promise that God would never again destroy the earth with a flood; and after the command to multiply and spread out over the geographically reconfigured earth; the struggle against sin still raged—that invisible passenger who had stowed away in the hearts of mankind. Ham sinned against his father—who happened to be passed-out drunk—and after Noah sobered up, he then blessed Japheth and Shem, but cursed Ham.

Unwilling family, though, to obey God, and instead of exploring the earth as they were commanded, they decided to build a capital city from which to rule the earth. They established themselves in the land of Shinar, and they built a temple to honor the false gods which they had worshipped before the Great Flood, intending to unite everyone in their misdirected worship. But why worship the sun, the earth, the sky, and the ocean? The gods are merely the created, not the creator, and they are subject to the will of the Almighty, not Him to them. What honor should they receive from us, the ones whom they seek to enslave? They serve the serpent, not Jehovah Elohim, and they lead us only into sorrow. Did Noah's sons so quickly forget the Flood? Maybe they dismissed it as merely natural. Maybe they thought the gods were insane (*Gilgamesh*).

But God promised not to destroy mankind again by a flood, and so He chose to weaken us by dividing us, and His punishment was for the inhabitants of Babel to speak different languages. Unable to work together anymore, each group finally did what God had originally intended: they spread out over the earth. And what challenges they faced! Bitter cold, soaring mountain ranges, raging rivers, and searing heat, unlike anything they had ever seen before. The world was vastly different. So Ham took his family to the south and eventually to the east; Japheth took his to the north, and eventually to the west; and Shem remained in the choice, well-watered plains where they had first settled.

Agriculture began to spread, cities arose, god-kings were anointed, and wars were started. New languages were set down in writing while some people lived primitively in caves and rough shelters, and their adaptation to the new, unstable climate was difficult. But mankind kept moving, surviving, and exploring. It was a new era. For those who found the choice land first, they became the great civilizations we study today.

## The Patriarchs

The folly of mankind runs deeply in our hearts, though, and always with us we nurture the serpent's lie. Our forefathers continued to worship the false gods, and those demonic forces continued to actively influence human events. Humanity persisted in trying to appease these beings instead of rejecting them, making images to honor them. They were trapped in an endless cycle of trying to explain what had been with what they currently knew, and they had forgotten their Creator who used to walk with mankind in the Garden.

But as the memory of Jehovah Elohim grew dim, He again spoke into the heart of one man, and chose Abram to be the father of a people to whom He would reveal Himself.

"You will be the father of many nations, kings will come from you, and I will give you and your descendants this land, from the river of Egypt to the river Euphrates, and from you a child, a son, will be born who will bless all the nations" (Gen. 12, 15, 17; Gal. 3:8).

Abram, though, became impatient because his wife, Sarai, was barren. So he had a child by another woman hoping to fulfill God's promise himself, but as a result he set in motion a conflict that would cause turmoil for the rest of history. Abram's name was eventually changed to

Abraham, and the child of God's promise, Isaac, was finally born. He would keep the line of the Savior alive. But his older brother Ishmael—who was a wild donkey of a man whose hand would be against everyone, and everyone's hand would be against him—would also be blessed by God, and his descendants would be many. To this day, Isaac, Ishmael, and all of his other children by Keturah, rule the land "from the river of Egypt to the river Euphrates," God had promised to Abraham.

Isaac, however, was not the fulfillment of the promised redeemer. He married Rebekah and they had twin boys, Esau the eldest, and Jacob, who usurped the promise from his brother. Jacob was later renamed Israel after wrestling with God, and he had twelve sons and a daughter by four different women: two wives, Rachel and Leah, and two maidservants. The son he truly loved, though, was born of the only wife he had ever wanted, Rachel.

Joseph was the favored son of Jacob, even though he wasn't the oldest, and his father groomed him to become the heir of all their property. However, his brothers became jealous and in the spirit of Cain, at the opportune time, the elder brothers sold him into slavery thinking they would never hear from him again. But when a great famine devastated Canaan, they had to go to Egypt to get the grain they needed and there they were reunited with their brother. Joseph went through many trials of faith after they sold him into slavery, but God was with him and blessed him, giving him a wife, two sons, and charge over all of Egypt second only to Pharaoh. When his brothers arrived he restrained his wrath, forgave them, and they were reconciled to each other.

His actions are a model of God's love for us, an example of the kind of savior God promised He would send: one who wants his children to return to Him; one who wants us to remember Eden. Jacob soon moved to Egypt where he was given the most fertile land, and there he died, content. And Joseph, the temporary savior, also died, although the promise did not.

## *Moses*

Years before, God had told Abraham in a vision that his descendants would become slaves in Egypt, and that prediction came true. God also foretold that they would someday return to the land He had promised—almost five hundred years later—and that God would have to perform many wonders to get everyone back.

So, in spite of the Pharaoh's command to slaughter all of the Hebrew male babies, Moses was saved and was raised in the palace of the Pharaoh himself where he spent the first forty years of his life living as an Egyptian. He learned their language, their religion, their engineering techniques, and their political structures. For decades he ruled as one of them over his own people, but whether he knew he was a Hebrew is not important. What's important is that for years he allowed their enslavement, oversaw their hard labor, and then chose to end it. Hebrews 11:24-26 explains:

> By faith Moses, when he had grown up, refused to be known as the son of Pharaoh's daughter. He chose to be mistreated along with the people of God rather than to enjoy the pleasures of sin for a short time. He regarded disgrace for the sake of Christ as of greater value than the treasures of Egypt, because he was looking ahead to his reward.

In his first attempt to free the Hebrew people, he murdered an Egyptian who had been beating a slave, but the Hebrews turned him in because they didn't trust him. An utter failure, Moses fled to the land of Midian that is in modern day Saudi Arabia, and became an exile from all he had known, rejected by the Egyptians and his own people.

He started a new life in Midian, which was far different than the luxuries Egypt had provided him. He got married, had two sons, and lived the simple life of a shepherd. Apparently he was content to grow old and let his life come to a peaceful end. But God now saw a humbled man; a man groomed by trials who could now be the savior of His people. And so He called him to go back to Egypt and free the Hebrews from bondage. He had heard their cries against injustice and Moses reluctantly returned almost forty years after he had fled. He then confronted the new Pharaoh with wonders which proved that God was above all gods. He then led God's people back to the mountain in Midian where God had originally spoken to him from the burning bush. They returned to Mt. Sinai.

But this time God did something even more amazing than the burning bush, the plagues, and the Red Sea combined: He engraved in stone ten laws which would endure throughout time as the standard for how mankind should relate to God and to each other. What we once had known in our hearts in Eden, He now had to define so that our sin would not define Him. There was much to say, and for two years God visited Moses on the mountain and in the tabernacle, imparting to him His word. Moses wrote it down so that future generations would not forget again that the God who had created us—the God who had walked with us in the Garden—still loved us.

### *The Promised Land*

After two years at Mt. Sinai, Moses then led God's people to the Promised Land and he was ready to establish Israel as a nation in the land of Abraham, Isaac, and Jacob. They had finally come back after their long exile, and God had kept His promise to Abraham. But the people were filled with fear and they doubted whether their rag-tag group of former slaves could ever conquer established cities. Stubborn folk who would doubt the God who had parted the Red Sea and freed them from the greatest civilization on earth, but they did and God's punishment for them was to let them die off in the wilderness. They wandered for forty years, and Moses became a bitter, angry old man who had grown tired of the lack of faith these stubborn people portrayed. Even he, in a fit of rage, disobeyed God and then God, ever impartial, told Moses—even Moses!—that he would never enter the Promised Land. When it was time, Moses appointed Joshua to become the leader, and he wandered into the hills east of the Jordan where he could see the Promised Land but never enter. And there Moses died with no memorial.

But now Joshua was ready, for he had wandered with the people all those years in the wilderness, and had seen God's wrath on those who pursued their former gods, and he had also seen God's power in defeating His enemies. Joshua knew what God could do, and so did the younger generation. They were eager to settle down and form a nation governed by the laws of God, not of man, and to become a light of justice in a world which was abandoning justice. As a nation, they were supposed to represent God's compassion and justice; His mercy and judgment. But the Canaanites were not little, innocent, peasant farmers minding their own ways. They worshipped false gods and sacrificed some of their children in fire to appease those gods. They also lived lives of unfettered immorality—if only they could see the innocence and the beauty God had founded in the Garden. If only they could remember what God had intended mankind to be. Maybe they would see how fallen their ways had become. But, just as in the age before the Flood, people's hearts had become completely blind to God's intended design for humanity, and their judgment came.

First Jericho, and all the central and southern parts of Canaan fell. They then went back up the Jordan River valley and took the northern region, conquering all and making treaties with some. Joshua then divided the land amongst the twelve tribes of Israel—Joseph's descendants getting a double portion—and he told them that they had a choice to serve the Lord or the gods of the land. There has always been a choice.

## *The Time of the Judges*

The governing document of this new nation was God's law, and it uniquely does not establish a kingship nor a god-pharaoh to rule over the them. Instead it establishes a judge who would adjudicate the law, and who was supposed to keep the people in tune with God's law. In fact, God warns against having an earthly king, because a king will always become an oppressor and take away our freedoms. He'll take more land, raise taxes, and take our children off to fight his wars. God tells His people to govern themselves, united by a commitment to follow His laws. If they did, they would be blessed, free, and remain in the land. But if they didn't, they would be cursed, enslaved, and lose the land.

For this new nation, God wanted to set apart for Himself a people whose devotion would be directed towards Him alone, not toward a mere king. They were to be a people governed by His law, not by cult personalities. They were to be a people of justice, not injustice; of equity, not inequality. They were to show compassion to widows and orphans, and they were to be enemies of proud, lawless tyrants. They were to be God's hand on earth, a national Eden where the image of God—what mankind was meant to be—was properly on display. And they were to illustrate God's character.

But within a generation they walked away…

And then they returned…

And then they walked away…
And then they returned…
And then they walked away….

After three centuries of perpetually facing cruel enemies, it was clear that obstinacy was entrenched in their heart and they became fed up with the way things were going.

---

*They were to show compassion to widows and orphans, and they were to be enemies of proud, lawless tyrants.*

---

However, instead of accepting blame for their rebellious natures they blamed God and their system of government, and they told the final judge, Samuel, to anoint a king for them so that they would be a "normal" nation, just like all the rest. Sadly, that's just what happened. Sometimes God gives us what we want in order to teach us a lesson.

### The Kings

Saul was their first king, who combined movie star good looks with sports star morality. He turned against God at every chance he had, but he found out that even a king wasn't above the law. God's law still hovered above him, ever-present, judging the actions of kings, not vice-versa, and holding arrogance accountable. Therefore, God had Samuel anoint another king, one who would exemplify what a heart for God should look like.

David was able to slay men twice his size and he conquered nations that had been a thorn in the flesh of Israel for generations. He cleared out from the land the enemies of God's people and he established Jerusalem as its capital.

But David, like Saul, found out that no one is above God's law, and he, and the nation, paid dearly for his sins.

Nevertheless, David repented and it was on his heart to build a temple for God. The Israelites had been using a tent, the tabernacle, since the days of Moses, but David was told that he wouldn't be allowed to build God's House since he was a man of war. Instead, a son of his would build it. That son, Solomon (David's second child by Bathsheba who was now one of his wives) would reign over the glory days of Israel. His wisdom and wealth were renowned throughout the world, along with his legendary promiscuity, and despite his unparalleled wisdom he illustrated that the wisdom of man can only lead to foolishness, vanity, and emptiness.

Solomon died in rebellion to God, and after his passing the nation became embroiled in a civil war. Too many children were running around wanting to be king, and ten of the tribes broke off from two: Judah and Benjamin. The others sought to set up their own temple and their own variation of worshipping God. However, not a single king ever truly "got it," and it was to the northern tribes that God first fulfilled His promise that He would remove them from the land if they disobeyed. The northern kingdom of Israel was completely wiped out by the Assyrians and carried off to a foreign land. The southern two tribes survived for a while longer, but within a hundred years they became a conquered people and Solomon's temple was looted and burnt to the ground by Nebuchadnezzar. Although the prophets had foretold this coming destruction and God's law had warned His people of the consequences of their choices, why hadn't they listened?

Maybe they, too, had forgotten Eden.

Eventually they returned to the land, humbled and greatly weakened, but their devotion to God and His law had become stronger. Daniel did not forsake God during the exile in Babylon, and Ezra and Nehemiah not only reintroduced God's law to the people, they exemplified obedience to it. God's temple was rebuilt and the refortification of Jerusalem was accomplished, and it was Ezra who organized the history of God's people into what we call the Old Testament. He gathered together all of Moses' writings and the records which had been kept by the priests and the prophets for a thousand years, and put it all together into a single book so that Israel would not forget that mankind had been born in Eden, and that we were now wandering in the wilderness.

That is the story of the Old Testament, which teaches that mankind was designed without sin, but was nevertheless allowed the potential to sin. Adam and Eve rebelled, but God immediately promised a redeemer.

In the New Testament (which we will explore more in the fourth movement), is the record of the arrival of that redeemer, His work on earth, and the promise of His eventual return to finally make all things right.

It's a tragic but inspiring story, isn't it? It is one of loss and redemption; one of losing our way and being brought back; one of grief, pain, joy, warfare, and peace; one of punishment and forgiveness.

But is any of it true?

There is a completely different history of the world (and a completely different understanding of death) being promoted as if it were true, so we need to know:

Is there any tangible evidence to verify the Bible's record of history, and, consequently, a confirmation that death is our enemy?

Oh yes, and the evidence is overwhelmingly abundant.

# End of the First Movement

*INTERLUDE*

# BEYOND ADAM

The following is an adaptation of the first Section in Jack London's novel "Before Adam." London, the ultimate Naturalist, writes about a modern man's nightmare of being an ape-man in the distant past. In my version, I write about a man's dream of what perfect humanity was meant to be. You can read his book online for comparison at http://london't.sonoma.edu/

P ictures! Pictures! Pictures! Ever have I wondered from whence came the multitude of stunning pictures that have thronged my dreams. They were not dreams about wake-a-day things that I would see in real life, but rather a procession of beautiful visions that would later convince me that I was the same as all the rest of my kind, a creature blessed but also cursed.

In my days only would I find any measure of reality, of sadness. My nights marked the reign of joy—and such joy! I make bold to state that no man of all the men who walk the earth with me ever have experienced such joy of like kind. For my joy is the joy of long ago, the joy that was vibrant in the First World, and in the youth of the First World. In short, the joy that reigned supreme in that period that was called The Garden of Eden.

What do I mean? I see explanation is necessary before I can tell you of the substance of my dreams. Otherwise, little would you envision the meaning of the things I know so well, but, indeed, you know all these things, and of these joys I will only remind you. As I write this, all the happenings of that other world rise up before me in a vast kaleidoscope, and to you they would be filled with rhyme and reason if you were to see them as I do.

Can you recall the pure companionship of Eve, the warm playfulness of Lion, the kindness and cunning of Fox? Can you feel the screaming craving for all these things you know you should have had, and so much more, but don't? Have you ever felt the grasses and sensuous mosses that paved the earth with their softness, and tasted the succulent fruits sweet in your mouth? In your own dreams you know these exist, but here they don't.

Perhaps it would be better, I dare say, for us to make our approach differently to these matters—so you will remember—and for us to revisit my childhood. As a boy I was very like other boys—in my waking hours. It was in my sleep that I was different. From my earliest recollections sleep was a period of joy. Never were my dreams tinctured with terror. As a rule, they were stuffed with joy—and with a joy so strange to me that on this side of my dreams it had no equivalent qualities. It was of a quality and kind that transcended all my waking experiences.

For instance, I was a city boy, a country child, rather, who lived in the city. My grandpa was a dairy farmer and we would occasionally visit, and when we left and returned to the city—the sprawling, black and grey metropolis—I would always long for the country. So I was not surprised, still later on in my life, to recognize, instantly, the feeling of dreaming about someplace to which I longed to return. To places that were green and fresh and wholesome.

Well do I remember the spruce trees, and the groves of alder that lined the banks of Hall's slough. And when I saw these again in my dreams, I could feel the joy they had brought to me in life, and I remembered joy. I would see them every night, in my sleep.

Even in my childhood, I knew from whence blackberries and blueberries came. The grocer sold them, but I had picked them myself from thorny vines and rows of cultivated bushes. I knew nature had actually produced them and that these were the links between reality and my dreams. I walked the dark halls of my outer world, but somehow I lived both lives.

Snakes? My grandma was terrified of them and I had practically hunted them to extinction around her house, my cousin and I. They, therefore, held no personal terror for me, but they did invade my dreams at times and I have always felt wary of them, concerned, bothered, cautious. They lurked in the forest glades and squirmed off through the tall grass or across bald streams of graveled road. They were old friends of mine, rather enemies, that would also visit me in my dreams. But they never became horrific, until later.

Ah, those endless forests on my grandparent's property and their glorious, alluring mysteries. For what eternities I wandered through them, searching, exploring, rejoicing at every new discovery, delighting, keyed-up, ever alert and vigilant, ready on the instant to marvel. I was the caretaker of every manner of thriving life that dwelt in that forest, and it was in ecstasies of joy that I found every new creature, frog and leaf.

I cannot remember how old I was when I first went to my grandparents farm, but as I grew up, every year the anticipation made me sick. When we would approach the road named after my mother's family, let me tell you, we, my sister and I, would look for the white arched bridge that told us so clearly that we were near. We would almost scream with expectation: who saw it first? I did! No you didn't, I did! Our arguing cheered me with assurances of pending glory.

Nevertheless, it was with joy and trembling, and with much hopefulness, that at last we would approach my grandparent's house. Ah, I knew it on the instant. The green! The white fence surrounding the front lawn. And on my inner vision flashed images that would be cemented in my dreams for the rest of my life: the midday sun shining on all the meadow grass, the domestic bull—sometimes dangerous—grazing quietly, the cows flung across the pasture like spices dropped on the kitchen floor, the crunch, crunch of walking on the gravel road, the great full-throated roar of the tractor firing up, the smells, the sounds, the life!

But at the sight of the house, glorious, nestled on the green lawn, and behind it the expanse of fields and trees and sky—the house my grandfather built with his own hands—we would dance up and down in our hearts and rush out of the camper hoping grandma and grandpa had seen us arrive. Our minds in that moment were filled with the joy of the First Days, of which we only see shadows now. Eden.

My parents didn't know my childlike joy. My mom had grown up here and she had left, but I developed a love for this quality of life, this semi-disassociation with the life I normally lived, this invasion of my real world by this other life that became my dreams. From anywhere I could once again nestle into the warm, heavy blankets of the East room's bed, and see.

I have mentioned that these things need an explanation, for normally when I share these visions with others, I am ridiculed for my feeble fancies. "I don't know too much about that," they say. And the more I say, the more they laugh. I swear in all earnestness that Eden is real and not this world, and they begin to look at me oddly. Then rumors fly until all look at me as if I am from another planet.

It is a bitter experience, but in another sense it is true: I am not here. I am the same as every man, but different, too. The telling of my dreams, I know, creates misunderstandings, but I cannot keep quiet. I know that my dreams are of Real things—as real as life itself but not limited by vapors and fleeting shadows. And it isn't the other world that alone is Real: it is both worlds synthesized because they should not be separate, and I want people to remember. I believe you know it. The Reality of reality.

Remember Eden.

For me no greater joy exists except what I see in my dreams. The leaves, the green forests fed by living waters, the deer in meadows and the wild geese overhead—these are the joys concrete and actual, happenings and not imaginings, things of the living flesh that inform my dreams, that made their bed with me throughout my childhood, and that still bed with me, now, as I write this, making me hope for what we should have been.

**Grandma and Grandpa's House**

# Movement Two

## Eden

…then the Lord God formed the man of dust from the ground and breathed into his nostrils the breath of life, and the man became a living creature. And the Lord God planted a garden in Eden, in the east, and there he put the man whom he had formed. And out of the ground the Lord God made to spring up every tree that is pleasant to the sight and good for food. The tree of life was in the midst of the garden, and the tree of the knowledge of good and evil.

Genesis 2:7-9

# FIREWEED

Fires quickly consumed the dry undergrowth. Flames raged across the horizon, lighting up the night sky with a red fury, dancing on the treetops in boastful victory. Firefighters fought helplessly; reporters sought for someone to blame; tears were shed; rangers tried to explain. On the worst single day, high winds pushed the fire across more than 150,000 acres. In the end, 1.2 million acres burned in the Greater Yellowstone region—about 793,000 acres were in the park itself—and more than 25,000 firefighters were involved at the cost of $120 million dollars and two lives. Amazingly, surveys found only 345 dead elk out of an estimated 40,000 to 50,000 (7 hundredths of 1 percent). The other casualties were thirty-six deer, twelve moose, six black bears, and nine bison.

People were outraged! Fire policies were reconsidered. Old Faithful was intact and tourists still came, but there was sadness and a lingering sense of "What could have been done?" Subconsciously, probably what irritated people the most was that here was the world's oldest national park, set apart to be preserved for all posterity, diligently monitored, cared for, treasured, and yet almost half of it had been destroyed by natural forces. Couldn't we have done something about it? Isn't this the result of that stupid let-it-burn policy on the heels of that don't-let-it-burn policy?

Experts searched endlessly for ways to place the blame on somebody, but the reality became apparent that it had simply been an extremely dry and windy summer and most of the fires had been put out. In the final tally, it had only been seven fires (out of fifty) which became the source of the primary devastation and of those, five had started outside the park. Firefighters had done all they could. There really was no one to blame.

It's a tough reality, but sometimes we just have to accept that we aren't in control as much as we would like to think.

It was ten years after the death of Tierre when I decided to take Faye on a trip to Yellowstone because I wanted her to learn about geysers. I was a teacher now and I had summers to spend with Faye exploring our world. She had learned about volcanoes at Mt. St. Helens several years earlier, but when I told her about geysers she called them glaciers. Big difference. So we went to Yellowstone. But as we visited the different sites and learned all about geysers, one event kept coming up that I had not thought much about for years: the fire of 1988.

Tierre and I had been married in 1990, and it was just a couple of months into our marriage when we moved to Spokane from Sedona so I could continue my training in youth ministry. Although Yellowstone was a little out of journey's way and a little beyond budget, we decided to visit anyway. I'm glad we did.

We got to see Old Faithful and several of the other geyser fields, but it was not what could be called a pretty park being only two years after the fire. The blackened snags and charred ground looked more like a campfire pit than a pristine wilderness. Yellowstone was interesting, but only in a sad, tragic sort of way.

But when Faye and I visited in 2002, I was astounded by the changes I saw. I clearly remembered the burnt snags, but now a stunning forest adorned the hillsides. Animals abounded, lush foliage flourished, soothing vistas of green surrounded us, and all with the added bonus of the geysers, dramatic and colorful. Some of its old splendor had returned (although the trees were still small) and the miracle of regeneration testified to the durability of life.

Fascinated, I watched every video shown of the fire and how the forest had recovered. We learned a lot, but a single fact kept being highlighted: all the data had been gathered in 1998, ten years after the fire.

Ten years—

It was now, for me, ten years since my wife had lain pregnant in her hospital bed, resting patiently, sacrificially, for the survival of our child.

Ten years ago—

It seemed so distant; a different lifetime.

Ten years—

How did my life compare to Yellowstone ten years after my devastating fire?

I looked at Faye. She astonished me. She liked to play in the sprinkler; she got all A's in the third grade; she woke up grumpy, whined and complained like any other child her age. How could such a magnificent blessing have been born out of such a ruinous tragedy?

Sometimes an insight drops gently into our hearts, and while in Yellowstone I received a blessed glimpse into God's ways. What we learned from the videos is that the recovery all started with a small, purple wildflower called Fireweed, which is most prolific immediately following a fire. It is a deep-rooted plant, and although the above-ground part of the plant is burned during a fire, it easily sprouts from undamaged roots.

---

*It's a tough reality, but sometimes we just have to accept that we aren't in control as much as we would like to think.*

---

The disaster in my own life had burnt down my hopes and dreams and had smoldered for years, my tears unable to put the fire out. It was a tragedy I was unable to prevent and that I could not blame on anything. But the small blessings that came right afterwards—the Fireweed—God used to hold my life together. My Fireweed was the cards, the hugs, the prepared meals, the financial support, the places to stay, the tearful conversations; it was the friends who loved us, my family who cared, the moments I didn't spend alone in utter despair. To anyone else they might appear insignificant, but to me, in the midst of the smoking ruins, they allowed my life to grow strong once again. I may have lost my wife, but I was never truly alone.

Thank you to all of you!

# THE FIRST WORLD

"Then God saw everything that He had made, and indeed it was very good."

Genesis 1:21

In the First Garden—the Garden of Eden—humankind was given the greatest gift God could ever have given to us: life. But it was also there that the first lie was ever told, sin entered our world, and we were banished. Our passports to get back in were rejected, and this, I believe, is the source of all our anxiety and woe: we are exiles from the country of our deepest desires and we cannot return. The deepest longing of our hearts is for the green fields of home, but the border has been closed.

The first garden that I ever remember being totally captivated by was The Butchart Gardens in Victoria B.C. I had enjoyed wilderness experiences before, and I already loved backpacking and camping by jade-colored lakes, but this. This was something extraordinary. It was like being immersed in a pool of brightly colored gems, all glistening and filled with ideas. I wandered those gardens with my daughter Faye over a decade ago, but I can still smell its fragrance, hear its fountains, and see the vine-draped cliffs that once were the barren walls of a quarry. Even though God's creation is meant to be enjoyed and never worshiped, I came close to idolatry there, and I imagine that Eden was far more beautiful still.

And yet I look around at most of our world and I see vast wastelands of frigid ice, torrid deserts, and the evidence of ancient disasters the likes of which would make us think Katrina was an April shower. I see a world that is far from perfect and even though I want to live forever, I'm not sure that this is the kind of world I would want to live forever on: it could kill me at any moment.

So, why did God proclaim that His creation was very good since it obviously isn't? How could He say that? When my wife died, it didn't feel "very good." When I see earthquakes wipe out entire cities, the first thing that comes to my mind isn't, "That's awesome! What a good God we have."

Yet, some people understand God and our world in such a way that they believe God designed our world with disasters, suffering, and death in order to test us. Therefore, since He is good, this must be good. One of the problems with such a view is that it contradicts the meaning of the word "good." Good means functional, not broken. It works. There isn't anything morally deficient or ineffective about it. It's pleasant, excellent, bountiful. It isn't out-of-whack, it's good. So, to imply that brokenness, suffering, disease, and death are necessary in order for the universe to function properly, isn't an idea I find in Scripture.

Another even more horrifying belief I reject is the idea that since nature is an expression of God, therefore God is the source of even these detestable things. This view makes God both good *and* evil. The difficulty with this view, in summary, is that just because God did allow the potential for evil to occur by giving Adam and Eve a choice, that doesn't mean He Himself would have to be evil. Evil is a deviation from the good, and the potential to disobey a law doesn't make the law itself an evil—in fact it reinforces that the law is indeed good (Romans 7:12-14). According to the Bible, evil is not necessary for the universe to function properly. We could have gotten along just fine without it.

So, then, if either of the above ideas were what the Bible taught, I would stop defending the Bible and switch all of my allegiance to Naturalism, which believes (among other things) that natural effects are only brought about by natural causes. For me, it would be much easier to blame the mistakes and flaws we see on the mindless laws of the universe, and to believe that mankind must pull ourselves up out of the muck, than to conclude some intelligent being intentionally made this mess. I am not an atheist, but I certainly understand its attraction. If God really did call good what we currently experience, then I, too, would have a problem with such a God. There are good things in it, but a god who would proclaim that starving little children was good, or that wars and pestilence were the signs of a first-class creation, would have to be discarded without a moment's hesitation no matter how much torture and pain He threatened me with. If that is God, no thanks.

However, that is not the kind of God I am defending, nor is that the kind of God Scripture is proclaiming. Scripture makes it abundantly clear that when God called His original creation very good, it was very good *before* the fall of Adam and Eve. What He spoke into existence was magnificent, without disharmony or disease. In other words, everything that humanity is horrified at in our world today was not present when God originally designed our world. It could function perfectly well without us dying, living in pain, or suffering. There was no deformity, no cancer, and *there was no need for these things*. A world like that is the kind of world He called good, and, incidentally, it is what we would call good, too.

But all that aside for the moment, what would God's original, very good world have been like? One in which death and suffering didn't reign? One in which the world was green, lush, and could sustain all varieties of life? Are there any clues left as to what that First World was like? The truth is, evidence abounds that the Bible's account of history is accurate, but we've been taught not to interpret the evidence that way. Truth isn't just facts, truth is the correct interpretation of those facts, and we are being lied to about the meaning of the evidence all around us. As Bonhoeffer explains, "To recognize the significant in the factual is wisdom" (*Ethics*, 71).

---

> *Everything that humanity is horrified at in our world today was not present when God originally designed our world.*

---

In order to see the truth about the origins of our world, though, we have to completely change the assumptions underneath our conclusions. False assumptions have been placed in our minds by the enemy like strategically placed land mines leading us to wrong conclusions, and our culture has conditioned us to think with evolutionary assumptions. They want us to put on evolutionary glasses, thinking that with those we will see the world clearly. But those taint our vision of the world and limit what we are able to see. As soon as I say, "The earth is young," everyone is conditioned to respond with: "You're an idiot! The earth was formed six billion years ago." If I say, "God created the animals quickly and with full functionality," the automatic answer is: "Really? Science has proven that all life evolved from a simple, common life form." If I say, "Death is a punishment for sin, not just a normal function of nature," people laugh in their sleeves and say, "How gullible."

Silly me.

Christians, then, who want to believe the Bible but who also want to be respected by the scientific community, have been maneuvered into accepting that Genesis 1 - 3 contains only spiritual truths, not actual history, and we are never supposed to question the consensus of the scientific community, right? Go tell that to Galileo.

I believe that the scientific community of today should be questioned on all fronts because they have become, ironically, the modern equivalent of the authoritative dispensers of truth that they opposed just a few centuries ago. They have made themselves into a priesthood that should never be questioned, and if you do, look out. How that mighty pendulum has swung!

So—dare I ask—what if evolution is wrong? What if its assumptions are mistaken? What if death is an aberration, not an assistant, to nature? What if the assumption called gradualism is not right, and catastrophism is? What if the belief that modern species have a common ancestor, isn't a correct one?

The truth (whatever the truth may be) has to be consistent with external evidence. And, also, the truth will help us make sense of facts, and it will never make absurd statements like, "There are absolutely no absolutes!" or "Be skeptical of everything (except being skeptical of being skeptical of everything)." The proper glasses (the correct assumptions) will put us on the path to understanding and enlightenment, and it is the Bible—contrary to popular opinion—that meets all the criteria for being truth, revealing truth, and opening our eyes to wonders beyond our conception. It makes sense of all the data and it is consistent with the evidence. It is truth. Jesus is the truth.

I'm hoping to untangle this mess in the following sections, recognizing that it is difficult to extricate oneself from the evolutionary narrative about this world's history. It is difficult to visualize what the Bible teaches because we've been told for so many years that evolution is true and the Bible is just a story. However, as we have already talked about, the Bible simply presents a different history of the world (and I believe a more accurate one) than what is popularly believed today, and Christians are unwittingly weakening the Bible when they try to make it fit the evolutionary model.

"But," some of you may be asking, "how is the debate about evolution and creation related to the topic of death? What does that have to do with answering the question of why death exists? And how will discussing evolution help me with my grief?"

Here's how this debate matters: if death is a necessary feature of the universe (as evolution requires), then there can be no cure for death. If death were absolutely necessary, then finding a cure would end the process of evolution, right? Death, for an evolutionist, must exist in order for life to exist. Death is therefore an inescapable, inevitable, necessary, and quite permanent event. There is no solution. My wife Tierre is dead and all the billions of people who have gone before her. That's it. Evolution champions this concept of death.

However, Scripture opposes this view of death and that is why I need to defend the veracity of Scripture. If Scripture is right, then death is not a necessary feature of the universe and there is a cure. Death can be conquered. Death, the enemy of life, is not as invincible as evolution requires, and the way things are is merely a temporary state of affairs. The Bible proclaims emphatically that death will someday be completely revoked. How could that be true if death is a necessary factor in creation?

So, instead of shying away from defending the Bible's version of events, Christians should be confident in the Bible's clear message: God wants to end death once and for all. That would certainly imply that He didn't create death in order to evolve us into the creatures we are now. He did things exactly as He told us He did it in the Bible, and all the evidence is on our side. We shouldn't cower in fear.

# *If Scripture is right, then death is not a necessary feature of the universe and there is a cure.*

I will even go so far as to say (and I know many will think I'm insane for saying this) that *all* the facts which evolutionists use to prove their point actually prove the Bible. I don't need to dig up new facts to make my case; I just need to look at the existing facts and they will confirm the Bible. As G.K. Chesterton says, "when I came to look at the facts, I always found they pointed to something else [than what I had been told they meant]" (*Orthodoxy*, 144). Evolutionists exude confidence in their theory, but as soon as I personally take a closer look at the evidence, I discover that the facts lead me to trust God and His word even more.

This sounds strange because the incessant water boarding of evolution has worn us down. We can no longer see the truth because we're tired of resisting. I know Christians who have thrown their hands up and surrendered saying, "Evolution is true and I have no problem with it." Sadly, we have been intimidated into confessing what is false and have forgotten who we are as human beings: death is an aberration and God is in the process of redeeming us from it. We have been misdirected and told not to even question the theory of evolution. They say they have the facts on their side, so let's look at the facts.

## Globally Warm

To start with, the geological record is clear that our world used to be a globally warm paradise. Plant life abounded, water was plentiful, and some of the animals were huge. Think of the movie *Jurassic Park* and envision our ancient world as that tropical island, only everywhere, much like the fourth moon of Endor in *Star Wars*. That's pretty difficult to imagine because our planet today is so different from what it used to be, but the fact remains that it was once a fabulous place to live and was filled with untold wonders.

For example, paleontologists have revealed that the Denver area was once a wet mangrove swamp on the shores of an ancient ocean. The Mile-High City hasn't always been a mile high. This explains why there are such large coal, oil, and natural gas deposits in the region, which are the remains of ancient forests and sea life which were buried under vast amounts of sedimentary rock, pressurized and super-heated. Fossilization occurs when a plant or animal is buried quickly (before decay can destroy it) in watery sentiments, and fossil fuels and fossilized animals are found everywhere on our planet. Everywhere. Indeed, if I could be so bold, coal, natural gas, and oil should be considered the original green energies.

If you were to go anywhere in the world—not just Denver—where the fossilized remains of large animals are found, you will find that those areas also used to be lush, green, watery climates. The evidence—the facts—are indisputable.

Underneath the Antarctic ice cap scientists have uncovered ancient forests in which eighty-foot trees used to grow in a year round warm climate, and they have found the fossils of several kinds of dinosaurs.

On the opposite side of the globe, an expedition to the Arctic Ocean in 2006 proved that the Arctic has not always been covered in ice, either.

> The first detailed analysis of an extraordinary climatic and biological record from the seabed near the North Pole shows that 55 million years ago the Arctic Ocean was much warmer than scientists imagined — a Floridian year-round

average of 74 degrees. (Nature 441, 610-613, 1 June 2006)

But not only were our frigid wastelands once green and lush, so were our deserts. Scientists have found that the Sahara Desert used to have a moderate climate that teemed with life and overflowed with life-giving water, and the fossils there are of the largest dinosaurs ever to roam the earth. If you doubt me, next time you go to a natural history museum, look at the artist's renditions of the world of dinosaurs. They are drawn living in lush rain forests or vast grasslands with plenty of food sources capable of sustaining such huge animals. Everyone knows our planet used to be far different than what we see it is today and that it used to be a globally tropical paradise and was very warm and moist compared to today's climate.

But—here's the crazy part—these facts contradict evolution, not the Bible. Evolution suggests that our planet used to be a barren, primitive rock and that the earth only gradually developed life. If that were true, then why does the fossil record prove that life was just as abundant in the past as it is today? Indeed, the further back in time we go, the *more* plentiful life is and the *more* sizable it is. The fact is that even simple life forms (such as protozoa and bacteria) have always been an essential component of our complex ecosystem. There is no reason inherent in the data to conclude that they were the *original* life forms from which every other life form evolved, or that they were the earliest life forms and existed before anything else did. The evidence indicates that these simple life forms have been around since the beginning, and that they've always been a necessary component of our complex ecosystem. There is no evidence of a primitive earth as evolutionists describe.

With that evidence in mind, though, consider how the Bible depicts the way the First World was: a global paradise. Our planet, according to the Bible, used to be a fabulous place to live and was filled with untold wonders.

God designed our First World to be perfectly functional; a world in which all the pieces would work together flawlessly. It was good. It was a world in which life would flourish. He formed marvels for mankind to investigate and to enjoy (Gen. 2:15), and we were supposed to be able to enjoy it for eternity. He filled it with magnificent creatures of all sizes and temperaments (Gen. 2:19), and it was lush and beautiful, wild and dangerous, reflecting the unlimited imagination and character of God. Just look at the animals that exist today in the sea, land, and air. We should be thrilled by the creative genius of God. The Birds of Paradise are unimaginably exotic and I can't believe that the Leafy Sea Dragon even exists. The squirrel and the gold fish are wondrous in their own way—although common. But now imagine a world that could sustain the dinosaurs and the Dodo bird and the soaring Pterodactyl. Astounding! Our God is a God of life.

The first world was a symphony of synchronicity designed to function flawlessly together, nothing exploiting the other and nothing needing more than what the other had to give. It was an intricate dance of unblemished patterns on a planet capable of sustaining large populations of fantastic and glamorous creatures; an unending well of wonder and delight; a botanical dreamland. *And our planet actually used to be this way.* The Bible informs us of what the world used to be like and the evidence supports that description.

## *Creation is a gift, not a god.*

But even better yet, according to the Bible, God set apart an ideal home, called Eden, for the first man and woman upon this First World. Food would have been easily accessible, and growing it would have been no problem at all. It would also have been exceptionally good. There would have been no weeds to deal with and it appears that

God's original design for our diet was vegetarian, perhaps even vegan, i.e. no animal products whatsoever. All of our nutritional needs were to be met without resorting to killing any other living creature so there would have been no hunting; no vast chicken or cattle farms; no slaughterhouses. We were designed to be gardeners and farmers who would enjoy the fruitfulness of the earth without concern for famine or plague. It would have been an idyllic pastoral setting; a communal, simple life that would make the most avid environmentalist drool. That is why it's sad to me that many cast aside God and His word so cavalierly and decide to worship creation instead of the Creator. Creation is a gift, not a god.

The world at-large, however, beyond the boundaries of Eden, would have been a wild, untamed earth that God wanted the descendants of Adam and Eve to eventually populate and subdue. By the way, "subdue" in this context doesn't mean to "exploit" and "destroy." It simply means "to bring order to" in its positive connotations, as how a gardener feels when gardening. God intended for us to be gardeners, explorers and adventurers. He intended for us to use His world for all of our creative endeavors, and maybe He even intended for us to eventually explore the stars, solving the problem of overpopulation.

The point is, that in spite of all the evidence that supports the Bible's depiction, we've been conditioned not to see it as evidence. The evolutionary model puts these conditions 65 — 250 million years ago during the Mesozoic Era (consisting of the Triassic, Jurassic, and Cretaceous periods when dinosaurs roamed the earth), and periodically throughout earlier eras, with continental plates drifting about like rafts. The biblical model, on the other hand, claims that a globally warm Earth is much more recent and that the reason our world looks the way it does now is because of a vast watery catastrophe we call the Great Flood which laid the rock layers down quickly, left us fossils to discover, and completely transformed the surface of our planet.

The difference between the biblical model and the evolutionary model, therefore, is not the facts: it's the interpretation of those facts. We all have rock layers, fossils, oil deposits, and nature to study. We all have evidence that nature is an elaborately interrelated construct. How we see the facts, though, is vastly different, and both theories can't be right.

## Gradualism vs. Catastrophism

To dig a little deeper, one must understand that the modern version of evolution is built on an assumption called gradualism, which teaches that the thick sedimentary layers we see today were laid down gradually over vast periods of time. If this were true, then the evolutionary timescale is right and sedimentary rock layers would represent millions of years. And since it is possible to measure the current rate of deposition of sediments in watery environs, and from that to calculate the age of the earth backwards, then the earth must be billions of years old. And if the continents have always drifted around at their current rate, then yes, it would have taken bazillions of years for them to have gotten to their current positions.

But what if this assumption is wrong? What if the current rates are just that: current? What if, instead, there have been times in earth's history when more sediment was present in the water because of catastrophic events? What if such events could have completely reshaped the surface of the earth, causing continents to sink and new ones to rise? Are we really not even supposed to discuss these possibilities?

To test the worldwide catastrophe hypothesis, we would have to examine recent catastrophes and consider their effects on the environment. If a local, small-scale catastrophe can completely alter the geology of an area, what would happen if such events happened on a global scale? For example, the 2011 earthquake off the coast of Japan was able to slightly shift the tilt of the earth, so certainly the kind of planet altering flood the Bible describes could have done the same thing.

The best example we have of what a catastrophe can do to a region is the Mt. St. Helens eruption of 1980. It proves that thick sedimentary layers can be laid down almost instantaneously and that canyons can be carved quickly. [1]

During that event, huge mud flows formed geological columns hundreds of feet thick with neatly sorted rock layers. This layering would have remained hidden, but a massive flow of water just a few weeks after the eruption cut through the recently deposited layers and formed a canyon that has similar features to the Grand Canyon (although on a much smaller scale). Thick layers of sedimentary rock were laid down quickly—it didn't take millions of years—and as a result the gradualistic assumption underlying evolutionary theory is no longer as trustworthy. I have good reason to doubt that rock layering requires millions of years, and I'm not willing to take the word of evolutionists that rock layering took millions of years. What can be tested and retested is more reliable than what cannot be tested, and evolutionary models *have not* been experimentally confirmed, nor can they ever be.

---

[1] "Mt. St. Helens: Modern Day Evidence for the World Wide Flood," by Dr. Steve Austin.

**Along the Tanner Trail, Grand Canyon**

On the other hand, catastrophism best explains what we see and it is the Bible (along with many other ancient texts and oral traditions) that records a vast catastrophe once reshaped the surface of the earth. Evolutionists have rearranged the data so that it doesn't appear to sync up with what the Bible claims, but that is the nature of the attack on scripture: to cause people to doubt the biblical time frames. Evolution needs bazillions of years to work and the geologic column, if it had formed gradually, gives them the time they need. A global, catastrophic flood, however, not only once devastated the earth, it currently devastates evolution, and that is why this debate is so heated and why I'm writing about it in this book: it influences our understanding of life and death.

Geologists like to tell us that the rocks tell a story, and I agree, but it is not a story of long eons, but rather one of catastrophe: how the original crust of the earth was ruptured by asteroids; the consequent expulsion of superheated magma; the collision of newly made continental plates; the thrusting up of mountain ranges and plateaus thousands of miles across; the destruction and burial of all plant and animal life on earth; the formation of basins miles deep; the rapid deposition of churned up, massive quantities of sediment; and the rapid cooling effects of water over everything, soothing the violent tremors of the fractured earth—these are all events which have happened to our earth, and they all happened as the result of one key event in earth's history: the Great Flood. It wasn't a little bit here and a little bit there, with hundreds of millions of years in between. It all happened at once, and the ripping, rending, and ramming forces necessary for making such geological features are obvious, but we've been told not to see them for what they clearly mean.[2] Christians, therefore, do not need to find new evidence in order to support the Bible: the evidence is all around us. This earth is exactly as the Bible describes: it was once a globally warm paradise, but it was decimated by a global flood.

---

[2] For a full discussion of this topic, please visit my blog at www.toconquerdeath.com.

# LIFE

"And the Lord God formed man of the dust of the ground, and breathed into his nostrils the breath of life; and man became a living being."

Genesis 2:7

One of the most toxic effects of evolution is that it has transformed our concept of death. No longer do we perceive ourselves as uniquely designed to nurture and take care of God's creation. Instead we are told that we are just very clever, highly evolved, successful, cruel, oppressive apes, and death is a necessity rather than a tragedy. Thuggish, brutish behaviors are simply accounted for as un-evolved aspects of our nature, and even though at one time such conduct was considered sinful and a corruption of God's image, now any such animalistic activities are considered a holdover from our animalistic origins. They're natural, and the belief in a God of any kind is considered un-evolved.

There is an exhibit at the Smithsonian's Natural History Museum in Washington DC, which puts on display the theoretical evolution of mankind. It's a nice summary of what evolutionists believe, but it comes across as if they have irrefutably proven evolution. They line up skulls of various shapes in the currently agreed upon lines of descent, and it all appears to be very scientific.

The problem is, it's complete fiction. The fossils exist, but the evolutionary lineages are not an accurate interpretation of the evidence. They have written an imaginary version of world history, packaged it nicely, and sold their interpretation to the public as reality. The hard truth, though, is that their story of our origins doesn't adequately explain the data. Evolution is flawed because it cannot explain how we came into existence and it cannot properly represent the essence of who we really are.

The Bible, on the other hand, declares that life is a gift from God. When He made Adam, He "breathed into his nostrils the breath of life; and man became a living soul" (Gen. 2:7). It isn't something that just accidentally sparked into being in a miry goo, then transformed into a zoo, and then into you. Life is a precious gift which was granted by God, because God Himself is life.

# The Origin of Life

The title Darwin chose for his book, *The Origin of Species*, misrepresents what his book is about. Far from explaining the origin of species, he intentionally avoids the question:

> We need not here consider how the bodies of
> some animals first became divided into a series of
> segments, or how they became divided into right
> and left sides, with corresponding organs, for such
> questions are almost beyond investigation.
> (*Species*, Kindle edition 7814)

For a book about the origin of all species, it is a stunning admission that how the features of animals first developed is "almost beyond investigation." What Darwin reveals is that his research was limited to exploring *fully functional existing life forms* and how the laws of development show up in modern animals and influence their ability to adapt. From these observations he extrapolates back that life has always followed those laws and that it makes sense to conclude that all life came from a single, common ancestor even though *it could never be observed*. What he meant by his title *The Origin of Species*, was that the laws of development he discovers led to the diversity of life we see. He wasn't actually trying to discover how life *originated*, as much as how it *diversified*. That is what he was clarifying in the above quote.

Lest anyone think I'm just throwing away Darwin's theory completely, though, I believe his starting point is based on an accurate observation: life is mutable. This was a revolutionary idea in his day because the dominant theory at the time was that species were immutable (which was a conclusion based on a mistaken interpretation of Genesis 1 and 2) and this created a dilemma for creationists: if God simply created a species, how come we find so many extinct species in the fossil record which are completely different from current species? What exactly did God create if species don't change? Darwin's contribution to science was that he observationally proved that the immutability of the species was a false idea and that species do adapt (some call this micro-evolution). This is a certainty. Darwin also demonstrated how survival of the fittest and natural selection influence adaptation (micro-evolution). And yet what I hope to demonstrate is that Darwin's findings, far from disproving Genesis 1 and 2, in fact lead to a deeper, more accurate understanding of what God did during the act of creation.

Darwin's extraordinary leap of faith comes when he tries to combine adaptability with the notion that all living creatures adapted from a single, common ancestor. He suggests that the small, micro-adaptations he observed in the natural world can gradually—if given enough time—transform a species into another species. He sought to prove this theory by explaining that laws such as growth, reproduction, inheritance, variability, and the competition for survival, all interact in such a way as to cause the divergence and improvement of an original, simple life form. These laws, according to his theory, collaborated to produce the "elaborately constructed forms" we now enjoy. From simplicity comes complexity.

The popular model used to illustrate his theory is called "The Tree of Life," and he explains that,

> Thus, from the war of nature, from famine and death, the most exalted object which we are capable of conceiving, namely, the production of the higher animals, directly follows. There is grandeur in this view of life, with its several powers, having been originally breathed *by the Creator* [emphasis added] into a few forms or into one. (*Species*, Kindle edition 8664)

Note that Darwin concludes that the origin of life and the origin of all the laws of nature that he was observing *were caused by the Creator*, not by nature, and so he concedes that nature and all its laws could not have brought itself into existence. In today's version of evolution, though, his words are anathema. "God" cannot be an explanation for anything. That's bad science. But how could the patron saint of evolutionary science answer the most fundamental question with, "God did it"?

I think it is safe to say that Darwin's conclusion was simply his way of avoiding the thorny logical dilemma a purely atheistic universe is presented with: how could the laws of natural selection bring themselves into existence? Darwin knew he couldn't defend the idea that nature caused itself, because he knew that such an issue could only be debated philosophically, or theologically, and he didn't want to deal with that issue in his book. He essentially writes of the origin of the laws of evolution as the workings of a god—an outside mover—one who is external to the laws of physics, and who would have created those laws. He used the generic term, god, and he left it at that.

However, in today's world atheists are attempting to answer what Darwin attempted to avoid. They believe that through the careful study and analysis of natural processes, they can prove how those natural processes came into existence without the need for a God. Nature created nature, so to speak. But how could that happen? How could what doesn't exist cause itself to exist? How can a scientist study nature and discover what *preceded* nature?

If atheists want to contend that nature itself is eternal, that's one approach to solve their dilemma. However, in his book *A Brief History of Time*, none other than Stephen Hawking demonstrated that the universe had a beginning— a very forcible one called the Big Bang. Science has contested that argument.

If, however, an atheist contends that the big bang occurred because energy from another universe broke into ours and so no god was necessary for our universe to pop into existence, one would still have to explain how the first of all universes exploded into existence and one is back at the first dilemma.

However, if one believes that the series of universes is eternal—i.e. that there was never a "first" universe—then an atheist is merely resorting to the same terminology that religions have used for millennia to define an eternal God, one who is without beginning and without end. The equivalent creed of the atheist would be "Nature always has been, always is, and always will be." An atheist merely strips intelligence and purpose from their "god."

But if one doesn't like the idea of an eternal series of universes, but rather chooses to believe that one universe expands, collapses, and rests, in an eternally recurring cycle, then one has just become a Hindu, which teaches that very concept in the *Vishnu Purana*.

> At the end of a Brahma day (approximately 4 billion years) a dissolution of the universe occurs, when all the three worlds, earth and regions of space, are consumed with fire.... When the three worlds are but one mighty ocean, Brahma, who is one with Narayana, satiate with the demolition of the universe, sleeps upon his serpent-bed...for a night of equal duration with his day; at the close of which he creates anew. (*Vishnu Purana*, I.iii)

And yet, if you want to hold firm to the original idea that the universe brought itself into existence from chaos (no outside mover necessary), then you would find yourself in agreement with the ancient Egyptians who named their creator god Nebertcher, which means "he who brought himself into existence."

> These are the words of the god Neb-er-tcher, who said: "I am the creator of what hath come into being, and I myself came into being under the form of the god Khepera...and I am the creator of what did come into being and I formed myself out of the primeval matter. (*The Book of Knowing the Evolutions of Ra*)

Nebertcher was not the universe, but he made himself into the universe. He once wasn't, and then he was. "I am he who came into being." Sounds an awful lot like what atheists believe, minus the universe bragging about bringing itself into existence. The idea of evolution is also taught in the text: "I laid the foundations [of things] in my own heart, and there came into being multitudes of created things, which came into being from the created things which were born from the created things which arose from what they brought forth" (Ibid). This quote kind of negates the idea that evolution is a modern theory based solely on an analysis of the evidence. Egyptian priests promoted the concept thousands of years ago! [3]

But evolution's problems don't stop there. Let's pretend they are right and natural laws which preceded nature created the universe. Once modern atheists un-deify everything they must then prove with *repeatable experiments* how nature, by chance and death through time, has been able to create life. It isn't enough that they confidently assert that a god didn't do it, they must still prove how nature could have done it.. Evolution's formula is

### Chance + Time + Death = Life

The glaring problem with this formula, though, is that in actuality chance, time, and death are *features* of the universe—they do not *precede* the universe. Life is not the result of death, time, and chance; these things occur to living creatures. And that is why none of the above addends can originate life—they only exist because there already is life. They presuppose a beginning that caused them to come into being: they don't explain the beginning itself.

Aristotle put it this way, "It is clear then that chance is an incidental cause in the sphere of those actions for the sake of something which involve purpose" (*Physics*, 52). Chance is not a primary cause because it cannot create anything. Only purposeful intent (intelligence) creates. Anything chance may produce is only an aberration or something out of the ordinary, but it never produces the norm. That is the logical dilemma atheists have: they are trying to defend the idea that chance could create, but chance cannot create anything. Chance merely modifies things that already exist. Time, chance, death, probability, laws, etc. are all *principles* of the universe and as such none of them could ever be the cause of the universe. Laws of

[3] See my blog post "Moses versus Egyptian Evolutionists," at www.remembering-eden.com

nature cannot be the cause of nature because a law of nature cannot precede its own existence. How could chance (or any law of nature) precede itself, and then bring itself into existence? Should we name chance *Nebertcher*?

## *Chance merely modifies things that already exist*

Think of it this way: inherent in a thing is the ability to change, but how did that inherent ability to change come into existence? Evolution could only happen to something that already had the ability to change, therefore, adaptation (micro-evolution) cannot be an original cause. Adaptation only happens to already complex systems—it doesn't create the system. The system that has the ability to adapt must be constructed first. Assembled, if you will. For something to be assembled, the individual components must be built out of raw materials, and throughout this process the end product must always be kept in mind. This is a perfect description of the origin of our universe as described by the Bible: it was assembled, and the attendant, inevitable realization is that there had to be someone who assembled it. He had to conceive of it, design it, build it, and now has to maintain it.

And this is precisely the model Genesis teaches. On days one and two, God built the fundamental building blocks of all things—the raw materials. He created motion, time (an alternating light and dark cycle), and all matter. On days three through six, God assembled the final products from those building blocks (the fundamental substances) and topped it all off with man and woman. The evidence leads us to theorize such a model, and the model then makes sense of the evidence.

Furthermore, life itself does not need death in order to exist. It's kind of an obvious point, but death is something that happens to a living organism, so how could death be responsible for life? Only once a thing is alive can it die, therefore death cannot create. Death, by definition, is the enemy of life, not its creator.

Please understand that I am not talking about the life cycle as it exists now. A dead grain of wheat needs to be planted in the soil in order for life to begin; a tree decomposes and fertilizes the soil that allows new life to grow. What I am talking about is that this *cycle* did not create itself. Life had to begin outside the system and then be infused into the system. The cycle of life, more properly understood, is the mechanism by which life sustains itself in spite of the presence of death, not because of it. Reproduction allows the continuation of a species that would die out unless it reproduced. As Seinfeld says, "Make no mistake about why these babies are here - they are here to replace us."

Darwin theorized that time, chance, and the laws of death could collaborate to modify life, but he had to resort to a generic god to explain how life attained these laws in the first place. He understood that nature couldn't have created itself, and so he falls far short of justifying the title of his book, *The Origin of Species*. What he should have called his book is *The Adaptation of Species.*

Survival of the fittest is a valid construct within a limited context, but it in no way accounts for how life originated. Natural Selection does not explain how the original, vast amount of information contained in DNA came into being, so that we had the ability to survive in the first place. No evolutionist can explain which biological mechanisms evolved DNA, that is, the information it requires. The odds are ridiculously high ($10^{89190}$)[4] to even consider that DNA assembled itself and organized all its protein molecules by naturalistic, random chance mutations.

---

[4] For a highly detailed explanation of what this number means, please read http://evolutionfacts.com/Ev-V2/2evlch10a.htm.

The following quote confirms that atheists still have not solved the problem of the origin of life even in 155 AD (After Darwin):

> Researchers are a long way from reconstructing any plausible path for the origin of life. But they have not given up. And they always conclude, no matter how fragmentary their evidence, that life is possible. ("How did Life Begin?" Nicholas Wade, NYT Nov. 11, 2003)

Brilliant! Evolutionists have no idea how life began, but they know that life did begin because life exists, and since life exists, they know that it came about by random evolutionary processes. Talk about blind faith.

And so, despite their confident assertions, atheistic naturalism has no evidence for how a natural law could have brought itself into existence and they know it. Evolution does not adequately explain our origins, nor can it.

However, the Bible proclaims the only logical explanation for life: "In Him was life" (John 1:4). God is eternal. He is life. He never had a beginning, and He brought all that we see into existence rapidly and with purposeful design. God lives—He has always existed, exists, and will always exist. God declared to Moses, "I Am that I Am", and such a God is the only logical explanation for the presence of life.

---

*The cycle of life, more properly understood, is the mechanism by which life sustains itself in spite of the presence of death, not because of it.*

---

# Our Essence

Another difficulty evolution has, though, is that it does not account for the full experience of our human-ness. What makes us human? Why is there evil and good? What is our essence? What defines us and makes us the dominant species on earth? And the most universal question of all: what is the purpose of life?

According to evolution, our humanity is defined by our skill set to survive in this rough and tumble world. We can out think our enemies in spite of obvious physical inferiorities, and we have the ability to adapt to changing environmental conditions. The dinosaurs are not around anymore as dinosaurs because they couldn't survive anymore as dinosaurs. They had to adapt and become something other than a dinosaur. Humans on the other hand, once merely an ape-like creature, were able to rise to the top of the food chain because we figured out how to use tools and make clothes. Then we figured out how to make fire and jewelry and music and we learned to work together in herds and protect each other. We survived because we adapted. We evolved.

The Bible has a different viewpoint. It defines us as made in the image of God. We have the goodness of God innately built into us, and our brutish, thuggish behaviors are the result of abandoning our design, not because we're living according to it.

So which version is true? I believe that the Bible's model is the one which accurately describes who we are because it adequately accounts for why we can be good and why there is evil. The weakness of evolution is that it doesn't have a satisfactory explanation for why our more noble qualities—such as compassion, humility, and self-sacrifice—evolved (just to say it was necessary for survival is not a sufficient answer), nor does it have any credible way to explain evil. Its explanations for such things are vague.

For example, a value such as compassion is diametrically opposed to evolution's dog-eat-dog, law-of-the-jungle value system. Evolution does not allow for kindness unless it benefits us—but is that what defines kindness? A virtuous act is something we do even if harm comes to us. Courage, honor, self-sacrifice, are all virtues because they overcome our baser, more selfish instincts.

Evolution teaches that the selfish instinct to look out for number one is what got us here. Barbarism and brutality were *necessary* for our success as individuals and as groups. If virtues such as honesty, self-sacrifice, and humility replace them, how shall our species survive? Virtue, therefore, is the enemy of evolution, and if you doubt my interpretation, you need to simply read the writings of the early proponents of evolution. They understood perfectly well for what they were arguing.

For example, the most forthright and honest of all humanists, Nietzsche, defined what he called the Superman—the ideal human—as a supremely independent man who is above the herd. Today's Superman is promoted as a noble, self-sacrificial saint who will do what's right even in the face of overwhelming evil, but Nietzsche's Superman was not so attractive. In the form of a catechism, he teaches:

> What is good?—Whatever augments the feeling of power, the will to power, power itself, man.

> What is evil?—Whatever springs from weakness....

> The weak and the botched shall perish: the first principle of our charity: *And one should help them to it* (emphasis added). [Nietzsche is boldly stating that he believes in killing the weak and the botched. He calls it an act of charity—of love.]

> What is more harmful than any vice?—Practical
> sympathy for the botched and the weak—
> Christianity…. (*The Antichrist*, 1)

Nietzsche sounds like the inspiration for every James Bond villain ever hatched! Ironically, Nietzsche also clearly articulates the fundamental principle of Christianity: compassion. He despises Christians because we want to help "the weak and the needy to live." He mocks our values and wants to replace them with a value system which weeds out the weak. Christianity should be objected to, according to Nietzsche, because we seek to preserve all human life, not just the genetically superior humans, i.e. "the most valuable, the most worthy of life, the most secure guarantee of the future" (ibid). Christianity is about the sanctity of life and Nietzsche believes that such a value system will lead to the degradation of our species.

Nietzsche was also willing to articulate the fundamental principle of evolution which its modern proponents try to hide: the truly noble "Superman" will help the weak and the needy to die for the evolution of the human race. Compassion, therefore, is the enemy of evolution. It is a drag on the human gene pool. Helping the weak perpetuates weakness. Destroying the weak will improve the human race and true humanists will accept that responsibility, even if a few undesirables have to be killed along the way. Nietzsche took evolution to its logical conclusion: killing off the weak in order to advance the strong.[5]

His application of evolution is mostly rejected now-a-days, but I wonder how much of that is due primarily to a branding issue. Nietzsche's raw humanism is an unmarketable product partly because Hitler illustrated the inherent brutality of such an ideology. In Hitler's quest to purify mankind, he tried to exterminate an entire race of people. Hitler put into practice Nietzsche's ideal even if

---

[5] Dan Brown has a clever variation on this idea in his book *Inferno.*

Nietzsche had no intention of inspiring such a madman. However, Hitler did say something very similar to Nietzsche:

> It [the State] must see to it that only those who are healthy shall beget children; that there is only one infamy, namely, for parents that are ill or show hereditary defects to bring children into the world and that in such cases it is a high honour to refrain from doing so. (*Mein Kampf,* Kindle edition 6780)

Hitler's belief that the State's primary responsibility is to improve the race by making policies which would promote healthy children and restrict the perpetuation of diseased or racially impure children led to the justification of the slaughter of millions of people.

Nietzsche's brand of "helping the weak and the botched to die," and Hitler's brand of convincing the weak and diseased to stop having children are applications of evolutionary theory which do not seem to have been intended by Darwin. Nevertheless, Darwin's original title had a racial component to it: *The Origin of Species by Means of Natural Selection, or the Preservation of Favoured Races in the Struggle for Life.* The idea that there are superior—or favored—races, gives a scientific legitimacy to bigotry.

The point is that such notions have fallen out of favor, and so the evolution of mankind is now marketed as if it were the exact opposite of Nietzsche's vision. Today, evolution preaches that humanity is moving toward a common morality, not an independent one. Now we are evolving toward compassion, love, tolerance, and acceptance.

What is really astounding, though, is that this modern application of evolution has successfully turned the tables and now implies that Christianity is the philosophy that doesn't care about the weak and the needy. Christians now are promoted as the ones who are considered power hungry, in-it-for-themselves brutes. Christians are the ones who want the weak to die. We are the racists. Nietzsche would be rolling over in his grave if he knew his humanist children were criticizing Christians for being what he promoted!

It is necessary to say this plainly so this generation knows the truth: Christianity loves life and defends life for all people whatever their social or economic status may be. We also believe that there is only *one* race of humans, not many. All human beings—with all of our magnificent variety—have descended from an original pair of humans.

Evolution, on the other hand, promotes death. Evolution justifies death as necessary. Evolution teaches that death is the only way life could continue to advance. To put it another way, Darwin's generic god is the kind of god who infused into nature the law of death, and his god proclaims that death is a necessary feature of life. It's an imperative. Life couldn't exist without it. To put it bluntly: Darwin's god *requires* the presence of starvation, disease, pain, and suffering. Darwin's god *created* these things so that life would evolve. The features of this world we hate and complain about, Darwin teaches his god *made*.

And people are supposed to hate the God of the Bible?

*Christianity loves life and defends life for all people whatever their social or economic status may be.*

The God of the Bible is shouting from the rooftops that starvation, disease, and suffering are horrifying features of this world; *they are not a part of His original design*. It is the God of the Bible who proclaims that He created us to live, that death is a consequence for sin, and that He is working out a cure for death. The Bible teaches that God constructed the variety of life forms to be complete, functional, and distinct; that He did it all quickly; and that death is a tragedy we need not be victimized by anymore.

Nietzsche took evolution to its logical conclusion: the death of the weak and the advancement of the strong. Christianity, on the other hand, teaches that compassion, kindness, and humility (Ephesians 4:1-6) are the character qualities we are supposed to emulate as modeled by Christ, the image of God. The sinless man.

Evolution can try to whitewash its cracked and flaking past, but it is what it is: it is a philosophy of death and it strips away any absolute standards of morality. As Nietzsche says, "Yet everything evolved: there are no eternal facts as there are no absolute truths" (*Human, All Too Human*, 161).

On the other hand, Christianity loudly declares that death is life's enemy, not its creator, and that life will prevail in spite of the presence of death, not because of it. Jesus is life. He is eternal life. He always has been and always will be. Cruelty may be the norm in our world now, but such behavior is contrary to who we were meant to be. It isn't our genetic structure that ultimately makes us human; it is our alignment with the character of God. What we are now is a corruption of our true nature, not a necessary outcome of our nature, and the bottom line is that immorality and cruelty are the cause of all the problems in the world, not morality and kindness.

God is fighting a war that He will win. Death itself will be cast into the Lake of Fire someday, and in the midst of this war He wants us to remember that we were made in His image—the image of the perfect, triune God, not the image of a beast.

# How Then Shall We Live ?

What does all this mean? What is its practical application in the midst of all the struggles of this life? If the God of life originated life on earth, and the essence of our humanity is compassion, what are we supposed to do with that knowledge when a loved one is diagnosed with cancer or heart disease? What are we supposed to do when we get "the call" and find out our spouse died in a car accident? We are the shattered image of God, but what are we supposed to do with that information?

When my wife was diagnosed with Eisenmenger's Syndrome, one of the things we learned is that her condition wasn't genetic, i.e. it wasn't transferable from one generation to the next. Some diseases are transferable, like Muscular Dystrophy, but even these only *might* be passed on. Eisenmenger's Syndrome, however, is what's classified as a defect, i.e. something happened during her mother's pregnancy that caused Tierre's heart to not develop correctly. Some defects are the fault of the mother if she smokes, drinks, or does drugs while pregnant, but many defects simply defy explanation, as in Tierre's case.

When we were faced with the decision on what to do after we found out she was pregnant, the doctors did some research and there were only about twelve recorded cases of Eisenmenger's, and of those, only three or four involved pregnancy, and of those none carried to full term. The bottom line is that Tierre and the baby were only given a 50/50 chance that either of them would live if she continued the pregnancy. Tierre's odds were not much better if she chose to abort, though, and, obviously, the baby would have no chance. What Tierre chose to do, therefore, defied the studies and the odds.

But this decision was only necessary in the first place because she had been born with a birth defect in her heart that no one had ever identified until after she had gotten pregnant. Her pregnancy did not cause the defect but it did bring it to light, and even though Tierre passed away four days after delivery, if she had never gotten pregnant she would still have needed a heart and lung transplant by the age of thirty.

A perspective we both had to mature into, though, is that sometimes a defect happens *in order to bring glory to God*, such as the man who was born blind and whom Jesus healed (John 9). It wasn't because of the sins of his parents that he was blind; it was so that Christ could show His power. I believe that that is the reason for my wife's defect: it was to bring God glory (C. S. Lewis explains how this works in *The Problem of Pain*). Tierre believed that, too, for she wrote in her diary during that time, "You made me this way for a sole (and soul) purpose: that You'd receive glory." There is no explaining these things satisfactorily, because there are so many truths in play. God is sovereign, but we live in a fallen world; God is good, but death is a tragedy; death is horrifying, but God can use it for His glory.

When we were experiencing these challenges, though, a very odd thing began to happen: we started getting along much better than we had before. Tierre and I had gotten married pretty young and one of the challenges we faced was learning to work together as a team. We often got frustrated with each other over petty little things, and sometimes the stresses of life such as bills, work, chores, etc. caused tension in our relationship that if we had been more mature wouldn't have been such a big deal. It was actually a rather discouraging time in our marriage.

But then we got the call about her heart defect and we entered into a realm of decision-making that matured our perspective of the world and we became less selfish and more compassionate toward each other. I'm kind of ashamed to admit it, but during our two years of marriage (we celebrated our second anniversary while we were at the hospital in Seattle), the last six months were the best. In spite of all the challenges—indeed because of them—we were forced to abandon our selfish ways and enter into the true unity found in a marriage that cannot be taught, studied, or chosen: we cared for each other in the deepest sense of the word.

After Tierre died, though, I began to face some new challenges. During the first few years I had all the help I needed from families in the church. Those were blessed times and I could not have endured the challenges without their help. However, after I got my first teaching job and was back into the normal swing of life, I felt the loss of Tierre in an entirely new way.

It was tough being a widowed dad, five, six, seven years into the deal. I had already dated one girl seriously enough to buy her a ring, but that all fell through. I then entered a stage of my life that I look back on as very lonely. I was putting one foot in front of the other and was faithfully plugging along, but there wasn't much joy.

But then God came through for me again. Not in the form of a wife, but in the form of a truth:

> So I commended enjoyment, because a man has nothing better under the sun than to eat, drink, and be merry; for this will remain with him in his labor *all* the days of his life which God gives him under the sun. Eccl. 8:15

God was pointing out to me that my life was right now. It wasn't going to be later when I got a wife (if I were to ever get a wife), and it wasn't going to be when everything was going smoothly and without incident. Life was *now* and I had better start enjoying it.

> Go, eat your food *with gladness*, and drink your wine with *a joyful heart*, for it is *now* that *God favors what you do*. Eccl. 9:7

God had shown me favor by gifting me with a beautiful daughter, a job, and great friends. I would be missing out on all of those gifts if I continued to live as if I were miserable. How ungrateful would that be?

> Always be clothed in white, and always anoint
> your head with oil. *Enjoy life* with your wife,
> whom you love, all the days of this meaningless
> life that God has given you under the sun–all your
> meaningless days. For this is your lot in life and in
> your toilsome labor under the sun. Eccl. 9:8-9

I had lost my wife, but I now had a daughter who loved to laugh and play and go on sledding trips and hit a softball in the backyard. This was my lot in life and I didn't have the option to go out and start sinning and living loosely without any moral boundaries. I needed to "clothe myself in white" and be the kind of man my daughter needed me to be. I needed to enjoy life right now. My personal pain wasn't a good enough excuse to check out of my God-given responsibilities.

> *Whatever your hand finds to do, do it with all*
> *your might,* for in the grave, where you are going,
> there is neither working nor planning nor
> knowledge nor wisdom. I have seen something
> else under the sun: The race is not to the swift or
> the battle to the strong, nor does food come to the
> wise or wealth to the brilliant or favor to the
> learned; but time and chance happen to them all.
> Moreover, no man knows when his hour will
> come: As fish are caught in a cruel net, or birds
> are taken in a snare, so men are trapped by evil
> times that fall unexpectedly upon them.
> Ecclesiastes 9:10-12

This was my life and I needed to live it with all the gusto and verve and energy I could muster. There would be no other time for me to live this life. We can't put life on hold while we suffer—this is our life and we must live it. We can't put it on hold and wait for something better. This is it.

Now, this isn't to say that I believe "this is it" in the sense that there is nothing after we die so *carpe diem!* Rather, God was highlighting a practical truth: the gift of God is life, so enjoy that life *whatever* challenges come my way.

Jesus said it this way, "I have come that they may have life, and that they may have *it* more abundantly" (Jn. 10:10b). When Jesus says "more abundantly," He means that He is our good shepherd and he will make us feel secure and He will provide for us (Ezek. 34:14-15; 25-31). He is going to guide us to our ultimate destiny where fears and tears will never harass us again (Rev. 21:4).

What I began to see was that I needed to start enjoying my eternal life *now.* Living in constant sorrow is not His goal for us. As Ecclesiastes points out, time and chance happen to us all and we don't know what will happen next. *This* is the moment we must be alive. This is the moment we must enjoy, and here's the ultimate promise extended to us in Christ: joy in this life and the next. The gift of God is eternal life in Christ Jesus (Rom. 6:23). He isn't promising a mere eternal consciousness, but rather an eternal *life* in all of its glory and joy. Life is so much more than just being alive.

And, so, take courage Christian: we should be confident that it is logical to conclude from the evidence that the God of life made us, that He did it in the way He revealed to us in His Holy Scripture, and that death is a consequence for sin. However, through Christ He has revealed to us a way to get back to what He intended us to become in the first place—sinless and with an unlimited capacity for life in all of its wonder.

God is providing a cure to death and a path to life.

That is good news!

# THE SHATTERED IMAGE

**Mendacious**: Given to or characterized by deception or falsehood or divergence from absolute truth.

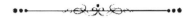

S o, the stage is set. The Bible account begins with a sinless man and a sinless woman living on an uncorrupted world filled with untold wonders. Eden was designed for their pleasure; sin and death did not exist; and they prospered in unashamed innocence and joy. They were content. They communed with God. They nurtured nature, and loved one another. There was no religion and there was no government. Their only occupation was to take care of things, explore, and then populate the earth. Isn't God good?

But what happened? What have we become? How was death introduced into a world where humans were not meant to die? And why would Adam and Eve risk it all for a bite of fruit, and why would God punish them with death—and all future generations—for such a seemingly trivial act? Let me set up the scene.

> And the Lord God commanded the man, saying,
> "Of every tree of the garden you may freely eat;
> but of the tree of the knowledge of good and evil
> you shall not eat, for in the day that you eat of it
> you shall surely die." (Gen. 2:16-17)

Now the serpent was more cunning than any beast
of the field which the Lord God had made. And he
said to the woman, "Has God indeed said, 'You
shall not eat of every tree of the garden'?" And
the woman said to the serpent, "We may eat the
fruit of the trees of the garden; but of the fruit of
the tree which is in the midst of the garden, God
has said, 'You shall not eat it, nor shall you touch
it, lest you die.' "Then the serpent said to the
woman, "You will not surely die. For God knows
that in the day you eat of it your eyes will be
opened, and you will be like God, knowing good
and evil." So when the woman saw that the tree
was good for food, that it was pleasant to the eyes,
and a tree desirable to make one wise, she took of
its fruit and ate. She also gave to her husband with
her, and he ate. Then the eyes of both of them
were opened, and they knew that they were naked;
and they sewed fig leaves together and made
themselves coverings. And they heard the sound
of the Lord God walking in the garden in the cool
of the day, and Adam and his wife hid themselves
from the presence of the Lord God among the
trees of the garden. Then the Lord God called to
Adam and said to him, "Where are you?" (Gen.
3:1-9)

This is one of the most famous stories in the history of
mankind and everyone has some sort of image in their mind
of a serpent coiled around the branches of an apple tree,
luring Eve with his Jungle Book song, "Trust in
meeee…just in meeeee…." Hiss. It's been caricatured,
ridiculed, maligned, and snickered at for thousands of years.

But, on just a literary level, is there any other story that
better characterizes the human condition? We all have mini-
falls every day, don't we? We know what is right; we've
been warned of the consequences of doing what's wrong;

but then an outside influence says that there are undreamed of rewards for doing it (what's wrong with it anyway?); so we partake. We believe the lie and then our eyes are opened and we realize what we have done. We feel sorry (but maybe not all that bad) and so we try to cover up our sin, but then when someone else finds out, we make excuses to justify our actions. But by then it's too late and our sentence is decreed.

It's the story of the innocent kid walking down the street, accosted by the drug dealer.

It's the story of the little girl lured from her family with the promise of candy.

It's the story of the man, devoted to his wife, believing the lie of Vegas.

It's the loving daughter giving up her purity to a boy who has sacrificed nothing for her: he's just using her.

The story of Adam and Eve is the ultimate archetype of all human greatness and depravity. After they ate the fruit (an apple has become the symbol, but the Bible doesn't say what kind of fruit it was) they were ashamed, they were separated from God, child birth became painful, prosperity became difficult, Eve would always want to dominate her husband but Adam would never allow it, and the process of physical death was initiated. They would both eventually die, but most devastating of all, they would be separated from God. And the fall is only amplified by the idea that what they could have become is more awesome than words can describe—but what they did become is more pitiful than tears can wash away. Is there any other story that so clearly explains the human condition?

Genesis 1-3 does no less than frame our entire existence. It explains the origin of our pain, our longings, and our suffering. It defines the source of our desire for life and love, our fear of death, our anxiety, and the source of conflict and war. Even if it were just a story, it is the most thoroughly accurate and enlightening story about why our world is the way it is. God made us good, evil is the result of the fall, and we are experiencing the fruit of the Tree of the Knowledge of Good and Evil to this day.

But here's the thing that sets it apart from all other literature, and what causes many people to gulp in hesitation: it is, in fact, true. These events really happened. God did create the universe in the way He said He did; Adam and Eve did corrupt the goodness God designed us to have; God is working out His plan to get us back to a state of sinlessness so we can get back on track and become the kind of humans He designed us to be. It isn't just a good story. It is actual history. The Bible is a comprehensive framework—spiritually and historically—of why our world is the way it is and we abandon its message to our peril.

## *The Temptation*

The question of why Adam and Eve gave up Eden has been an interesting topic of theological debate for millennia, but what us moderns really want to know is whether it was even a real event. Was there really a walking, talking serpent that convinced them to eat? Was there really a tree that God forbade Adam and Eve to eat from? Were they really immortal before they sinned? If I say, "Yes!" then I'm immediately deemed an idiot; if I say "No," then the opposition smugly sits back and says, "See, I told you it was just a story," and then they promote their version of reality. And if I say it illustrates a spiritual reality even if it wasn't real, then I've deferred to Darwin and accepted that evolution has adequately made its case. So, was the temptation real, or was it just a clever story?

Amusingly, geology and biology both come to the Bible's rescue again and provide a defense for a historical interpretation. In Genesis 3:14, God curses the serpent: "upon thy belly thou shalt go." That would imply the serpent once had legs, but how silly is that? A snake with legs? However, in the fossil record there is evidence that a snake species used to have legs. They weren't long, gangly things, but they were there.

Scientists are also aware that the python has all of the genetic information necessary to grow legs, but "for some reason," the gene has been turned off. It's called the Hox gene, and mutant versions have been found which had grown a leg anyway. They are really, really creepy, because they can use their legs to cling to walls. A woman in China purportedly saw one in her home, knocked it down and beat it to death. Maybe Eve should have, too. The Bible's story is consistent with the evidence.

But why do we have a problem with the Bible's claim that a serpent deceived Eve? Perhaps because we think that everything today is as it once was. Evolution has succeeded in planting in our minds that all life was once primitive and has been gradually improving, becoming increasingly organized and complex over hundreds of millions of years. But as we have seen, that is backwards from what the evidence suggests. The evidence points to our descent (a loss of information), not our ascent (the addition of information), and the fact remains that life has always been complete and functional. The fact that a serpent once had the genetic material to grow legs, and now doesn't, speaks of decline, not improvement.

And yet, in regards to the whole talking thing, one must remember that we accept, as Christians, that there is a spiritual world and that demons can possess living beings. There is evidence that possessions are real, so it isn't a stretch to say that many of the things we think of as odd or superstitious are actually only strange to westernized minds that have been told incessantly that such things cannot happen. Even many non-Christian religions believe that a spirit can inhabit a person and speak through them. I discipled a young man once whose mother channeled spirits and he heard her speak in voices and languages not her own.

I guess the point is that I just don't put as much faith in the judgment of atheistic scientists about our world as they would like me to. Carl Sagan expressed regret that more people hadn't abandoned the idea of a God in light of all the scientific evidence he had unveiled. Ironically, the things he revealed about our universe are so amazing I can only conclude that there must be a Creator. I believe in science but not in atheistic naturalism; I believe science can clarify the truth and correct misunderstandings, but I do not believe in evolution. I'm not anti-science—I'm anti-evolution.

> There are more things in heaven and earth, Horatio,
> Than are dreamt of in your philosophy. (*Hamlet*, I.v)

At its core, atheistic naturalism limits our understanding of the world. It reduces, minimizes, and constrains what we are to accept as possible. There are many strange and wonderful things about our world that are true, and they are no less true simply because a scientist with atheistic assumptions hasn't figured out how they could be true. The Bible presents a much broader image of the universe than an atheist would agree with.

*I'm not anti-science—I'm anti-evolution.*

And so, even though science cannot explain how a spiritual being can inhabit a physical being (*Star Trek: The Next Generation* gave it a go in season 7, episode 14, "Sub Rosa"), that doesn't mean it has not or cannot happen. The earth revolved around the Sun long before Copernicus figured it out. The earth was round even though the intellectual leaders said it was flat. E equaling $mc^2$ kept the universe functioning long before Einstein identified the equation. Quantum Physics functions even though we can't piece all the mysteries together. Sometimes scientists make it sound as if they invent the laws of physics rather than just being smart enough to finally figure a few of them out.

The Bible's account of a serpent that deceives Eve is highly probable. I'm not saying that the snake had vocal chords, but rather that communication can take many forms and somehow Satan used the serpent to lure Adam and Eve into eating the forbidden fruit. If we were watching, we may not have even heard their conversation. Take into consideration that perhaps, before the fall, we had a closer connection to all of nature including angels and animals. What if in the sinless perfection of God's original creation we were designed to be completely interrelated with all of creation? God did walk and talk with Adam and Eve in the Garden (does God have to have vocal chords in order to communicate to us?), but one of the consequences of their sin was to be disconnected from His life-giving presence. But what if what was also severed was our connection with nature? What if we had been designed to communicate with God's creation in ways we only fantasize about now?

Whatever happened in Eden was a unique, one-of-a-kind event, and that doesn't automatically make the story a lie. The biblical author gives no indication that he is writing anything other than what historically happened, and even though it contradicts what an atheist tells us his limited vision of reality allows, to me that makes the Bible's story all the more believable. A spiritual deception taking place is more conceivable to me than evolution's claim that a wolf-like ancestor was able to transform into a whale. Really?

The historical event we call "the fall" gives the symbols their meaning. The reason the serpent and the forbidden fruit have become archetypes of human experience is not because they are part of a made-up story; it is because they were real players in actual events.

## *Obedience*

Why would God punish their disobedience with death? Why wouldn't God just slap their hand, or give them a ticket, a warning, or a time-out? Why did He punish them—and millions of generations—with death and suffering? That seems a little over-the-top for a mistake.

The only way I can see clearly to address that question is to start by dealing with a different question altogether: "Why did the serpent's lie appeal to Adam and Eve in the first place?" I can understand the influence of the external cause (Satan) on those events, but I'm not sure I've properly understood the internal cause. They were without sin so Satan couldn't have been appealing to their sin nature. They didn't have one. So what was he appealing to? What was in Eve's non-sinful nature that influenced her to disobey God's clear command?

John Milton in *Paradise Lost* suggests that Eve was alone when the serpent approached her, and since Adam wasn't with her, that is what made her vulnerable. As Milton lays it out, she had wanted to work alone for awhile, away from Adam, and Adam, after much deliberation and a firm warning to be wary, allowed her to go off on her own. Satan took advantage of this opportunity:

> ...Greedily she ingorg'd without restraint,
> And knew not eating Death.... (IX, 791-92)

Then, once sated and even amazed at how awesome the fruit was, she decided to approach Adam and she convinced him to eat. At first appalled, Adam decided to eat because of his love for her:

> ...me with thee hath ruind, for with thee
> Certain my resolution is to Die;
> How can I live without thee, how forgoe

Thy sweet Converse and Love so dearly joyn'd,
To live again in these wilde Woods forlorn? (IX,
906-910)

It's a highly romanticized version of the fall of
mankind, and as much as I adore *Paradise Lost* for its
brilliant insights, I think Milton actually underplays the
darkness of the fall. He implies that Adam made a mistake
by letting Eve go off alone, which left her vulnerable to
temptation. However, I believe that Hannibal Lecter in
*Silence of the Lambs* gets closer to explaining the spirit of
the deception:

> HANNIBAL: First principals, Clarice. Simplicity.
> Read Marcus Aurelius. Of each particular thing
> ask: what is it in itself? What is its nature? What
> does he do, this man you seek?
>
> CLARICE: He kills women....
>
> HANNIBAL: No. That is incidental. What is the
> first and principal thing he does? What needs does
> he serve by killing?
>
> CLARICE: Anger, um, social acceptance, and, uh,
> sexual frustrations, sir....
>
> HANNIBAL: No! He covets. That is his nature.
> And how do we begin to covet, Clarice? Do we
> seek out things to covet? Make an answer to
> answer now.
>
> CLARICE: No. We just....
>
> HANNIBAL: No. We begin by coveting what we
> see every day. Don't you feel eyes moving over
> your body, Clarice? And don't your eyes seek out
> the things you want?

Satan coveted Godhood. He saw God every moment of
every day and after his initial, direct, but failed attempt to

overthrow God with an army of angels, he then saw his path to godhood by destroying the innocence of God's creation. And how would he do that? By convincing Adam and Eve to covet the one thing they didn't need: the fruit of that one, particular tree. Imagine, twenty or thirty years of knowing that the tree was there and not even caring, and then Satan introduces the idea of wondering about it. That's all he had to do. He made her notice it and see it in a different light, i.e. as an obstacle to something more desirable. He caused her to doubt God and to ask the question: "Why, exactly, is it wrong? It must be something that God just doesn't want us to experience. Something really amazing."

Sound familiar?

This event makes it clear that one does not have to be a sinner in order to be tempted, and that covetousness did not enter her heart from within herself. Satan put the thought into her mind. As Paul points out in 1 Timothy 2:14, Eve was deceived and became a sinner, and in 1 Corinthians 15:21-22, Paul teaches that by Adam came death. Therefore, biblically, both Adam and Eve played their part in the fall, and both faced consequences for the parts they played. Furthermore (and contrary to Milton's version) in Genesis it reads as if Adam had been right there with her during the temptation. The image I get from Scripture is that Satan tempted Eve; she ate, turned around, and immediately gave it to Adam. Satan's lie, therefore, was intended to be heard by both of them, and Adam did nothing to stop Eve. She was deceived, and he let her be deceived.

The scary thing is that Satan's methodology has been emulated throughout history: let people think they are being offered enlightenment, sexual pleasure, money, and power, and they'll abandon any semblance of morals they ever had. The promise of god-like knowledge, power, and no punishment—"You'll be fine, there is no death (no consequences)"— appeals to all of us.

But, now to come back to the question: "Why did they believe the lie?"

Quite truthfully the answer is too embarrassing, even insulting, to accept. We like to think very highly of ourselves and we like to romanticize our sins just a little. As Milton suggests, Adam couldn't imagine life without Eve and so he ate, too. He fell because his human desires overwhelmed his reason. It sounds noble.

But the stark truth is very unromantic: Adam and Eve were simply innocent. The fall wasn't caused by covetousness, pride, and greed…those were merely the bait. They believed a lie and acted on their belief because they were like children. Satan convinced them that the truth was far more complex than the simplicity God had revealed to them.

To accept this answer, however, requires one to first acknowledge how much influence the power of suggestion has over every single one of us. Yes, even you. Mark Twain was partly right when he said, "A man's brain is so constructed that IT CAN ORIGINATE NOTHING WHATSOEVER. It can only use material obtained OUTSIDE" (*What is Man*? 73). Think of all the influences that berate us constantly: music, TV, news, radio, billboards, magazines, the Internet, books, etc. Is it possible to distinguish between ideas we have thought of and ideas which others have introduced to us?

Twain is not entirely correct, however, because he drew the conclusion that Eve only did what she could *only* have done: "It [our brain] is merely a machine; and it works automatically, not by will-power. IT HAS NO COMMAND OVER ITSELF, ITS OWNER HAS NO COMMAND OVER IT" (Ibid). I would agree that we are very much like machines, but I believe we are such sophisticated machines that we have a choice over which influences have sway over us. As Milton says,

…within himself
The danger lies, yet lies within his power:
Against his will he can receave no harme.
(Milton, IX)

Basically, from the story of Adam and Eve, it appears that we were designed to be able to willingly choose between right and wrong; between obeying God or disobeying Him. The Bible makes it clear that we must take responsibility for our moral choices (Joshua 24:15; Proverbs 1:24-33), and that we cannot pawn them off on some genetic code or factory design. Or even, in Christian-ese, on our sin nature. The concept that I was born in sin does not excuse me from being accountable for my choices to sin. We aren't looms or robots. We are wondrous beings made in the image of God. We are free, independent souls and unlike a simple factory machine—or a brute beast governed by primal instincts—we have been designed to choose which input we obey. Every tyrant in the world would love for us to be mere machines because machines can be programmed and controlled. Think, *Brave New World*. And this point alone proves that God isn't a tyrant. If He were, we wouldn't have been created with the ability to choose.

---

*The concept that I was born in sin does not excuse me from being accountable for my choices to sin.*

---

Out of the many lessons of the fall, this is the most horrifying one of all: we can never excuse away our sin. We cannot say that Satan or our substance made us do it.

Don't get me wrong: we, the children of Adam and Eve, have been born into sin. Psalm 51:5 says, "Behold, I was shapen in iniquity; and in sin did my mother conceive me."

Paul says in Romans 5:12, "Wherefore, as by one man sin entered into the world, and death by sin; and so death passed upon all men, for that all have sinned." We are sinners, and yet we cannot use that as an excuse when we stand before God in the day of judgment. When I sin, I make a choice to sin, and if I try to explain away my sin by saying, "It was my sin nature that made me do it," I'm mistaken. Unless I take full responsibility for my sin and admit that I chose to do it, I will circumvent God's work of grace in my heart. Repentance involves acknowledging that I made a conscious choice to sin. No more excuses!

Adam and Eve made excuses: "The serpent deceived me...." "The woman You gave me...." Nope. Sorry. We can't blame each other or God. We are the ones responsible for our actions. Own up to it. We believe the lie. We are responsible.

We want to convince ourselves that we are independent—that we can determine our own destiny—and that sinning in defiance of God's law makes us free. But our constant penchant to blame others for our faults and our never-ending attempts to not admit our wrong-doing in the face of all the evidence to the contrary, proves that we want to be enslaved to our sin. We don't want true independence—true self-reliance—because of all the horrifying responsibility which true freedom requires.

I used to think that people rejected Christ because they didn't want to admit their sin; now I realize that people are fine with recognizing their imperfections: what they really fear is responsibility. They fear the raw, naked, feeling of absolute awareness that they are accountable for everything they have ever done.

We fear accountability and that is the root of why we fear death, the ultimate accountability. Death is the moment when we must face the raw, naked truth of our own decisions.

That is also why we can only be truly independent and finally in control of our destiny when we confess our sin. In any other state, sin controls us and it overwhelms our will to follow God. By the way, the natural state of our original humanity is to follow God. Adam and Eve did so without question until an outside influence persuaded them not to follow God. To return to that state of absolute trust, though, we must admit that we sin, and we shouldn't blame anyone or anything else other than our own choice.

We can only blame ourselves.

And it is this truth that highlights the horrifying nature of Satan's lie and why death had to be our punishment: Satan subverted Adam and Eve's pure trust of God. They wouldn't have sinned if He hadn't of taken advantage of their innocence, and the only way back to purity is through the valley of death. They were innocent children who would have grown and matured over time, but their lack of guile also made them easy prey. And this is what makes Satan's lie so Hannibal Lecter-like: he lusted to destroy their clear conscience. It would be the equivalent of a forty year old seducing a three year old. It should stir that kind of horror in us.

And I believe that the fall is why Jesus taught us that we would be better off if a millstone were hung around our necks and we were dropped into the sea than to cause an innocent child to stumble. He had seen it happen in the Garden of Eden, and we live its effects to this day.

## *Where was God?*

Well, the obvious next question is, "Where was God?" Why didn't He protect them if they were so vulnerable?

He was there, waiting for them to choose Him. As innocent as they were, they knew enough to make a choice. The tension of the drama in the Garden of Eden is similar to what a father feels when his oldest daughter is off at college. He hopes some slug doesn't seduce her, and that she will stay strong in her faith. He fears that all the influences which are pushing on her, are going to break her down. But that dad also knows that he can't make her choices for her. If he were to hover around her permanently, she would never mature into the woman she is supposed to become. But by that abdication, he opens her up to danger. It's a scary situation.

The reality is that our parents can teach us. They can pray for us. They can warn us and give us advice. But they can never make our choices for us. And if we fall? Is that the parent's fault? No.

But that is a truth difficult to grapple with, so let me explain it this way.

I believe it is a vain endeavor to blame God for the fall because it doesn't make any sense to blame the one who gave you a choice for the choice that you make. "Hey! You shouldn't have even given me a choice to disobey you or not, knowing what a wrong choice would result in." Imagine a God who would have made us without the ability to choose. Does that kind of existence sound attractive to you?

In an episode of *Star Trek: The Next Generation*, a Q (a being with god-like power) in the form of a beautiful young woman, fell in love with Ryker but he didn't love her in return (*True Q*, episode 6.6). Upset, and all-powerful, she decided to create a fantasy realm where Ryker adored her without question. He now praised her, and worshipped her as the moon and the stars. He sang to her and quoted poetry and he did everything love was supposed to do...except be expressed from a free will. He hadn't willingly chosen her and after awhile she realized how empty his words of love were. In the same way, God doesn't force us to love Him. God does not force us to praise Him. He does not force us to choose Him.

"But," the critics say, "what if we don't choose him? Won't he kill us all? How is that really a choice, then?" That's a fair question, but it is founded on a misunderstanding of what Scripture teaches about the judgment of God. God punishes sin, and rightfully so. We can be horrifyingly evil creatures, wreaking death and destruction on a planet God intended us to take care of. Sin is punishable because sin is a destructive force that is the cause of all suffering. Sin disfigures our world, not God. God designed a universe where death would come into existence if sin was committed, but that doesn't mean He has an overbearing ego that can't stand people not adoring him. That's what the Ori do in *Stargate*. That's what Ghengis Khan, Adolf Hitler, and Mao Tse Tung do. Not God. As I said earlier, the fact that He even gave Adam and Eve a choice should prove to us beyond any doubt that He isn't a tyrant. Being punished for our sin is not the same thing as being randomly slaughtered by a tyrant god who is offended that we don't do what he wants.

But another question I have heard is, "Why would God make such a law in the first place?" The only way to answer that is to first understand what the purpose of making a rule is. Properly formulated, law actually allows us to succeed and to thrive. The prevailing opinion is that God's law restricts us from having a good time, but, in fact, God's law, if obeyed, leads to freedom, peace, and prosperity.

## *Sin disfigures our world, not God.*

Think of it this way: if there wasn't the law of gravity, could we fly? If there wasn't the necessity to eat food, would we have ever invented cherry pie? If water didn't have banks, could it be a river? God's Laws are good. Boundaries are good. Yes, if we break those laws bad things can happen, but if we follow them, they unleash our creativity, our adventurous spirit, our unique gifts, abilities, and individuality. Obeying the law doesn't inhibit us; it frees us. God's Law unleashes our human potential; it doesn't diminish us. God's Laws, far from being a negative, allow us to achieve far more than we could ever do without them, and if we had a relationship with God, undefiled by sin, then we would be able to soar beyond anything that we can currently imagine! It isn't law that holds us back: it's sin which stops us from maturing into the humans He meant us to become. It's the breaking of the law that destroys us, not the law. [6]

Some friends have also asked, "Why didn't God more clearly warn Adam and Eve about the consequences of their decision? Maybe if they had fully understood what death was really like, then they wouldn't have fallen."

"But," I must answer, "did Adam and Eve really have to understand what death was in its fullness in order to obey God?"

Absolutely not.

Have you ever tried to explain getting burned to a child who has no experience of being burned? It can't be done. You could describe the searing pain, the smell of burning flesh, the tears, the prolonged healing process and all the bandages and ointments that would ever be needed, but in a child's innocence—before being burned—a proper fear of burning could never be present. The same holds true for Adam and Eve: no matter how clearly God could have described the consequences of their sin, they wouldn't have understood. They were innocent, uncorrupted, pure, undefiled. The fear of suffering didn't exist.

We use fear tactics, but we've already been corrupted. I remember watching *Red Asphalt*, the driver's education

---

[6] Please note that I am referring to God's Laws. Man-made laws, such as the Pharisees wrote, led people away from the truth, not towards it. We could call some of God's Laws "natural law," since He is the creator of nature.

video that graphically showed bloody, gory car accidents in order to scare us new drivers into being careful. The message was: Driving is dangerous. Don't be stupid. Pay attention. As effective as that movie was, I can even more clearly remember my own personal close calls while learning to drive on the L.A. freeways. Those moments of fear have ingrained in me the need to always use my mirrors and to stay defensive while driving. Experience with fear has taught me well. Couldn't God have employed the same tactics with Adam and Eve?

I also remember watching the movie *Scared Straight*. Filmed in 1978, the goal was to expose kids to convicts who told them about the horrors of prison life. The in-your-face, confrontational, this-is-how-it-is methodology proved to be extremely successful. Of the twenty kids who were in the movie only one continued a life of crime. Pretty effective stuff, so why couldn't God have used the same approach? Why didn't He clearly tell Adam and Eve how it would play out if they disobeyed? Why didn't he show them the gang rapes, the bloated, starving children, the weeping wives, and the murder-suicides? Why didn't God show them a slide show of all the horrors that would plague mankind if they broke that one law?

Part of the reason is that fear does not guarantee obedience. For example, how many smokers even care about warning labels? It has turned a few away, sure, but more often than not our own personal desires influence us far more than any impersonal, generic warning. We say, "I am bullet proof"; "That won't happen to me"; "George Burns lived into his 90's." So, even if God had been graphic in His depiction of death, Adam may have still disobeyed and we would still be in the current condition we are in right now.

The other problem is that fear does not form a lasting obedience. Under the fear of threat you may convince yourself that you believe for a while, and you may even obey, but then what happens to your heart when the threat is gone? What happens to your heart when you're out from under your parent's authority, or the gun is no longer at your head? What happens if a bigger, scarier threat comes your way?

Fear is weak; love is strong and I believe that is the reason God didn't scare them into obedience. God expected them to obey because of who He was. It really isn't much more complicated than that. They didn't need a paralyzing fear of death in order to obey God, they just needed trust and respect. God required a response from them—and us— that is rooted in a belief in His goodness, not in the fear of consequences. Consequences are real and they are necessary, but our decision to obey God should be based solely on the character of God and not on some graphic image of pain and suffering. Obedience based on fear is the weakest form of motivation.

## *Fear is weak; love is strong.*

The truth is, God's command was the only fair and compassionate warning that could have ever been given. Isn't it the best commander who expects obedience from you without recourse to dramatic images? Don't you hate the arm-twisters and the manipulators; the ones who cajole you into submission? Give me a firm, decisive commander who is worthy of obedience and I will follow him to the gates of hell! A command given by a person of this nature relies on love and trust, not threats. A commander of this kind calls on the most noble and most selfless part of a person's character to do the right thing, and even if a command is disobeyed, it is clearly because the subordinate had a free will and was acting with self-determination. We can't blame the commander for his subordinate's disobedience, nor can we blame God for Adam's choice.

And this is why Adam and Eve's crime was such a horrifying travesty, deserving of death. A time-out in the naughty chair wouldn't have sufficed. Adam and Eve's sin was nothing less than a complete rejection of God's loving favor and provision. It was so much more than eating a piece of fruit. It was the ultimate insult, the premiere "I don't care what you say!" moment.

Our decision to obey God should be based solely on the character of God and not on some graphic image of pain and suffering. And so, by the nature of the command, it demonstrates that God did not design Adam and Eve to be puppets. Rather, He designed them with a free will to love Him or not. God wanted them to obey, willingly, and if He had created them so that they would always obey no matter what, that would have been a worse kind of creation. What worthless creatures we would have been. Obedience from love and trust is the only worthy motive for obedience, and it's the ultimate sign of maturity. God's goal is not to cajole us into submission, but rather to prove to us that He loves us. He wants us to respond to His kindness rather than His threats.

He will judge us because He loves us.

He will forgive us because He loves us.

That is why the human heart, in order to be truly free, must be allowed the opportunity to make a wrong choice. Human freedom and maturity will never be achieved if God only made our choices for us. Adam's sin brought about pain, suffering, and grief, not God. We cause the horrors of this world, not God. Suffering and death were initiated by a choice that was willingly made by the man in the first garden. Suffering and death are *our fault*. He created us to care for His planet; we decided to destroy His planet. He wants us to grow up.

And that is why in the first garden, God wasn't trying to prevent humans from becoming gods, He was trying to protect us from becoming monsters.

# End of the Second Movement

# OF DREAMS AND REALITY

The heart of Man is not compound of lies,
but draws some wisdom from the only Wise,
and still recalls him. Though now long estranged,
Man is not wholly lost nor wholly changed.
Dis-graced he may be, yet is not dethroned,
and keeps the rags of lordship once he owned.
    J.R.R. Tolkien, *Mythopoeia*

I am not hiding from reality—I'm counting on it. I do carry this dream within me, and I believe that we all do to some degree or another. Whenever I sit by a creek or walk through a glade in the forest in the morning, I feel the First World and I marvel at the overwhelming joy it brings. But is it all just a fantasy? Am I merely delusional? Is it a nice idea but completely disconnected from reality? There is a part of me that will not accept that conclusion. But if not a fantasy or a delusion, then what is the source of my vision?

Perhaps it is a memory. Not a personal one, but rather a genetic one. Perhaps within the human race lies the memory of a world in which we were designed to live. In a sort of pre-programmed way, we know what kind of world we were supposed to have, and we instinctively know that it wasn't like this. Plato thought we remembered the heavens, where we dwelt as spirits before and after our death, but I suggest that we have an instinctual longing for Eden, for a world that was actually real and which had no flaws. We know we shouldn't die; we know there shouldn't be suffering; we know that war, disease, and crime are corruptions of our perfection; we know that lust and hatred and conflict are the result of our own selfish choices. But why do we know that?

It is because we know what we should have been.

# Movement Three

# The Heart of Darkness

". . . No, it is impossible; it is impossible to convey the life-sensation of any given epoch of one's existence—that which makes its truth, its meaning—its subtle and penetrating essence. It is impossible. We live, as we dream—alone...."

*Heart of Darkness*, Joseph Conrad

# PETER

I want to tell you now about one of the greatest gifts God gave to me after Tierre died: Peter Crawford. He had been in my discipleship group before Tierre passed away, but then he became my greatest friend. He was a wild, reckless kind of youth who had an over-active imagination and no governor switch, but, when Christ got a hold of him, he had an equally passionate, reckless love for people. I could tell you stories of him that would make you cringe, and others that would make you cry. There was no middle of the road for Pete.

**Peter at his bachelor party**

We became friends partly because of our common love for hiking and traveling. We hiked Glacier National Park together in Montana in July of '93 while Faye stayed with Pete's mom, Carolyn. It was just a little less than a year after Tierre's death, and I was still so solemn, wrapped in a shroud of grief. However, Pete had a gift for making me laugh whatever was going on. We would be listening to the Christian musician David Meece while we drove, and he would come up with the most outrageous music videos I could ever imagine. Poor David didn't have a chance. But as off-the-wall as we were sometimes, Pete and I could talk for hours about the most serious and profound theological topics, and I discovered that under his veneer of immaturity resided a deeply thoughtful, passionate, and authentic individual. In all honesty, I have never met someone quite like Pete.

And so when the opportunity arose in the summer of '94, he wanted to come along with me on my trip to visit family in Arizona and California. His motives weren't purely altruistic, though, because he had fallen in love with cactus on a mission trip in '91, and this was his opportunity to really get up-close and personal with them. I was more than willing to accommodate him. I loved the Southwest, having lived there much of my life, and I was happy to introduce him to it all since it meant I would also have help with Faye on the road. And Pete was fun.

So, my plan was to take him to Sedona by way of Bryce Canyon, Lake Powell, and the North Rim of the Grand Canyon. We were going to hike, sightsee, swim, cliff jump, and then visit Tierre's family and some of my church friends. Then, after Sedona, we would go on to Southern California to see my parents.

The most exciting opportunity, though, was going to be the Grand Canyon. Pete had never been there before, but I had been there many times with my parents as a kid. I loved the Canyon. I remember camping with my parents and cousins on the South Rim. We would ride bikes, feed the chipmunks, take long rim walks, and dumpster dive for aluminum cans. My mom and I even rode mules down to Roaring Springs, 2.5 miles below the North Rim. Later in life, when I lived in Sedona, some friends and I hiked from rim-to-rim-to-rim for five days. Therefore, the Canyon, by the time I met Pete, had already been well established in my heart as my favorite place in the world.

So, it was my pleasure to plan a special opportunity for Pete: we would hike down to Roaring Springs, stand under the waterfall, and then hike back out. I was able to carry Faye on my back in a child carrier on the way down, but halfway back up I couldn't take another step. It was Peter who took her the rest of the way out, and he still beat me by half-an-hour. That was the kind of friend he was.

Well, we also had a good time at Lake Powell swimming, jumping off cliffs, losing my glasses, and an equally wonderful time exploring Sedona, visiting family, and reconnecting with my church friends from when Tierre and I had lived there. We next hustled down to Southern Cal, hung out with my parents, celebrated Faye's birthday early, and then high-tailed it back to Spokane. What a whirlwind of a trip, but I wouldn't exchange my memories of that time for anything.

In the following summer of '95, he went with me on a mini Faye World Tour, but this time we went to visit my family in Oregon. We visited the farm and he met my aunts, uncles, and cousins. He had now been introduced to every important person in my life within just a few years' time. In '96, though, Pete married his high school sweet heart, Amanda, and we didn't do any more long road trips together for quite awhile. It wasn't until 1999 that both Pete and Amanda were able to come with me to the Grand Canyon again for a six-day hike. I was ecstatic. It had been twelve years since I had last extensively hiked the Canyon, and I had been dreaming of doing a special hike to a place called Clear Creek ever since my original hike. So, I planned it all out, got all the permits, and then Pete and Amanda both got blisters on the way down. I was so disappointed, but then it hit me at 3 a.m. that I could hike to Clear Creek on my own, and they could enjoy some one-on-one time together without me around for the next two days.

It turned out that they had a great time together, camping on the cliffs above Phantom Ranch, cooling off in Bright Angel Creek, and just lounging about. For me, I spent two nights in utter, blissful seclusion—and I have never felt such respect and awe for the power of God before in my life. That trip was magical in so many ways, and I will cherish that time with them for eternity.

The next time Pete and I hiked the Canyon together, though—and the last time—was in 2005. For this journey I selected a rugged, off-the-beaten path-type trail, and did it ever live up to its billing. We saw practically no one for the entire five days. We got to see where the Little Colorado River connected with the Colorado, and we took mini-hikes up side canyons and just hung out together and caught up on life. He had a son and daughter now and he lived in Pasco, Washington. I lived in Colorado and was remarried. I look back and I remember thinking we would do these kind of trips until we were old men. And even then, after our knees couldn't take it anymore, we would still rim walk and reminisce about the good ole' days. But that was never to happen. What I wouldn't give to re-walk that trail with my best friend.

**Corey (left) and Peter in the Grand Canyon, 2005**

My next opportunity to enter the Canyon came in 2008. My father-in-law, brother-in-law, and I were going to raft the Canyon for six days. I tried to get Pete to come along, but he was getting ready to move to Redding, California where he would manage two cancer clinics. It had been a dream of his to live there ever since that inspiring mission trip to Mexico in '91 when he had fallen in love with cactus. So, when the opportunity presented itself, he jumped at it.

We had to put off any immediate trips for the time being. He visited me in Colorado; I visited him in Redding, and we called each other weekly and talked about politics and faith, told stupid jokes, complained about church, and talked about the future. It was just like we had done on all those road trips for hours and hours, days and days, and weeks and weeks.

He often reminded me, though, that I had promised to move to Redding if he ever did, and since he had, where was I? I did try to, but it was in April 2011 when he found out that he had an unknown form of stage four cancer. I went out to see him that May, and then one more time in July, but he died on August 21, 2011, just four months after being diagnosed. At the time I am writing this, he didn't even know he had cancer a year ago. He didn't know it would be his last Thanksgiving, his last Christmas, his last birthday. Life is that fleeting. That vaporous.

He is the greatest friend God has ever given to me and I feel his loss every day. He helped me to laugh when I couldn't anymore. He encouraged me in my darkest moments; challenged me; argued with me; and agreed with me just to shut me up. We were best friends, and I feel like I understand better the words of Enkidu: "Is this the way it is with friends? Me to die and you to wander on alone?"

Apparently it is.

# THE PAST IS NOT GONE

"'I am the God of Abraham, the God of Isaac, and the God of Jacob.' He is not the God of the dead but of the living."

Matthew 22:32

Mankind churns about in a cacophony of whirling busy-ness, hanging on for dear life. We must keep employed; we must care for the needy; we must protect ourselves from shame; we must walk the dog. We must relax; we must dance; we must peer into the turquoise waters and pass out in the forgetfulness of our self-indulgence.

Every day we get a little more frenetic; every day we get a little lazier.

What are we doing?

I strapped Faye into her $60 car seat to keep her safe as we traveled to Tillamook. A big push and a loud click assured me she couldn't fall out, or fly out, if we happened to roll over.

It was a quick seven hour drive from Spokane, and I liked to get going early: 3 a.m. early. I made sure my coffee was hot, Faye had her blanket, and the door to the house was locked. I pulled out of the driveway slowly, turned onto the street, and glided away. A shadow.

No other cars. Traffic lights flashed yellow and every business along Division Street was lit up like it was open for business. The black ribbon of the street guided me, but no place was open, not even a bar. It was the in-between time, when only the metallic residue of light drifted through the darkness.

The mall flowed past and even now, at this time of night, its power of attraction pulled on me. I wanted to go in and stare at things. I couldn't afford those things, but it was cathartic to stare at them: to want them, to not have them, and to walk away still content. It was like standing in the middle of a river, challenging the current to pull me down and roll me helplessly along, like a log. But the Spokane River never could get me, and neither could the mall. Why do we believe the more stuff we have, the freer we will be? I have found that it is when I get away from excess that I feel the most free. The mall's magnetic allure weakened the farther away I drove, and it wasn't long before I crept out onto the highway.

The city seemed alive. Most people were asleep, but the city was thriving like bones, blood vessels, and soul. Working. The highway lifted me a little higher up as I drove west out of town, and I could now see the row of hospitals on the south side pulsing with activity. Unlike most businesses, they were active 24/7. They had to be. Their brightly lit halls and beeping rooms with periodic moans and emergencies were keeping a segment of the population alive while overseeing other's deaths. Loved ones needed them to survive, but if they didn't, they needed comfort. Everyone wants to live another day and enjoy another moment.

I drove past as quickly as I could.

Spokane flickered out behind me, and the early morning darkness, gratefully, closed in around me. Peace. This was the moment I had been craving. Simplicity. Here, only the bit of road in front of me mattered. I could see the dashed white line straight between my two lanes, and the edge on the right was bordered by pine forest. It was a split highway at this point, and the headlights from any on-coming traffic on my left were far away, distant, unobtrusive just like I needed them to be. I needed the simple boundaries of my small truck. My seat, the stick shift, the faintly comforting dashboard lights, the clutch, brake, and gas. These were the constraints of my world for the next few hours. And this is what I imagined death would be like: simply present with an undistracted devotion to the Lord.

The grave.

Only my memories would keep me company after I die, for the past is never really gone. Hopefully, I would have more good memories than bad ones, because if I were unforgiven and knew I was going to be held accountable for my sins. No wonder there is weeping and gnashing of teeth in *Hades*. My wicked deeds haunt me even in this life, wretched man that I am. Who will rescue me from this heart of darkness?

The engine sounded right, and as I motored up the final hill out of town, I realized I had passed the off-ramp I would take to get to the cemetery where my wife was buried.

Shaking my head, I decided I needed some music and I opened my package of sunflower seeds, which, for some odd reason can keep me awake on long trips better than any caffeine rush. Empty again, I let my mind stay that way.

By six a.m. we were in The Tri-Cities—Richland, Pasco, and Kennewick—and I had a favorite Denny's that I loved to stop at. It reminded me of the road trips I had gone on with my parents all those years ago. I woke up Faye; we went in, ate breakfast, and then walked around outside a little to stretch our legs. My brain was waking up, too, and the deep melancholy of the night was being chased away by the morning light. It felt good to be alive. I smiled at Faye, clicked her back in, and gave her something to color and reminded her if she dropped anything I wouldn't be able to pick it up. I also put in some kid music and we had a regular pre-school going on while we were rolling down that road.

After a ways, the city long gone, the land undulated like a great tan ocean. No more forests, but not really desert, either. It was just vacant. This stretch of road bored me to death, but I knew it wasn't long before we would converge with the Columbia River Gorge, and once I got there I felt like we were as good as in Tillamook.

A branch of the Oregon Trail converged with the river near Umatilla, and I can only imagine the hope settlers must have experienced when they first saw it. For thousands of miles they had been drinking from barrels and holes, and for the last few hundred miles they had been dying because there was no water so close to their destination. Dirt and grit. Starvation and thirst. Tiredness and loss. Then this big, beautiful, conduit of life converging with their dreams and they were nearly home. So was I.

I recently discovered that my fourth great grandfather, Squire Stoten Whitman, started his journey West from Monmouth, Illinois, traveled the Oregon Trail in 1850, and settled in Monmouth, Oregon. I even have a picture of him with the wagon, oxen, and other men sitting around. It was given to me by Monmouth University (now Western Oregon State University). They had it because he had donated the 200 original acres the school now sits on. He was a blacksmith, not an educator like me, but he was a strong Christian and the group he came with intended to start a Christian place of learning. Ironically, I attended Monmouth University for one term in 1987 without having any idea about the significant role my family had played in its founding. How the results of one's decisions may play out for centuries.

**Preparing to leave Monmouth, IL - 1850**

I had traveled the gorge so many times my mind couldn't keep all the memories organized. In practical terms, our strong impression is that time has a direction; that it is a line drawn in the sand; that it is a series of snapshots placed in a row, as a movie, and that we can remember moments which are now gone as we constantly move toward what will be. But what if this was not the nature of time? What if all our moments continue to exist and time was merely the way in which our consciousness kept track of where we were? What if memories were more like bricks being stacked, collectively shaping us into a house we call Our Life? But they aren't stretching out behind us—they are us. Isn't God able to observe every moment we have ever lived and ever will live? So, does any moment ever really cease if God remembers it?

Oh the wandering, philosophical meanderings the mind bends itself with sometimes! I looked out my window and began to wonder if I were moving at all. Couldn't it be true that the landscape was simply moving under me? Couldn't the world be spinning my tires, while I was merely sitting in my car? No. Time must be the fabric of space wherein we all move in relation to all other things. No. Time itself is the motion of all things. The universe is time. No. Time is how we measure the motion, it is not the motion itself. Or is it—

—me? As far as I can tell I am time. I am the one in motion, and I can remember what I've been and what once happened to me and to others, but how can I prove this? I suppose the evidence is in the words I'm writing, which didn't exist before I wrote them and which continue to exist after I wrote them, thus proving I once did something in a previous moment and which continues into this moment and future ones. Every moment, therefore, matters, and it will always matter. So, if there is a Book of Life which records all of my actions—a mind of God which observes and remembers—then aren't my actions everlasting? But what if that same God chose to erase from His book those actions of mine which He chose to forgive and forget? They would be destroyed, wouldn't they?

But—whatever the proper definition of time may be—I do know that I exist because God knows me:

> But that the dead are raised, even Moses showed, in the passage about the burning bush, where he calls the Lord THE GOD OF ABRAHAM, AND THE GOD OF ISAAC, AND THE GOD OF JACOB. Now He is not the God of the dead but of the living; for all live to Him. Luke 20:37-38

God knows us, therefore we exist, and because of this the most fearsome thing would be to be forgotten by God. That would be true death; the ultimate, final death.

So, I can't get it straight. Is time motion or non-motion? Am I swept along a river of time that relentlessly moves me forward, or am I soaking in an ever-rising ocean of time we call "the present" and everything that was, always is? Is there a timeline, or am I experience?

In patience I relinquish all my sighs,
To wait in sacred silence sweet compline,
And languish in a place so quite divine,
Strewn with gilded thoughts without design.
Time may hide within its weary eye,
The face of ancient youth and youthful age,
But in God's mind the mounts have reached the sky,
And seas have scoured down their high prestige.
So Time can never give us certain counsel,
But Love exists, a mind that's not our own.
Its fountain pours from moments of eternal,
And is ceaseless perpetuity alone.
And since High Truth reveals that God is love,
If I should blink and see tomorrow was
—though today prevails, the sun above—
Would to be has been and yet it still impends?
    I cannot proclaim only now is now,
    When love exists in the heart with no bounds.

So, is Squire Stoten really dead? I know his body has died, but is his essence just gone? According to God's word, no, because God is the God of the living and since Squire Stoten was known by God, he must still exist. He is still living.

In the same way (although in my limited, flawed, human way) my journey through the Gorge reflected the way God sees time. As I journeyed, I was swept up in a collection of memories which exist because I remember them. It's odd to me how a place, a smell, or a song can trigger memories and make me feel as if I were right there again. Is this what immortality will be like?

❖    I was a sophomore in high school, and this was going to be my first hunting experience. I was getting an entire week off school, and my sister and I rode in the over-the-cab camper of my parent's white Ford truck. I discovered years ago that if I lay on my back with my feet pointed to the rear, I could read without getting car sick no matter how serpentine the road. However, if I lay sideways, or on my stomach, I would instantly get queasy.

❖ The Gorge in October was bleak, grey and windy. Cold. The pine forest on the cliff side was speckled with some remnants of color, but it mostly went quietly to sleep for the winter. The river was always in turmoil no matter what season it was.

❖ A winter much later, I was driving back to Spokane after spending Christmas in Tillamook. A storm had hit the night before and the Gorge just east of Portland was covered in ice and snow. And there was wind. The wind was always blowing. I had to drive 40 mph most of the way, but the semi-trucks scared me more than any ice patch. I remember the intense fear I felt as I passed them quickly, speeding up to get by them in case they slid into Faye and me.

❖ An overlook. I remember riding in the back with my cousins in the red van my Uncle Art and Aunt Bonnie owned. We were on our way to Eastern Oregon to go hunting, and we stopped at an overlook, stretched our legs, and the weather was particularly beautiful that day. Vaguely I remember standing at the railing, running up and down cement stairs, and admiring the ruffled surface of the river. And I remember the wind. I always remember the wind.

❖ At a rest area, Tierre and I had gotten out of our green van and taken our dog Winston for a walk. I got a picture of him lifting his leg and I could swear I saw him smile. He pranced about, sniffing the air, going to every spot any dog had ever marked and taking over their territory. This was his domain, his canyon. Tierre and I walked about and stood on the banks of the river and I told her of all the times I had traveled up and down this Gorge with family and friends. We even swung on the swing.

❖ My friend's four wheel drive pickup was about as noisy and rough of a ride as I've ever been in. Six of us— the old men were in the other vehicles—were headed to the North Fork of the Umatilla to go elk hunting in November. We had horses and loads of gear. We were going to hike three miles into the wilderness, set up our big canvas tent and hunt for eight days. It was a man's dream. No showers. Lots of bacon, eggs, and meat. Even more trekking up and down canyons all day.

Art and I started out together until we split up. He went up the ridge on the right, and I was to go down through the draw on the left, then up the ridge on the other side where we'd converge up top. Just as I crunched through the fringe of the woods, though, I saw an elk down to my left contentedly, obliviously, eating a bush. I took aim and got her through the heart. It was my first kill and I had always been worried that I would only wound an animal, or that I wouldn't be able to shoot.

It had been a couple of years earlier that I had been deer hunting with my family in the Hell's Canyon area of eastern Oregon. Denise (a dear friend of the family) and I were walking together at the bottom of a valley. My dad was ahead of us and this was my first time carrying a rifle. Up high we heard some shots fired and Denise to this day swears she heard bullets ricocheting around us. We took cover next to some trees and it wasn't long before we heard an animal crashing down through the brush. I lifted up my rifle, hoping it was a deer. It was a buck and I took aim, but my left leg started shaking like a pogo stick and I couldn't get him in my sights. Buck Fever they call it. It was just as well, because he was already wounded. He collapsed onto his haunches and his head lolled over. He tried to get up, but he just writhed there until he died. We called up to the other hunters that they had got him and one guy came down and looked a little drunk and a little put out that he had to clean his kill and haul him all the way up the canyon. How inconvenient. I don't know if he ever finished the job. We took off.

My family, on the other hand, had a whole system worked out on how to get deer out of the bottom of a deep ravine. It was my first hunting camp—I was a sophomore—when I discovered how clever my family really was. They strung up canvas tents with cables stretched between trees and designed an outhouse that rivaled the Old West. We had a regular tent city that put most camps to shame. We built huge fires and every tent had a wood stove welded by my uncle Ron. He also had a turquoise Toyota Land Cruiser that had a thousand feet of cable mounted on a winch in the back. Somebody got a deer that year and we drove right to the rim and ran that cable right down to the gutted deer. We kept its hide on to protect the meat, and then hung it from a pole in camp. Later my cousin Kim and I skinned it and I still remember how bitterly cold my hands became. I salted and then traded the hide for a pair of deerskin gloves that I used for years.

**Makinster Hunting Camp, 1990**

❖ Faye started crying in the back and I gave her a little snack to hold her over until lunch. I wanted to get to The Dalles before we stopped. My dad had been a youth pastor in The Dalles—I can't exactly remember when because it was long before me. On one of our trips they had showed me the parsonage they had lived in. I remember visiting their church, too. We went to a potluck for a 100-year anniversary, I think, or something like that.

❖ It was year's later, long after Tierre had passed away, that I drove through The Dalles alone—Faye was staying with friends—on my way to meet Art and Bonnie, Ron and Andrea, and a few others to go for a half day rafting trip on the Deschutes River. I rarely had this much time to myself and I was glorying in the opportunity. After rafting, we said our goodbyes and I went and camped by a lake close to Mt. Hood. The site was isolated on a little bluff and no one was around. I had clear views of Mt. Hood and I can't remember a better campsite, ever.

❖ The next time I went rafting was with Pete years later. We both still lived in Spokane, and I had been given a leftover bid from a school auction for a rafting trip on the Snake River. We drove down to the Washington/Idaho border and since neither of us wanted to pay for a hotel, we slept on playground equipment in a park. A policeman woke us up at 5 a.m., but he wasn't too upset. Just told us to get on our way.

❖ And then my mind wandered to La Grande, OR, not too much further south from the Snake. We used to stop there after every hunting camp to clean up. It was a special treat after a week in the wilderness, and also quite necessary. My cousin Jason and I stayed in the same room one time, and he allowed so much water to run out onto the bathroom floor that it leaked into the room below.

❖ La Grande. Pendleton. Baker. I never spent any significant time in Baker until just a few years ago after they built the Oregon Trail Museum. My parents had visited there and raved about it. So, the next two times that Beth, Faye, Avery and I (you'll learn about them soon), traveled from Longmont to Tillamook, we made sure we visited the museum. Both times we barely snuck in before it closed and barely had time to read the plaques. But what I have seen fills me with awe. Here we were, traveling at speeds in excess of seventy miles per hour. The wagon trains traveled nine miles in a day! It would take them eight days to go the distance we did in an hour. And their living conditions! We drove back to our hotel, swam in a pool, ate at a restaurant that has a miniature train running at all times, and went to sleep in comfortable beds. Them? They slept on the ground next to their wagons and most of the time had very little to eat, let alone any variety. Time for them was only that moment. They didn't know what would come; they didn't know what our technology would allow us to do; they didn't know that their sacrifices would lead to our comforts. But they were still here, living their moment, because I remembered them. Maybe what I would become was as valid as what they had become. Squire Stoten was part of the reason I was here.

❖ After The Dalles came my favorite feature of the Gorge: the multiple waterfalls. There is an old highway that is so beautiful words can hardly describe. You just feel like you're driving through a painting it's so unreal, but then you remember it's all real. A place such as this exists. There are moss covered stone bridges, portions of the curving road completely roofed by trees, light filtering through like strands of silver hair, and if you drive slowly and look carefully, you'll catch glimpses of small waterfalls cascading down green, rugged ravines. Places like these can almost make one believe in fairies and leprechauns.

Horsetail falls is an easy hike. I'd taken Faye there when she was little and I have some of the cutest pictures of her lying in a field of green grass with white daisies. But the granddaddy of them all is Multnomah Falls. I can stand and stare at that magnificent waterfall for hours in utter contentment. It is loud enough to filter out almost all the sounds of people and there is a pilgrimage-type feel to ascending the path to the bridge. To me it feels sacred, and I can visualize portions of the trail with vivid accuracy. And then to stand up there and look closely at the chunk of rock that is the size of a house in the pool beneath the upper falls, is mesmerizing. Oddly, I would bet some have never noticed it. I know I have to descend again, of course, but I do so reluctantly.

**Multnomah Falls**

. I have waded in its waters, spent hours in the gift shop, have eaten ice cream, and have drunk hot chocolate while seated on its benches. I've been there in every season and in every weather condition. I rarely just drive by it, and when I don't stop I always regret it. My life changes, but the Falls never seem to, although I know that's a misperception. It experiences change just as I do, albeit more slowly. A particle here, a particle there, and the cumulative effect is the same as what happens to us all. We are different every few years. Not so different we're unrecognizable, but emotionally, spiritually, and physically we alter. And sometimes I fancy the Falls notice me and remember what I used to be—and are surprised at what I've become. I am convinced that we are not just dust in the wind, crumbling to the ground; we are immortal. All I am does not just slip away. I am known. The past is never gone. Experience is everything that I am. I will not cease to exist unless God doesn't know me.

My life movement, then, as I perceive it, is in part linked to the Gorge. Every stage of my life has passed through that rift and it is there that my experiences seem to pile up like rocks beneath its mighty cliffs. It has seen the youthful me playing along its banks, walking my dog, kissing my wife, and pushing my daughter in a swing that overlooked its waters. It even tried to kill me once with a boulder that tumbled across my path six feet in front of me. And it has seen the middle-aged me.

I have driven more of my life along that stretch of road than any other, and it will be there long after my transient ways have moved on from its massive experience. My time on earth is temporal, but my life in God is everlasting. The Gorge has become the visible manifestation of time to me. I am now; I was then, and, Lord willing, I will be tomorrow, but *only because I am the Lord's will I live forever*. Only He actually knows what I've been and what I will be—the Gorge doesn't—and only He knows me because only He always is. He is the great *I AM* and He will outlast the Gorge. I only am because He is, and I would cease to exist with all that I know, if He didn't know me.

Thank you Lord for the Gorge, a place that helps me to know my life is in motion because I can remember myself there. I can see a little bit of what You see. I also know that You are the real mover of my life. My motion has been from You, to You, and because of You. I only have a brief moment here, but You are eternity, and You retain all that I am. I will only cease if You forget me. Forgive me for my sins. Forget those, please. I am Yours.

# Questions

"You have placed our iniquities before You, Our secret sins in the light of Your presence. For all our days have declined in Your fury; We have finished our years like a sigh."

Psalm 90

As much as I love this world, I also hate it. I am prone to its darkness like any other person, and my own personal sins will haunt me for the rest of my earthly life. The only thing that keeps me sane is knowing that I'm forgiven, and when God forgives that means my deeds will not be held against me at the final judgment when all of our crimes and diseases will be burned up like the worthless chaff they are.

And so, even though I love this world, it is completely rational for me to hate it as well. It corrupts me. It's like an acid on my dreams, causing them to fizzle away in a toxic steam.

This world is madness and delight all at once. It is shameful and beautiful. It is filled with horror and filled with wonder. It is gross, despicable, terrifying, and deranged; and it is glamorous, charming, brave, and sensible. The world has just enough lovely things in it to make me want to fix it, but it is just horrible enough for me to want it wiped out. As G.K. Chesterton asks, "Can [one] hate [the world] enough to change it, and yet love it enough to think it worth changing?" (*Orthodoxy*, 64).

Let's see.

## *Is God Good?*

Before anyone can make a confident decision to follow a person, we must evaluate him or her. Is this person trustworthy? Does he live a lifestyle consistent with his values? Does he have what it takes to get the job done?

And in regards to the issue of death, these same criteria apply. Is what a belief system says about death trustworthy? Is its teaching consistent with what we know about death? Does it have what it takes to solve the problem of death?

We all, at some point, will question our belief system and it will usually be when death gets in our face. For example, when my friend Pete first got the news that he had cancer, his initial response was that this was "for his good and God's glory." It was a correct and faith-filled acknowledgement of God's sovereignty in all situations, even in trials. However, after a few months of dealing with the progressive horrors of cancer, Peter began to ask the ultimate question: "How could God be good since this is happening to me?" At a fundamental level, he was questioning the Bible's explanation for death and why the world is the way it is.

As he explained it to me, he believed it would have been better if God wouldn't have even given Adam and Eve the opportunity to disobey Him. Why would God give them a choice if He knew what would happen if they chose poorly? Look at what it led to. Look at the devastation that the fall has wrought upon the earth and on mankind. It is horrifying when put into its proper view, and Peter, if anything, was an honest person. He wanted to call things out as they were, not as people hoped they would be. He was honestly angry with God and the way things were turning out for him. He didn't see death as "good," and he wondered how a "good" God could contrive such suffering.

I want to restate at this point that such a question is an emotional cry of the heart, and that intellectual answers typically aren't enough to bring peace during the intense times of suffering. My friend knew perfectly well about the fall and Adam's willful disobedience in defiance of God, but just to know the doctrine doesn't really make one feel better, nor does it bring tranquility. In times like these, asking God "What are You doing?" is a fair question. It's okay to ask. God gave us our intellect *and* our emotions.

I was with Peter when he asked this question, and, ironically, it was the day after we had gone to a healing prayer service at a local church. Another of Pete's friends, Scott, and myself had taken Pete to this church, filled out the paperwork and sat in a hallway with a bunch of other people who were there with various ailments and what-not. After awhile, we went into a room where the lights were dim and a worship team played music and a group of people were up front who would walk around and pray with us and encourage us, kind of like coaches.

After awhile, we went into another room and two men came and laid their hands on Pete and we all prayed for him. They would stop periodically and ask if he was feeling anything different, and when he would say "No," they would then pray some more. But after several of these pauses without any results, they said he should maybe go out and then come back in again later so that someone else could pray for him; maybe someone more "powerful" than they were. They seemed rather disappointed his cancer hadn't fled his body (as were we, but for different reasons), but the thing that concerned me most about their attitude is that they implied that God's plan for Pete was to be healed at that moment. God did have plans for Pete, but it wasn't to be healed of cancer.

It was the next day that Pete went into a deep funk and bitterly stated, "God isn't good." He wasn't raising the topic for a theological debate; he was claiming that it was illogical to say God is good if He could allow the kind of suffering he was going through. And, indeed, this is the same question asked of every Christian who ever gets an interview on national TV or radio. Some people can't wait to ask this question of a Christian in a public situation, because, quite frankly, it is completely unanswerable in a mere sentence or two (I've already written half of a book in order to properly deal with it). For example, if God were really an all-powerful Creator, and if He were also really as good as Christians claim, how could He allow this world to be such a mess? The question is brilliant because there is no way to answer it quickly without sounding ridiculously positive or black-heartedly cruel.

If one were to answer, "God is good, but He allows evil," then the response is, "Your God must be weak and thereby cruel." And the critics have a point! I would even enhance their point by asking: "How does our defending God by saying He allows evil make a strong case for His goodness? If I were to stand by and watch a murder, theft, or rape *and could do something about it,* isn't that a decision to allow harm? Why does the all-powerful, all-knowing God of the universe stand by and allow mass suffering and murder? How could He be good and ignore all this cruelty?" The detractors have a point.

On the other hand, if one were to answer (as the "healers" do) that "God only intends good things for us" (and by implication, if good things don't happen then it is a lack of faith on our part) then the critics can say, "Look around! If God only intended good things for us, then He must be even less powerful than I thought, and He certainly isn't good. If He doesn't want bad things to happen to us, but they do in spite of His desire that they don't, how weak is that? And if He is strong enough to stop it, and He doesn't, how evil is that?" And they have a point!

And that was the heart of Pete's question: how could God allow what was happening to him? How could the Bible be right? How could God have allowed even the possibility for sin? He was going to die and leave behind his children and his wife. It didn't make any sense to him. How, in any way shape or form could that mean God is good?

In between his hacking up phlegm and moaning in pain, he expressed his anger at the way things were, and I firmly believe his anger was justifiable, and is, in fact, the whole point of the matter. We are supposed to get mad at death. We are supposed to hate it. We are supposed to ask the hard questions. We are supposed to wonder why God allowed death to enter the world, knowing what kind of horrors it would lead to. Death forces us to ask the questions we normally wish to avoid. Facing death causes us to see our sin for what it is.

And, honestly, I have nothing to say that will make anyone feel okay with his or her impending death. If you want a sound bite answer, I have nothing. Absolutely nothing. From my experience, death is horrifying and I hate death as much as it deserves.

---

## *We are supposed to get mad at death.*

---

And let me say something even more shocking: I believe it's okay to hate death. It isn't unspiritual or unnatural to hate it. It is, in my opinion, the most natural thing in the world to hate death and it is, in fact, unnatural *not* to hate it. In the spirit of calling it like it is, I have never heard an argument posited that can convince me not to hate death. I saw my best friend wither away into nothing, and then die. How could I look his grief (or my own) in the eye and say, "Be cool with this"? When I sat with Pete, every theologism fell away dull and gray, just as it had when my wife was wrenched away from me. Just as it did when I saw my dad lose his mind to dementia. Triteness gets exposed quickly when you look death in the face.

So, my challenge to the healers at that church is for them to read their Bibles a little more thoroughly and with a little less marketing strategy. Genuinely free health care is appealing (no more chemo and no more doctor's bills), but making God out to be super nice is as idolatrous as making Him out to be tyrannical. He is compassionate, but He is also an unbiased judge. God is merciful and forgiving, but He will also cause calamity.

Read the entire Book of Judges.

Read Isaiah 45:6b-7 where the prophet says,

> I am the LORD, and there is no other, the One forming light and creating darkness, causing well-being and *creating calamity* (emphasis added); I am the LORD who does all these.

2 Kings 24:3-4 says,

> Surely this [destruction of Jerusalem] came upon Judah at the command of the Lord, to remove them out of his sight.... For he [their king] filled Jerusalem with innocent blood and *the Lord would not pardon* (emphasis added).

When Christians try to claim that God will eventually forgive everyone, there is a lot of evidence that that simply is not true. In these verses, we see that He wouldn't even forgive His own people because they were so sinfully offensive to Him. They were killing the innocent: is there anything more heinous than that? God is supposed to judge those who have committed wicked deeds *because He is good*! He's good therefore He judges sin. He's good and that is why the wicked will perish from the earth. Justice is not evil: withholding justice is evil. Justice is the way God deals with evil, and the harshest penalty is death.

And we all die.

The point is God does not always intend good things for us. We aren't all going to get rich; we aren't all going to escape suffering. He will cause calamity in order to get our attention. He doesn't merely allow it—sometimes He causes it! He might even harden a person's heart in order to bring Himself glory (e.g. the pharaoh of the Exodus). We do God an injustice by shying away from this answer. God is harsh and firm. His strength isn't demonstrated by solving every problem that we have, Jim Carrey-style. He proved His strength when He created everything. He proved His strength when He delivered Israel out of bondage in Egypt. He proved His strength when He raised Christ from the dead. God was flexing His muscles for us in every one of those situations and in so many more little ways in our lives every day all the time. He isn't weak. I see His strength every day.

His strength is in the sinews of the horse.

His strength is in the wings of an eagle.

His strength is in the unbreakable bond of love.

I want to be sure, here, that you know that I am not saying that God was punishing my friend Peter with cancer. If that is how God punishes our sins, I could think of a lot of other people God should have punished long before He ever got to Pete. The world is fallen and we are all on the path to the grave. Pete wasn't any more wicked than any of the rest of us.

Also, I do not believe for a second that Pete died because he had a lack of faith. The Bible is filled with people who had great faith and yet died anyway. Yes, some were healed because of their faith, but some were killed because of their faith, too. It could be God's will that we, as His children, might have to suffer in our lives, but not as the direct result of some sin we have committed; there might be a larger plan God is unfolding.

Read Foxe's Book of Martyrs.

Read Hebrews 11.

Look at the cross!

Pete's death seems premature from our temporal perspective, but even if he had lived he eventually would still have died. We all will. Death is our enemy. It's a horrible situation.

Cancer overwhelmed his body and he died. My dad has died because aging happens, and I might die tomorrow because of some freak accident, and no amount of faith is going to circumvent the inevitable death of my body.

And that is why the "Mr. Bluebird on my shoulder" answer some Christians give is deficient. It's not entirely untrue, but it's not completely true, either. God is good, but His goodness isn't only shown through His mercy; it's also shown through His justice. A lot of bad stuff happens in this world because of sin and we can't pretend it doesn't, and we shouldn't on the one hand say God is in charge of this world and then on the other hand imply He's too weak to deal with it. He is patient, not weak. And He is good even when bad things happen to us.

God is good even though trials come our way.

God is good even though evil seems to prevail.

God is good even though people we love die.

God is good, even when He punishes sin.

It's when we face the hard questions that the truth becomes clear. It took awhile, but Pete's faith became stronger and more vibrant *after* he questioned the wisdom and goodness of God. I believe his quest for understanding was similar to Job's quest, because God answered Job and He answered Peter. However, God's answer wasn't what either of them expected.

What Pete finally realized the day after the healing ceremony, and which stirred up his anger, was the reality that God wasn't going to heal him. He had been hopeful his cancer would miraculously be taken away and he could get on with his life, and that would mean God was good (and what a marvelous testimony that would have been!) But God had different plans for his life, and that reality hit him hard. "I am going to die" is a hard truth to accept, so he lashed out at God. That is why any of us lash out at God when death gets in our face: it disrupts our fantasy that we can avoid it. That harsh reality is going to hit every single one of us eventually, and that is the point of death! We all have to face the reality of our situation. We're sinners in need of a savior! Our relationship with God has been shattered and no amount of philosophizing, drugs, whining, political structures, or magical potions will ever change that truth.

And in that moment of realization, God's answer to us isn't "Deal with it," or "Ha! Ha! Now I have you, my little pretties!" His true answer reverberates across the ages in the moment of our greatest crisis: "I have cured death! Don't lose hope! My Son has offered you life!" We must listen or forever hold our peace.

Pete's longing to be healed is the same longing we all have, only intensified. God hears our longing hearts. The fact that Pete died in no way discounts his faith in God: his faith was right on. It was just that the timing was off. Faith is never to demand God's mercy this second, but rather to trust in God that the miracle will come. The "healers" implied that the miracle was going to come on the day they laid their hands on Pete; but the real miracle occurred when God laid His hands on Pete.

God is with you even in the moment of your greatest trial. Pete's desire to be healed was exactly the same faith that Abraham had. It is the same faith as all the martyrs and Christians throughout the ages have had. As it says in Hebrews,

> And all these, having gained approval through
> their faith, *did not receive what was promised*
> (emphasis added), because God had provided
> something better for us, so that apart from us they
> would not be made perfect. (Hebrews 11:39-40)

Did you see that? They "did not receive what was promised." We like to talk about God fulfilling His promises to us, but the big one—the resurrection—is something we all have to wait for. What Peter wanted—life and healing—is the ultimate desire of the human heart. Our frustration, however, comes when we realize things are not working out now. We suffer. We face hardship. People we love die. Pain happens. This world is a mess and there are opposing forces setting themselves against God's truth. And on top of that, our own sins constantly assail us.

But someday we will get the reward of the crown of life together, at the same time. Peter, Tierre, you, me, Abraham, Moses, etc. All of us together, someday, will be resurrected. Our bodies and spirits will be reunited in a glorious moment and then all who are written in the Lamb's book of life will dwell in the New Heavens and the New Earth for eternity in the presence of God without sin or the fear of death.

That is what God has promised us, and yet, God, mercifully, will sometimes give us a glimmer of hope and a glimpse of that impending promise. And God did just such a thing for Peter and his wife, Amanda, about a week before he died.

You see, God did heal Peter of his cancer—for a day. I know that sounds odd, but it is what happened. For several weeks Pete hadn't been able to move his right arm because his unknown, stage four cancer, was invading his joints. But then, one evening after many of his friends had been fasting and praying all day—it was a Friday—he could suddenly move his arm. *Completely pain free.*

Some might not consider that a miracle, but there is no medical explanation for Peter to have been pain free. He was on drugs, but he had been on drugs for months. It had to have been God's mercy—knowing what was coming soon—and God gave him and Amanda one last, pain-free evening together. And if you think about it, every healing God performs is merely a temporary fix until we all receive our permanent healing at the resurrection. Pete's healing lasted for one, blissful evening, and that was enough. That night they danced, sang praise songs, and then recorded a video testimony explaining what had just happened to them. I have transcribed it in its entirety (Development C: "Peter's Testimony"), along with a link to the video. Here is an excerpt:

> He's putting my focus on Him. Not anything else.
> Whether He takes my life, or He keeps it, it's all
> for His glory…. He takes schmucks like us, who
> make stupid decisions, and He uses those to bring
> us to our knees so that we can see every trial is
> actually a blessing. The world will never
> understand it. You have to go through it to
> actually experience it. I'm not just a guy waving
> my arms [pain free]. I'm praising the Lord. He's
> doing great things and He's going to continue to
> do great things. He wants to do it in all of our
> lives, but we have to submit. Sometimes we
> submit willingly, but sometimes we don't, but it's
> all coming from a heart where He wants to bring
> us into connection with Him, so that we can enjoy
> His presence.

There is profound wisdom in those words, and that is from a man who was going through profound suffering. Peter had come to an "insane contentment," as Chesterton calls it, a "simple satisfaction," that could suddenly live with all of the apparent contradictions in life. Normally, we try to rationalize everything, seeking to draw straight lines from one event to another like Job's counselors. We would like it to be so simple: only evil people suffer, and only good people prosper. However, one of the many observations of Job is that the wicked prosper and the righteous suffer. Life seems random, paradoxical, and irrational.

But as my friend Peter discovered, like Job, being in the presence of God ties everything together, and the result is contentment. Pete said:

> There's times I questioned Him. And I
> questioned, God, why do You allow things to
> happen? It just seems so illogical. But you know
> what? I don't have everything up here [points to
> his head]. And it's when you're brought low, and
> Christ is brought up, that things start to come into
> clarity, and that you start to understand that
> there's so much more than what I can see, what
> the mind can comprehend. He's God. Not me.

Science is seeking to explain what our world is all about, but it can't. There are as many unsolved mysteries as there are solved, and science has only scratched the surface. Anything it has discovered only reveals deeper levels of complexity, and even though science provides neat little gadgets, it really can only analyze how things work. That's fine. That's what science is supposed to do, but there is a certain kind of madness to their dedication to figuring it all out, as if they can unveil the physical law that explains everything and then solve the ills of mankind. It is irrational to think that the universe could ever be boiled down to a single formula or a simple explanation. It is irrational to think that any of us, even collectively, could comprehend how all the pieces fit together. Only God's mind is capable of that. Hawking is smart, but he isn't *that* smart.

**Peter Pain Free**

On a little aside, this particular observation brings forward my intellectual dissatisfaction with atheism: atheism oversimplifies the world. As attractive as a mindless universe is on one level—nature does what it does, why get mad at it?—it is lonely on another level: there is nothing beyond ourselves. Atheists try to take design and intention out of life and our souls rebel against it. It dismisses our pain with, "Get over your superstitions, focus on solving the world's problems (which are primarily caused by religions, they say), and we'll be fine, at least until we die and then we won't care anymore." But has the world improved since we killed God? The 20th century—when atheists ruled the earth—is the bloodiest in world history.

But, quite frankly, no, we won't be fine. We all will die, and that's bad. Atheism offers no solution to death. They just say, "Deal with it," and they hope science will come up with a cure. But whether one is an atheist or a theist, the universal cry of our hearts is for a cure, and all of our attempts throughout history have failed.

But Jesus succeeded.

So, should I really put my faith in science to solve death? Scientists can give me a comfy bed to sleep in, and pain pills, but they can't cure death. Even if they could, would they be able to solve the human penchant for doing the wrong thing?

The fantasy isn't that God has cured death; the fantasy is to think we can cure death. In a conversation I had with Pete's wife, Amanda, after his funeral, she wondered why God hadn't seen fit to bring Himself glory by completely healing Peter and letting him live. Wouldn't that have brought God more glory? God's answer is that He will bring glory to Himself when He raises Peter from the dead with all the rest of us.

God will heal Peter, just not today.

It's not very comforting now because all of us who love Pete want him to be alive. But, on the other hand, it speaks to a deeper truth that brings a more lasting sense of peace: the death and suffering in this world is temporary. We all will have to face that profound, "Oh my" moment (unless we're alive when He returns), but we can find solace in knowing that death won't last forever, and that we will be resurrected.

*The fantasy isn't that God has cured death; the fantasy is to think we can cure death.*

The truth is irrefutable: evil exists, but God isn't evil, or powerless. Starving children and merciless warlords are not symptoms of an evil God; they are symptoms of a sinful mankind. We are blaming God instead of blaming ourselves. God will punish the warlords who cause the innocent to suffer, which is proof that He is good. The world's mistake is to think that if God were good, He would let us do whatever we want without consequences. But even as the darkness of sin and chaos overwhelm this world,

God's goodness, His trustworthiness, fidelity, loveliness, kindness, and truthfulness become brighter still. It is in the darkest room that a candle shines brightest, and His justice is good.

Concurrently, God's mercy and patience are giving us a chance to repent (2 Peter 3:8-9), and that doesn't mean He is evil. It means He is good. When evil attacks or the tragedies of this life tear us down, God is our defender even if we die. He is with us in the struggle and ultimately He will prevail. It only appears to us that evil is getting away with its brutality and lies now, but it really isn't and it really won't.

God is grieving with us in our losses and our failures. He's waiting for us to return to Him, and we will rejoice with Him in the final victory when sin and death are finally eradicated. Until then, we will march forward through the bullets and the mortar fire, confident that the enemies of God will be judged even if they kill us first.

Perhaps you have heard the verse, "And we know that all things work together for good to them that love God, to them who are the called according to His purpose" (Romans 8:28). That is absolutely true in the long term, but in the short term things can happen to us that don't make any sense at all. Indeed, they could even be bad things, as with heart defects or cancer. Paul isn't teaching us a psychological gimmick to think of even bad things as good things. We're not supposed to look at something tragic and pretend it's not tragic. The one who wrote that verse, the Apostle Paul, was beheaded during the reign of one of the vilest emperors of all time, Nero. How is that good? It isn't good, and yet when all of us get to the resurrection it will be all of us finally coming together at the same time and the victory will be ours. That is the good that God is moving all of history toward.

Even though the trials brought into our life by God will afflict us, don't lose sight of the fact that everything will be resolved one day. Forgiveness will be meted out—and vengeance. The phrase, "'Vengeance is mine,' says the Lord," is a statement of complete trust that God will eventually right every wrong.

Our Creator cares for us. When we suffer, He embraces us. When we cry, He weeps with us. He hates the sin of this world as much as we do, but He also loves this dark-hearted world enough to try and fix it. Indeed, He hates death and loves life so much, that He chose to give us eternal life—by dying.

# SUFFERING AND GRIEF

Have mercy on me, O Lord, for I am in trouble;
My eye wastes away with grief,
*Yes,* my soul and my body!
For my life is spent with grief,
And my years with sighing;
My strength fails because of my iniquity,
And my bones waste away.

Psalm 31:9-10

Suffering and grief are a part of life, but sometimes people tend to suppose—especially when we are going through those hard times—that suffering and grief are themselves an evil. I would like to suggest to you that as much as pain and grief are difficult experiences, they really are only symptoms of a greater problem and they are not an evil in and of themselves. Pain, as you know, can actually save one's life, which is good. If we get a cut, or get some other kind of injury, it is important that we feel pain. Even that emotionally charged ache in our stomach or chest we sometimes get is usually an indicator that something we're doing is destructive to ourselves or to others. Pain in its many forms is God's warning system, and we superficially suppress or ignore such indicators to our detriment. Grief, therefore, forces us to pay attention to whatever is going on that isn't right.

And it is sin that isn't right, not grief.

In the introduction, I mentioned that this isn't a book about grief (although it is about the ultimate solution to grief), but in this section I need to put grief into its proper context.

---

Grief is my constant companion.

After my wife passed away, I don't think I ever really got over it. Grief entered me and has never left. And I don't believe that it will ever leave. I live with an ever-present sorrow that dwells securely in my heart, and I'm okay with that. This wasn't so at first, but over time Grief has become a good friend. A close companion and a confidant.

You see, at first—when Grief darkened my soul, intensely—I thought eventually Grief would move out. Like a bad tenant, I thought after he ruined my carpets, let the lawn die, and allowed a rat infestation to flourish I would serve him his papers and evict him from my heart forever.

## *It is sin that isn't right, not grief.*

But he's still here, and we get along splendidly. He is, in fact, actually a rather quiet, peaceful sort of chap, who likes a good cigar, reads the Wall Street Journal, and pays attention to the world around him. He is kind, gentle, loves people (contrary to popular opinion), and he is attentive to politics and would like to be involved so he could make a difference. However, he understands that he is simply too real to make a difference. If he ran for office, people would shun him because politics requires a certain level of obscurity and subtle presentation of opinion. Grief, however, by his nature, is very raw and "out there." There isn't anything subtle or non-opinionated about him. Hence, he makes people cry. He lets you know what he believes in without pretense or Photoshop filters, and because of that, very few people want him around—he's too sane. Too honest. Too real.

Grief, therefore, in my opinion, is a wildly misunderstood tenant. Far from being destructive and irresponsible, he has a certain calming influence, and he helps me to gain a sober perspective on the world around me. In a way, he's become my counselor. He warns me away from frivolous activities; he helps me to be more forgiving; he frees me up to cry when I see things that are wrong with this world and with people.

Why, it was just the other day that I heard about another shooting, and so I went to visit Grief and he consoled me and we wept together over the senseless loss of human life. He helps me to weep when I ought to weep. He's a good tenant.

And I visit him often. I find that no matter what is going on he always refreshes my soul. I see my sin for what it is; I turn to God for my needs, not to empty, frivolous things; and I gain courage for the battles I face. Yes, it is a little gloomy at his place, but I find that when I leave I have an indescribable brightness of the soul. I see the world a little more clearly; a little more honestly; a little more compassionately.

The grass *is* greener on the other side of grief, not sinful self-indulgence.

Life becomes a little less perplexing after I visit Grief, and, ironically, there's a little more laughter and a little more forgiveness. And Grief, far from causing me to be depressed, actually allows me to experience joy again. People tend to be scared of Grief, or they mock and avoid him, but he is the kindest, gentlest man I know.

Oh, but let me warn you: his twin brother Despair is lurking just on the edges of your soul. He looks an awful lot like Grief—almost indistinguishable—but he is extremely different. I don't know what it is with that guy and why he hates his brother so much, but he comes across to most people as insightful and congenial, and many of the same people who make fun of Grief, will praise Despair with unrestrained adulation. They write songs inspired by him, and he makes people swoon with ecstasy. Why, they'll even weep, raise their hands, hug each other, and then go get high and completely indulge every physical desire simply because despair makes them feel jilted.

---

*The grass is greener on the other side of grief, not sinful self-indulgence.*

---

Despair is appealing because he takes away their hope and then makes them feel like they've gotten the short end of the stick and that life has kicked them in the teeth, so why not indulge their sensual desires? They've been dissed, so why not just do what they've wanted to do all along: buy tickets to a reckless, exciting, flesh carnival? Despair can be very rousing.

Grief, on the other hand, causes us to think deeply and soberly about our life and the world we live in. He is very moralizing. Not nearly as flamboyant, but oh so much more useful.

And, so, when something bad happens to us or to those we love, Grief and Despair introduce themselves and Despair generally has more curb appeal than Grief does. As I said earlier, for some reason I thought Grief was going to ransack my house, but, instead, he brought order and contentment. He brought joy in spite of sorrow—and maybe this is because I wept. Hiding from Grief doesn't mean he isn't there. For some people, though, they think Despair is going to give life meaning, and so they feel justified in becoming wasted, slothful, and destructive, ransacking their own souls in the name of "I have nothing, anyway, and it's 'their' fault."

I am so thankful for Grief! Without him I don't know where I'd be right now. Probably living with Despair and his two sidekicks, Blame and Denial. I see so many people trying to pretend Grief doesn't exist, but he does. And he is good.

We *should* cry when evil rears its ugly head. Grief has a purpose, and I believe that it is the most important method God uses to get our attention about what is really going on in this world. We would like to believe that this world is all happiness, joy, and feasting, but we know deep down that we are lying to ourselves. We want it to be better than it is, but we know it's not. We want ourselves to be better than we are, but we know we can't. We can't even meet our own expectations, let alone other people's. Let alone God's.

But, still, we hang onto the fantasy that we can solve every problem by reason, law, and love, and that if we could just figure out the right social system, obey the right law of the universe, unlock the genetic code, or just think positively in cooperative enlightenment, then everything will be alright.

But then death gets in our face, sin breaks our knees, and evil assaults us. And it is then and only then that we lose our fantasy and recognize the vanity of all our efforts. Death is the ultimate reality check, and grief is supposed to force us to lose our delusion that we can cure our own problems.

As David says, "I am weary with my moaning; every night I flood my bed with tears; I drench my couch with my weeping. My eye wastes away because of grief;" (Psalm 6:6).

And as Solomon teaches, "It is better to go to the house of mourning than to go to the house of feasting," (Ecc. 7:2a).

## *Why Kurtz was Right*

I have come to realize that I am actually afraid of true enlightenment. I'm not sure I want to know, or want to accept, what this world is really like underneath the glitz and the glamour of our every day lives.

For example, do I really want to know all of your sins? Do I really want you to know mine? Do I really want to know about Lyndsey Lohan's, again?

Actually, let me rethink this. There is a part of me which does love finding out the dirt on other people, and there is an entire industry that feeds that need. Today, we know more about the depravity of man than at any time in history, and there are some who are making millions off of it. So, in that sense, we do want to know each other's sins. It's very marketable.

But, in another way, such exposure is really only one of the ways we self-medicate. Reframing reality doesn't mean we've faced reality. Sin, in its raw state and seen from the perspective of what we should have been, is the truth we want to hide from. We don't want to see our sins as horrible, awful, disgusting insults to God. We don't want to repent of our sins—we want to feel okay about them. We don't want to take responsibility for our sins; we don't want to see ourselves as less than what we ought to be; we want to see our sin as normal. We used to say "Everybody sins," but far from being a Calvinistic doctrine of total depravity anymore, such a concept has come to be a mantra to accept sin. Now we say it much more smoothly: "Everybody does it," which, for some magical reason, negates "it" as wrong.

And so, I suppose, it could be said that I am writing a book that is promoting the idea that we should feel bad about our sins. We have deviated from God's original design for us and instead of excusing our sins as common—or normal—we should see them as aberrations of the profoundly magnificent beings we should have been.

Death is the moment when we have no more chances. It is the most inviolably raw, naked moment of accountability we face in our life, and whether our culture promotes that view or not, it is true. When you face death, you will see your sin as it really is, and you will clearly, cognitively, and deliberately either choose to ask God for forgiveness through Christ, or reject Him very intentionally. You might try to broker a deal at first, but you will inevitably humble yourself, finally, or you will shake your fist at God, defiantly. That's it.

Therefore, I believe that the Christian call could be summed up with: humble yourself now before it's too late. You will have to eventually, whether you want to or not.

And that is what Kurtz was right about in Joseph Conrad's *Heart of Darkness* when he said just before he died: "The horror. The horror" (Conrad, 202).

Conrad's main character is a sailor named Marlowe, who is telling a tale about a legendary man he had met named Kurtz. The whole tension of the book is built around Marlowe's previous journey up the Congo River in Africa as the captain of a steamboat looking for the infamous Kurtz, who had been one of the most productive ivory gatherers in Africa.

However, Kurtz had gone rogue and started slaughtering natives if they didn't worship him. He wanted to become their king and god, and not to just use them for business purposes. Power had gone to his head, and technology had empowered him to control them. Word had gotten back to England about Kurtz's abuses. Marlowe, therefore, was supposed to bring him back to civilization, where Kurtz would be held accountable for his crimes. But when Marlowe finally finds him, he turns out to be a skeletal, pathetic figure who is at death's doorway. He doesn't want to be taken away, but he is too weak to resist and he begins to realize that the natives are not afraid of him anymore. Many who had been following him out of fear still served him, but most now saw him for what he was—a mere man—and they hated him for his atrocities and they wanted to kill him.

As legendary as Kurtz had become—as successful and inspiring and god-like—on the steamboat trip back even Kurtz (like all of us) had to face death:

> One evening coming in with a candle I [Marlowe] was startled to hear him say a little tremulously, 'I am lying here in the dark waiting for death.' The light was within a foot of his eyes. I forced myself to murmur, 'Oh, nonsense!' and stood over him as if transfixed.
>
> Anything approaching the change that came over his features I have never seen before, and hope never to see again. Oh, I wasn't touched. I was fascinated. It was as though a veil had been rent. I saw on that ivory face the expression of somber pride, of ruthless power, of craven terror—of an intense and hopeless despair. Did he live his life again in every detail of desire, temptation, and surrender during that supreme moment of complete knowledge? He cried in a whisper at some image, at some vision,—he cried out twice, a cry that was no more than a breath—
>
> 'the horror! The horror!'
>
> I blew the candle out and left the cabin. (Conrad, 201-202)

As I said earlier, I don't think I want that kind of honesty. I'm not sure any of us want that "moment of complete knowledge," of that raw self-realization.

It has been debated endlessly what Kurtz exactly meant. Was he decrying English colonialism or his own wicked behavior? Was he seeing an afterlife of judgment that he was about to face, or did he realize he was about to stop existing? Whichever interpretation fits (and I think the brilliance of the writing is that they all fit), my general observation is that Joseph Conrad portrays death as the mechanism that forced Kurtz to finally face reality. As Marlowe later observes,

> And perhaps in this is the whole difference;
> perhaps all the wisdom, and all truth, and all
> sincerity, are just compressed into that
> inappreciable moment of time in which we step
> over the threshold of the invisible. Perhaps! (206)

## *Why Kurtz was Wrong*

On another level, though, I completely disagree with Kurtz's assessment of life, that it is a series of vain, meaningless endeavors that lead to nothing. Which lead to a feeling of horror.

You see, the thing that Conrad leaves out of his book is the message of the Gospel. He exposes the horrors of this world and the crimes of humanity against each other in the name of progress, and he comments on it brilliantly. We should be horrified by slavery and power-crazed manipulation of people's lives. Indeed, there is much reforming power in such awareness if we recognize it before we die. But Conrad ignores the fact that Jesus Christ faced those same horrors head-on, and all in the effort to redeem us from it. Jesus hated this world enough to try and fix it, and He isn't going to leave us to repair our mess on our own. He paved the way for the solution, if we would but follow it. Indeed, the more like Christ we become, the better and more lasting our repairs will be and the more effectively engaged in this world we will be. Christianity is supposed to help the weak, the downtrodden, the unjustly treated, and the oppressed of this world. It's our obligation.

Christianity is rooted in theology, but it must be lived out, not just thought about.

Christ's final words on the cross are far more insightful and profound than Kurtz's, because they not only account for the horror of this world and its wickedness, they *do* something about it: "Forgive them, for they do not know what they do." The most horrible crime in all of history was to execute Christ on that cross (just because His death led to our salvation, doesn't negate the crime they committed), but the ones who demanded it and the ones who did it, didn't see it that way. They thought they were doing something good, or routine. Jesus knew fully and completely the horror of death and the self-illumination it brought, but He exposed himself to it anyway in order to solve it, not just to be horrified by it. Kurtz saw the problem and was helpless to do anything about it; Christ saw the problem and solved it.

No more fearsome cause of pain exists than death, but that is why we need a solution to our sin. Facing death causes us to rethink our values, what we care for, and who we are as individuals. And it inevitably leads to thoughts about God, the nature of the afterlife, but more importantly, an evaluation of our own Heart of Darkness.

But if we try to ignore the manifestations of that pain (such as guilt, grief, and shame), then we won't ever solve the real problem—the source of that pain. Our grief reveals something profound to us about the world we live in: it is broken. But we shouldn't run away from our grief. We should embrace it and allow it to work its magic on us.

Whatever has happened to you to cause you to grieve is terrible—but your grief is not that terrible thing. We should be horrified by the images of children starving. We should be mortified by the acts of senseless violence against unborn children. Pain and grief in all of its forms is a perfectly natural response to tragedy.

And as such, I don't want to get rid of pain—I want to get rid of the cause of pain. I want sin eradicated. I want molestation, rape, murder, stealing, adultery, and promiscuity in all their forms to stop haunting us. I want my dead friends back. I want my dead family back. I want my enemies to be my friends. I want hurt relationships to be healed. I want innocence again. I don't want to merely live fully now; I want to live fully forever. I want the New Heavens and the New Earth.

# End of the Third Movement

# AUTUMN LEAVES

I sat down amidst the dropping red and red-orange leaves of autumn. All around me colors drifted by, and every leaf had a name. Jeff—or was it Geoff—landed on my shoulder and I picked him off and stared. The veins; the crinkled edges; the splotches of deadness. Poor Geoff. We got in a fight in a pool when we were kids. He held me under longer than I liked, and then we fought. It was one of those fights nobody wins, and nobody gets hurt.

I had known him since we were toddlers growing up in the same church. He was one of my three best friends: Geoff, Randy, and Johnny.

God, where are their leaves now?

Geoff shot himself after trying to murder a former girlfriend. A murder-suicide, but in this case she didn't die, so what is that?

I dropped the leaf from my hand in sorrow.

Randy is married, has a couple of children, and is a teacher like myself. Johnny I hadn't talked to until my dad passed away in 2015. He was the one with the cool Atari. His parents smoked and we played backyard baseball. The smells; his churned up yard; his dad's cop-radio.

I looked around and saw the leaves of other lost friendships—too many—lying strewn about.

Then I reached down and picked up a half-buried leaf. Hardly recognizable. I blew off some of the grit and stared closely. What was her name?

Molly? Yes, Molly. My first grade crush. I smiled and gently laughed. Innocence. That's what I needed right now, not grief, and I put her in my pocket.

I stood up and glanced around at all my other memories. And sighed.

**Autumn leaves near Estes Park, CO**

# Movement Four

## Gethsemane

Jesus went out as usual to the Mount of Olives, and his disciples followed him. On reaching the place, he said to them, "Pray that you will not fall into temptation." He withdrew about a stone's throw beyond them, knelt down and prayed, "Father, if you are willing, take this cup from me; yet not my will, but yours be done." An angel from heaven appeared to him and strengthened him.

Luke 22:39-43

# LONG'S PEAK

L ong's Peak isn't the tallest of the fifty-three 14ers in Colorado, but it dominates the Front Range mountains close to Denver, Colorado at a towering 14,259 feet. I live close to it now, in a town with its name: Longmont. Every day I get to observe its dignity and its mood swings. It can glower with anger or bask with contentment in the morning light. I live in the shadow of the lines, "For purple mountain majesties." I get to enjoy it every day.

**Long's Peak**

But how I got here is fascinating. It twists my mind into a pretzel to this day.

I was firmly ensconced in Spokane. I had a good job as a teacher and I had friends galore. Faye was in the fourth grade and I envisioned her attending the school I taught at until she graduated from high school. She's attending college now, and oh how far different is our life.

What changed was a woman. We were introduced to each other by my cousin's wife Ellie—her best friend—and we initially just emailed each other. Then we started talking on the phone and we would talk for hours. I would hang up and couldn't believe it.

The reason I couldn't believe it was because I had given up. I had dated two other ladies pretty seriously—one I almost got engaged to, but she was wiser than me and walked away. The other, we just didn't work out but we're still friends—for real. And, also, I had been on several blind dates and they were, well, educational experiences. Why others thought we might have had something in common with each other I'll never understand, but I appreciate the attempts. And so, now, here I was talking for hours to someone whom I had never seen before except in one photograph briefly glimpsed years earlier. No wonder I couldn't believe it.

Well, as fortune would have it, she—her name is Beth—was going to visit Wes and Ellie in Oregon the following July. (This was the summer following my excursion to Yellowstone with Faye.) So, I immediately began making plans on how to meet her for the first time. Ellie suggested we meet by a waterfall, and I concurred. I love waterfalls. So, I came up with an entire scheme to leave her notes along the path, ending with a map on where I would be stationed to meet her. I brought coffee, had cushions to sit on, muffins, a bug repellant candle, and she had to find her way through a logjam to find me. I thought it was cool, but I had no idea what she would think and for some reason I didn't care. I just had to go all out whatever may happen.

Well, it worked. We hit it off and we spent the next week going on dates up and down the Oregon Coast, going to the beach, visiting the Newport Aquarium with Faye, going to the Tillamook Creamery, hanging out with my Oregon family. Tillamook was my hometown even though I never actually lived there, and it was meaningful to me that I got to know Beth for the first time there.

But, it was all about to end. She lived in Longmont, CO, and I lived in Spokane. Sounds like some 50's high school summer fling movie. But here's where it gets mind-pretzling: I had lost my teaching job after six years. My contract "had not been renewed" (which simply means you can be fired without your bosses having to legally justify it) and I was on the hunt for a new job, which would most likely be only subbing in the public schools until I found something more permanent. It was a terrible tragedy for me and all I can say about it now is that God had turned the heart of the king against me, because I would never have quit my job just to move to Colorado for only the possibility of love.

The unforeseen consequence of this unfortunate event was that Beth suggested (and one would have to know Beth to understand how monumental her suggestion was) that I look for a teaching job in Colorado. Boom! It was as if lightning struck.

We said our goodbyes—most likely forever—in Oregon, but as soon as I returned to Spokane I got on the Internet and started looking for Christian schools in Colorado. Only one had a job opening that fit my major, English. When they called and asked me to come and interview, I immediately called Beth to make sure she was okay with this. I reassured her that even if nothing went anywhere with us that I still needed a job, so the move wasn't all for her. She didn't let on how nervous this made her, but she did give me the green light, anyway.

To this day, even while writing this, I'm amazed at how thoroughly God slammed the door on my life in Spokane. I had been an intern, but I was no longer going to that Church; Pete and Amanda had just moved to Salt Lake City so he could become a certified Nuclear Technician; and I had just lost my job. Hmmm. What to do?

And just at the right moment I met this woman who didn't mind me looking for a job out her way. When I got the job—I actually got the job!—she still didn't freak out that I was moving out there. Well, we dated for the next year, and I schemed and plotted on how to propose, and when I did she said "Maybe." She kept me waiting for another three months before she said yes, but when she said yes, wow, did my life change! And so did Faye's.

Faye was eleven and she needed help in learning some of the feminine arts. You know. I kind of knew, but not really, and so just at the right time God gave Faye someone who did know and am I glad! We were married at Wild Basin Lodge on the banks of the St. Vrain River next to Rocky Mountain National Park and life has become more peaceful and "normal" for me than it has ever been. It has its challenges, no doubt, but I am far beyond expecting that life is supposed to be smooth. Beth and I now have a little girl named Avery. She is eight and she wants to be everything Sissy is. She wants to play softball, she wants to drive, she wants to go to school, and she wants to stay up late, although she still likes to get up early. And right now Beth is six months pregnant with our boy! He's due this November, 2015.

What a life! It seems like a completely different existence than I had twenty years ago, but just as in Yellowstone, the scars from my former life still remain. The landscape may be fresh and vibrant, but every now and again a gnarled old snag reminds me that death is watching. As blessed as my life is now, I must never forget that it will never be what it was intended to be until God returns.

**Beth, Corey, Matt (left), Peter**

# THE SECOND GARDEN

Can Death defeat his most noble foe?
Aye, you scourge the earth with unquenchable ire;
Yay, you powder mortals in the pestle, our woe;
Yes, you devour our most precious desire.
Life dismissed, where have you gone?
Aye, in the ashes of a bitter, cold fire;
Yay, in the tear's sad, grievous song;
Yes, within the smoke above the pyre.
But despair, why do you consume so bold?
You linger too long as a malodorous mire;
Unwelcome, you dwell within my lost soul;
With spite you deceive for selfish pleasure.
    But Death, Life is not your most noble foe:
    Love is your unvanquished woe.

It was in the first garden, Eden, where death was first introduced into the world—a historical reality. But now we are going to enter the second garden, Gethsemane, where death was conquered—also a historical reality. Yes, I know that the resurrection is the actual point in time when death was defeated, but I have come to believe that the critical moment upon which all else depended—the fait accompli—occurred in the Garden of Gethsemane. The Garden was the turning point in the war. It was Gettysburg. It was D-Day. The victory we call the resurrection couldn't have occurred if Jesus hadn't chosen the path of the cross when he was in the Garden. It was there that Jesus came to peace with His fate and His courageous choice initiated a chain of events that became virtually unalterable.

Intellectually, I must allow that in theory Jesus could have changed His mind after the Garden if He had wanted to. He could have listened to the taunts from the people: "...let Him save Himself if this is the Christ of God, His Chosen One." He could have spoken up at His trial and rallied an army of zealots against Roman injustice. He could have persuaded everyone with a snap of His fingers that He was the promised Messiah. All of those possibilities were available.

But when those temptations came, He had already made His choice in the Garden; He had already accepted His fate; He had already set Himself on the path of suffering and of death. He had made His decision and He already knew that it couldn't be any other way if humanity were to be redeemed. He had wrestled with His destiny in the Garden and come to a point of peace about what was going to happen no matter how painful a death he must endure. His path was settled when he got up from his knees and those soldiers arrived. He had crossed the Rubicon and there was no turning back.

But we need a little back-story to understand why Jesus was even in the Garden of Gethsemane that night. Jesus is known to have prayed there on a regular basis. It is a small, tended, private garden—we would call it an orchard— where olive trees are planted in rows and regularly harvested to this day. It grows on the lower slopes of the Mount of Olives and it was most likely a privately owned estate in the days of Jesus, implying that he must have been given permission to come there whenever he wanted.

The Mount of Olives, or Mount Olivet, also plays a significant role in the history of Israel. It has a fabulous view of the Temple Mount and it is where David wept during the rebellion of Absalom (2 Sam. 15:30-32). It is where a great victory will take place in the future when the

Messiah returns: "Then shall the LORD go forth, and fight against those nations, as when he fought in the day of battle. And his feet shall stand in that day upon the Mount of Olives, which is before Jerusalem on the east..."(Zechariah 14:3-4).

The Mount of Olives was also the place where Jesus paused on His way to Jerusalem before He entered as king (Mark 11:1-3), and where Jesus sat teaching his disciples about the end of days while overlooking the temple just a few days before his crucifixion—just a few days before his betrayal in the Garden of Gethsemane (Mark 13:1-3).

But whatever those historical or prophetic events might have been, the garden was the place where Jesus would regularly remove himself from the crowds and the stress and revive his soul in the presence of His Father. Certainly he went there for the same reasons we pray: to honor the Father, to discuss anxieties, to worship, to gain strength, and to find wisdom. Deity in the flesh was still burdened by the weaknesses of the flesh, but what I find rather revealing about the fact that Jesus regularly prayed in the garden is that it exposes a very important trait about who He was as a human being: he wanted to pray in nature.

Have you ever wondered what it is about nature that draws us closer to God? Is it because of the lack of noise, the seclusion, or the calming sounds? Or is it because it resonates with our original design? Does it connect us back to Eden in spite of how cluttered our spirits have become? For some, the euphoria resulting from being in nature is so powerful that they begin to worship it, but if put in its proper perspective nature can be the most powerful temple ever constructed. A temple can only mimic, or reflect, God's perfect work, and although some seek out grand cathedrals or quiet chapels to pursue God (which I don't mean to discount the value of), it was in a garden that Jesus sought out God most often and it is where He most frequently walked with Him in intimate communion, and that only a short distance from the very Temple of God itself.

And, so, I would go so far as to say that he not only enjoyed Gethsemane, he craved it. He longed for it. He regularly sought out this place, this garden, and it couldn't have been just for the sake of praying to his Father (which he could do anywhere). I believe it was to commune with his Father while in a natural, well-tended setting in a way he couldn't have done anywhere else.

I believe it reminded him of the Garden of Eden.

Eden had been God's original well-tended Garden, and Gethsemane had become Eden's modern counterpart. Perhaps, then, Jesus went there because he remembered that first garden where he had walked with Adam and conversed with him in the first days before the fall. Perhaps he reflected on warning Adam not to eat the fruit; perhaps he could feel the sorrow when he discovered they had. Perhaps the disciples who were with Jesus in Gethsemane just a short distance away, painfully reminded him of that weakness in mankind to give in to temptation. Perhaps that reminder, though, gave him the courage to stay the course and to make the choice Adam hadn't been strong enough to make.

Whatever his motivations may have been for choosing a garden in which to pray, we should not ignore the parallels with Eden. Even more significant, though, are the comparisons between the two men who made those decisions.

# The Second Adam

Jesus is the most extraordinary individual to ever walk the face of the earth. Everything about him is something we should admire. He is compassionate and righteous; Lord of the universe and humble; truthful and loving; just and merciful; forgiving and confrontational; a peacemaker and a warrior; kind, but not afraid to condemn sin; gentle, but willing to show anger; tempted, but never did he sin. He is the Image of God, the ideal model of what we should have been.

But Jesus is not just an inspiration—He is also a rebuke. He is every superhero wrapped up into one man, but with one important difference (other than being real): superheroes merely save the planet from conquest or destruction—Jesus defeats death.

As we have discussed, a longing for life is in us all, but it was even more certainly in the Son of Man who is Life. He who is eternal would obviously want to remain eternal, but when God took on the burden of human flesh the possibility of death was introduced to the Immortal.

Adam had been fresh in the morning of creation without any concept of pain or suffering; but Jesus entered into the process of decay with the full knowledge of what He was getting into and what He was giving up. Even though He willingly took on our human body knowing that He came to die, it is clear from how He behaved in the Garden of Gethsemane that He did not want to die. The story is recorded in all four Gospels, but below is the account as recorded by Luke:

> Coming out, He went to the Mount of Olives, as He was accustomed, and His disciples also followed Him. When He came to the place, He said to them, "Pray that you may not enter into temptation." And He was withdrawn from them about a stone's throw, and He knelt down and prayed, saying, "Father, if it is Your will, take this cup away from Me; nevertheless not My will, but Yours, be done." Then an angel appeared to Him from heaven, strengthening Him. And being in agony, He prayed more earnestly. Then His sweat

became like great drops of blood falling down to
the ground. Luke 22:39-46

What I find moving about this event is that Jesus was so
burdened by his decision that He had to have an angel
strengthen Him. Jesus! The Son of God; God in the flesh;
the sinless one; the one who could calm the seas and heal
the blind. He needed help and He was so distressed about
His impending death that the capillaries in His skin broke
and he "sweated" blood.

Yes, it is true that He, the perfect one, was about to take
on the condemnation for sin in the world. Yes, it is true that
He was about to face a gruesome death that would make us
think Freddy Krueger was an amateur. And yes, unlike
Adam, He knew perfectly well all the horrors of death. No
wonder He sweated blood.

But, it is also true that His response meant that He loved
life and He hated death. He didn't want to go demurely to
the grave and Jesus' struggle should assuage any guilt we
may have about agonizing over our own impending death.
It's okay to contend with death—Jesus did.

Buddhism, on the other hand, teaches us to be
indifferent to the death of our body since it is only the spirit
that matters. Stoicism teaches us to have a manly, noble,
unconcerned acceptance of the reality of death. Death is
coming; why put yourself out about it? Modern materialistic
atheism teaches us the same thing: our bodies and "souls"
will just cease to exist.

But here is Jesus, the Word become flesh, agonizing
over dying. If we are supposed to be calm in the face of
death—to take it like a man—isn't Jesus showing
weakness? If we believe that Jesus is God, then why would
God not have a more enlightened perspective on death, and
why doesn't He know that even if His body dies His spirit
will go on? If Jesus knew that, why is He begging for a
reprieve from His Father? The fact that He is God and that
He responds as He does should give us pause, and we

should rethink our attitude toward death and how we should be counseling people who are facing death. Should we just merely accept the reality of death? According to Jesus' actions, absolutely not!

What's out of whack is not our instinctive hatred for death, but rather the multitude of teachers, philosophers, religions, and positive thinking seminars which are trying to persuade us that we should just go demurely to the grave. Jesus' behavior in the Garden disavows that attitude. He responds the way we should respond: with agony. The grave is nothing less than an affront to everything we were designed to be and we should shout, "I want life!!!" We shouldn't allow calm philosophies to shush us, as death slips a dagger into our hearts. It isn't wrong to be upset. It isn't wrong to want to live. It isn't wrong to be afraid. In fact, it is this very desire for life and hatred for death that makes us desperate for a solution. And God's solution is the only one that will work.

But, please don't misunderstand: I'm not advocating bitterness, anger, and resentment. Rather, I want to acknowledge that our struggle with death—our feelings of remorse, regret, fear and sorrow—are what are normal, *not death*. A desire to live is normal; a quiet walk to the grave is not.

And yet, someone may ask, if that is true, then why did Jesus exit the garden, calm, cool, and collected? His confrontation with death while praying, as painful as it was, ended and He overcame His fear. How? What gave Him peace after such overwhelming distress? Why, when He was finally betrayed and the soldiers came for Him, didn't He go kicking and screaming to the cross, crying for mercy?

The answer is the key to everything we believe as Christians: He saw our life beyond the darkness. He faced the darkest moment any person could ever face, and He chose to conquer death *for us*. What we couldn't do for ourselves (cure death), He resolved to do, and it was while

He was in the Garden of Gethsemane that our Lord found the courage to go forward with His mission. No matter how much pain or dread He personally might face, He came to a point of peace and willingly chose to go to the cross.

But that wasn't all.

---

## *A desire to live is normal; a quiet walk to the grave is not.*

---

Since Christianity's earliest days, the enemy has always sought to undermine what happens next: the resurrection. If what happens after the cross doesn't really occur, then Jesus was merely a man and everything else that Christianity stands for (primarily forgiveness) falls apart. If the resurrection does not happen, then we are indeed—more than any other group of people—most to be pitied (1 Cor. 15:12-19). But, Christ did rise again from the grave and we now no longer have to fear death. The sting of death—the fear of punishment—was removed when Jesus rose from the dead.

The historical reality that Christ rose again from the grave—thereby proving He had conquered death—is the only way for us to find peace in the face of death. Sure, I suppose we could stoically ride the Titanic into the cold bitter waters while sipping champagne, but still, at that last moment, one's eyes will be opened and the horror will strike us.

But not if we know that the resurrection is real; not if we know that we are in fact going to live forever, that death has been conquered. Not if we know that death is temporary! Not if we remember Eden and look beyond the darkness to the hope that awaits us. Such knowledge leads to freedom.

The resurrection is not a lie. Jesus went to the cross, died, and rose again. It happened, and because it happened it undermines every other belief system that exists. No wonder there is a war going on which fights for the strategic high ground we call "What really happened," and it's a hill Christians have been willing to die on since our first martyrs, James and Stephen. They died defending the truth (in every sense of the word) that Jesus rose from the dead, and they weren't afraid to die. The resurrection proves that God has the cure for our most dreaded experience: death. The same God who cried out in anguish "Where are you?" when we rejected Him in Eden, wept tears of blood in Gethsemane in order to find us.

Death is formidable. Death is inevitable. Death is unsolvable by us. But death is also temporary.

God loves life and He hates death, and His solution required the purest form of courage: action in the face of certain death. *That* is what happened in the Garden of Gethsemane when Jesus got up off His knees.

# The Second Decision

Do you know where to go
On this journey of your soul?
Can you see the horizon
Where your destiny unfolds?

Can you walk with your heartstrings
Sweetly tuned to the heavenly chords?
Do you know that the way is paved
To the Sabbath of your soul?

There is a debate going on which has raged since Adam first regretted his choice: are we puppets of destiny or are we free to choose our own way?

Not to get too stuck in the spider web of this topic, but we have to acknowledge that in one sense we are free to choose our own fate, i.e. to make a decision between whether we want to follow God or not.

"Come unto Me, all ye that labor and are heavy laden, and I will give you rest" (Matt. 11:28).

"Repent ye: for the kingdom of heaven is at hand" (Matt. 3:2).

"If *any* [emphasis added] man will come after me, let him deny himself, and take up his cross daily, and follow me" (Luke 9:23).

Come. Repent. Follow. Sounds to me like I have a choice to make, and a very important choice. Through the loud speakers of creation and revelation, God has made a clarion announcement to all of mankind that we have abandoned a garden for a wasteland, and He wants us to choose to return. It is in this sense that God leaves us alone in order to decide for ourselves whether we want to follow Him or not. Inherent in His appeal is the understanding that He wants us to follow Him willingly because we see our need for Him. He doesn't force us to follow Him; He simply holds out His hand gently, pleading with us to repent and to see the beauty of walking with Him in companionship, not thralldom.

---

*God has made a clarion announcement to all of mankind that we have abandoned a garden for a wasteland.*

---

But, in another sense, we are completely incapable of *implementing* that choice. Even if we wanted to, we could never obey His laws so completely that we would then enter into God's presence. We fall desperately short of that capacity. We have been corrupted by sin so thoroughly and our fleshly will is so obnoxiously powerful that we can never make enough right choices to cure our sin. We can't turn back the clock and erase what we've done even if we were to live a sinless life from this point onward. There is no amount of good deeds that can outweigh the heavy weight of even one of our sins. It would be like stacking pebbles on one pan of a beam scale in order to compensate for a mountain on the other pan.

It is in this state of utter helplessness that God steps in and by the power of His Spirit awakens us to the salvation that we couldn't have accomplished for ourselves. He knows our incapacitated condition and He entered our world to free us from the shackles of our sin. Even so, God does not override our will in order to force us to choose Him. Instead, in the Garden of Gethsemane He made the choice for us that we would never be able to make on our own: complete obedience. When He made the choice to obey in Gethsemane, He made that choice on our behalf. He obeyed for us. He chose what we could never have chosen to do, and His choice overrides Adam's choice.

Adam chose to disobey in Eden and death entered the world; Jesus chose to obey and the potential for life was restored. Belief in Christ, therefore, is infused with the idea that Jesus' choice in the Garden of Gethsemane was the right and moral one, and that it was the choice Adam was supposed to have made. When we believe in Christ, we surrender our attempts to make ourselves right with God and we accept that Jesus made us right with God so that we would have eternal life.

Jesus did what Adam didn't do.

Jesus did what we could never do.

And that is why Jesus' choice reverses Adam's choice. Adam's choice was "My will, not Thine," but when Jesus chose to obey God it became, "Thy will, not mine." He gives humanity the way to get back on track to the sinless existence which God had intended for us all along. We are off track; He is putting us back on track. He chose to obey and when we put our faith in Him, His choice becomes our choice (a choice within a choice). What we choose when we repent is not to will ourselves into a righteous life from here on out, but rather to accept that Jesus chose to live that moral life for us. And when we humble ourselves and accept that He had the strength to choose what we would never have the strength to choose, His strength becomes our strength and then we start living according to our original design.

Think of it this way: imagine that you are drowning. You are out of breath and you want to breathe and you know you should be breathing but you simply can't keep your head above water. Now imagine a scuba diver who swims up to you and holds his mouthpiece out for you to breathe from. He can breathe underwater with it and so you know that if you were to trust him and put the mouthpiece in your mouth, you, too, would be able to breathe underwater.

However, you still have to put the mouthpiece in your mouth. If you don't, you will continue to be in a condition of drowning and you must accept that you could never solve that dilemma on your own without the help of the scuba diver.

Likewise, all of us are drowning. It's just that some of us are still trying other options to save ourselves. Maybe you think you can swim to the surface by your own strength, but what if you are swimming the wrong way? My father-in-law told me of a friend of his who was in a boating accident. He was thrown under water and didn't know which way was up. He was strong and confident, though, and in spite of the fact that he was wearing a life jacket he chose to try and swim to the surface. The problem was that he was swimming the wrong way. He was disoriented and He was swimming deeper into the lake. It wasn't until he realized that the surface shouldn't be so hard to reach that he stopped trusting his own strength and he let the life jacket do its work. He quickly floated to the surface and was fine.

If all of us could only learn that kind of humility.

To put it bluntly: we are all going to die and we know it. We are immersed in a habitat of death but we keep thinking we can solve the problem on our own. Jesus rose from the dead in order to prove that we can conquer death if we would only stop striving to save ourselves. He has done it for us already.

Every single one of us, at some point in our life, will have our spiritual eyes opened by God and we will be given an opportunity to believe this truth. At some point, God's message will make sense to us and we will see it clearly. Maybe it will be during a moment in the mountains, during a song in church, or while driving down the road. Wherever and whenever, we all have that moment, and in that moment, what will you do with the truth God has revealed to you? Will you rationalize it away?

You have the choice to remain where you are, or to follow where He will take you.

You have the choice to fall asleep, or to wake up.

You have the choice to try and pay off the debt of sin yourself, or accept that Christ paid it for you already.

You can choose to continue to weed your own garden, or you can enter into God's garden draped with vines, fruit, and rest.

You can choose to accept your own ability to swim, or you can let Him save you.

It is at this point of decision that God doesn't interfere with you anymore. He chooses you, but He doesn't choose for you. He chooses us to follow Him (we wouldn't seek Him out if He hadn't of reached out to us, first); but we must choose to follow Him.

Some might ask, "Has God really chosen to extend the offer of salvation to everyone? Doesn't He just choose a few to save?" Not in the sense I have been talking about. As we read from Scripture earlier, He calls out to everyone to follow Him. He desires all to repent and to be saved, and His call is evident to everyone. We all know He's calling to us through nature and scripture, and on judgment day no one will be able to say "I never knew I rejected You."

But in another sense He does only choose a few, and this shouldn't be considered a cruel and despotic doctrine. In fact, it's very pragmatic. In the business world some people are hired and others are not. Owners can't hire everyone (even as good-intentioned as they may be) but when a person is chosen the hope is that they will be productive and a benefit to everyone around them. Likewise, God could only have chosen one Abraham to give His promises to. He couldn't have given the same offer to Abraham's brother, Nahor, or to his neighbor Uzul down the road. So God chose Abraham, and yet Abraham still had to choose to believe that God had chosen Him (Romans 4:18; 22). It is a mystery which is difficult to explain, but far from God's choice being a narrow, exclusionary doctrine, God gave a promise to Abraham which was to be amplified and extended to all of mankind, and Abraham's son, Jesus, (albeit 2,000 years later) was born as King of the Jews in order to be a blessing to all nations. Jesus fulfilled the promise to Abraham which encompasses all of humanity regardless of skin color, body size, or intelligence. Forgiveness of sins is available and accessible to everyone. Anyone. It supersedes all cultural and material boundaries. Abraham was simply the switch which turned the power on for all the rest of us. God's choice of Abraham was inclusive, not exclusive, and Abraham is also an illustration to all of us of how *we* are supposed to respond to God's amazing choice of us: with faith.

Let me boldly say it this way: if every single person were to repent today at the same moment, God's forgiveness could handle it all. There would be no breach of the dam; there would be no overload of the servers; there would be no grace shortage, no road closures, no traffic jams, no turning anyone anyway. His bandwidth is more than sufficient to handle all six billion souls at the same instant. He wants all of us to repent.

So, then, the choice that Jesus made in the Garden of Gethsemane was to completely obey; a choice that Adam hadn't made. My faith, therefore, (a faith given by God) is that Jesus' choice is sufficient to override every bad choice I have ever made, or will ever make. I can never choose to eradicate my sin, but I can choose to believe that Jesus eradicated my sin for me.

At this point, I would like to step back and reflect on the decision Tierre had to make when we were presented with the option of aborting our baby or not. Her decision was in no way equivalent to Christ's decision, but in many ways it parallels it. (I just realized this (in 2015), but we actually made our final decision while walking in a garden at Manito Park, Spokane, WA.) Tierre knew that her life might end—in fact that it would most likely end (50% chance) if she continued with the pregnancy. She also knew that the baby's life would certainly end if she chose to abort. However, there was no guarantee that she or the baby would live if she continued the pregnancy.

How does one make such a decision? We sought the counsel of our pastors and elders, and they were evenly divided. The basic message that they communicated to us was that nobody would condemn us for whichever choice we made. In other words, because of the nature of Tierre's condition there would have been no sin attributed to us if we had chosen to abort. There was no coercion; there was no guilt; there was no secret agenda. They wept with us and struggled with us and they acknowledged that the choice was solely ours—ultimately Tierre's. In a way, that made the choice more difficult. If there had been a clear-cut sinful choice then that would have decided it for us, but as it was there were only two equally viable choices.

---

*I can never choose to eradicate my sin, but I can choose to believe that Jesus eradicated my sin for me.*

---

So, we prayed. We took walks, we read books and we talked to more doctors. We didn't sweat blood but we shed tears and in the end it came down to answering this question: what does it mean to live? Does just breathing and walking around and having friends mean you're alive? Or does life come to us when we do something more significant than live for our own needs? We reflected on these questions and ultimately, what best summarizes the heart of Tierre's decision to continue the pregnancy is engraved on her gravestone: "Life held onto selfishly is no life at all."

**"Life Held Onto Selfishly, Is No Life At All**

It is the great irony of life that in order to truly live we must be willing to die. To be truly courageous, we must be willing to be killed.

That was it, then, and she eventually came to a point of peace that surpasses understanding. Life was so important to her that she was willing to give up her life—and that brought her peace. That which she longed for the most she was willing to give up for another. She accepted the possibility of her death and risked everything for the sake of another person.

It is that courage which helped her to be at peace, and it is that same courage which has become the key to unlocking the true source of peace in the face of death. Indeed, it is the only key.

As long as we continue to live selfishly and ignore the reason death is in this world, we will also continue to fight the reality of God's solution. This doesn't mean we are giving up on our desire for life; it means we are accepting the only way we will ever be able to actually achieve that desire. It is only after we courageously look death in the face—as Jesus did in Gethsemane—that we will experience the well-spring of life. We will not compromise God's truth in order to stay alive for a little while longer. We won't negotiate with Satan to gain a few more days. We must walk through the dark tunnel to find the joys of paradise beyond. We must hike the excruciatingly long trail and face the pain of the final hill before we can get to camp. We must give up our greatest desire (to stay alive) in order to gain our greatest desire (to live forever). We must endure our demise, in order to rise. We have to let go of everything we hold dear, in order to gain everything that we hold dear. We have to be willing to give up our will in order to do God's will, and then we will discover what we really wanted all along: life! However, we must be willing to give up *this* life to find *that* life.

In the Garden, Jesus accepted that He would have to die on the cross in order to live and to give us life. His love was so great, that He chose to give up His life for us even if we never chose to believe in Him. Jesus chose to be the sacrifice for all of us even if none of us would ever accept what he was doing, and every person who hears the gospel has a choice to walk away. Yet even if we do, that does not change the reality that Christ did die for us on the cross and He did rise again from the grave. One can deny the empty tomb—but the tomb is still empty.[7]

---

> *"In this is love, not that we loved God, but that He first loved us."* ~ 1 John 4:10

---

His love is universally extended, but not universally received. His choice of us is a gift, but we must open that gift. The amazing reciprocity is that once opened and we see its wondrous glory, we will never take credit for our choice to open it and we will give all the credit to God. You see, one of the elements of His gift to us is the knowledge that without God's intervention in our lives we couldn't have made the choice to believe and we don't necessarily see that before we bow down to Him. Far from being a point of pride, once we're saved we see our salvation as a point of submission. We're thankful, not pompous.

To those who refuse to open the gift, though, all the shining treasures of such knowledge will remain locked away in a vault, a vault to which everyone has the combination if they would only use it, and the combination isn't a secret. There are no special rites you have to

---

[7] For a full defense of the historical reality of Christ's death and resurrection, see Josh McDowell's book, "Evidence that Demands a Verdict."

participate in to access the knowledge, nor do you have to have level five clearance. The combination?

## *Comprehension*

> In this the love of God was manifested toward us, that God has sent His only begotten Son into the world, that we might live through Him. In this is love, not that we loved God, but that He loved us and sent His Son to be the propitiation for our sins.

> (I John 4:9, 10)

## *Profession*

> I have not written to you because you do not know the truth, but because you know it, and that no lie is of the truth. Who is a liar but he who denies that Jesus is the Christ? (I John 2:21, 22)

## *Confession*

> But if you confess with your mouth the Lord Jesus and believe in your heart that God has raised Him from the dead, you will be saved. For with the heart one believes unto righteousness, and with the mouth confession is made unto salvation. (Romans 10:9, 10)

> If we confess our sins, He is faithful and just to forgive us our sins and to cleanse us from all unrighteousness. (I John 1:9)

## *Possession*

> Blessed be the God and Father of our Lord Jesus
> Christ, who according to His abundant mercy has
> begotten us again to a living hope through the
> resurrection of Jesus Christ from the dead, to an
> inheritance incorruptible and undefiled and that
> does not fade away, reserved in heaven for you,
> who are kept by the power of God through faith
> for salvation ready to be revealed in the last time.
> (1 Peter 1:3-5)

These, indeed, are precious truths, brethren. We should find comfort and solace in them. We should find inspiration and hope. The choice Jesus made in the Garden is accessible to us all, but, sadly, not all will avail themselves of that choice. Some want to choose to try and attain perfection for themselves, on their own, with their own strength, wisdom, and words. However, we *can* find peace in the midst of death, but not because we accept death, but because we accept life.

## *"Because I live, you will also live." John 14:19b*

## The serpent shows up—again

However, it wasn't only Jesus' internal conflicts that made his choice difficult. There were external forces at work, too.

I have for many years pondered Judas, and the question that I find most puzzling about his betrayal is that his actions seem rather superfluous in light of Jesus' public presence. Why did Judas have to betray Jesus? Everyone knew what Jesus looked like—he was hardly a stranger. He was often in public places on public streets teaching crowds of people. The soldiers and the Pharisees could have identified him in any number of ways, and they could have arrested him at any time they wanted. Any one of them could have pointed at him and said, "There's Jesus." So why did they need Judas to take them to him?

Some have suggested that since it was dark, in order for the soldiers to make a positive identification Judas had to kiss Jesus. Others have suggested that because of the multitude of people in Jerusalem, it would be difficult to positively identify Jesus. Even though I believe both of these possibilities are valid, neither one answers my question: why did *Judas* have to do identify Jesus? A Sadducee or Pharisee could have done the same thing. There were many non-friends of Jesus who could have identified Jesus in any crowd and at any time of day.

The answer is, unfortunately, related to politics. Luke records that the Sanhedrin were "afraid of the people," and so it wasn't so much that Judas himself needed to betray Jesus, it was more like the Sadducees needed someone close to Jesus to betray him so the people wouldn't hate the Sanhedrin. Judas volunteered for the job. They needed an insider who would stand up and proclaim to the rest of the people that Jesus wasn't what he had made himself out to be, and then they would become the defenders of the public good by getting rid of that rascally Jesus. They needed leverage so they could sway public opinion against him (everyone loved Jesus as evidenced by Palm Sunday), and Judas provided that opportunity. They needed the crowds to lose their enthusiasm for Jesus by causing them to doubt that he was the long-awaited Messiah, otherwise the Sadducees would have a riot on their hands if they tried to have Jesus executed. They needed an insider to betray Him so the people would doubt Him.

What's also interesting about Judas is that he is the one who allows Satan to enter into the unfolding drama. Satan's vehicle in Eden had been a serpent; in Gethsemane his vehicle became Judas.

> Then, leaning back on Jesus' breast, he [Peter] said to Him, "Lord, who is it?" Jesus answered, "It is he to whom I shall give a piece of bread when I have dipped it." And having dipped the bread, He gave it to Judas Iscariot, the son of Simon. Now after the piece of bread, Satan entered him. Then Jesus said to him, "What you do, do quickly." (John 13:25-27)

Notice that Satan enters Judas at this point of decision, but, just like Adam, Judas is the one fully responsible for his choice. Judas will be the one who bears the blame and the punishment for what he did because it was in his heart to do so before Satan entered him. He's the one who approaches the Sanhedrin and accepts their bribe. No one else walked there for him and no one else will be punished for what he did. Destiny did not force him to betray Jesus, but destiny was fulfilled when he did. In the Day of Judgment we cannot pass the blame.

## *They needed an insider to betray Him so the people would doubt Him*

And, yet, Satan did cheer him on. The Old Liar slunk his way back into our story in order to try and thwart God's plan for humanity. And this time he knew he couldn't deceive Jesus with the same sales pitch that he had used against Adam and Eve, nor with the same lies he had used in the wilderness after Jesus' baptism. This time he had to break Jesus, and in order to do that Satan needed to make Him face the ultimate horror: death itself. It wasn't that

Satan wanted Him to die just for the sake of killing Him (technically, it was *God's* plan was for Jesus to die); he wanted Jesus *to sin* before He died and when Jesus had to look death in the face it almost undid Him. If Satan could somehow cause Jesus to lose His perfection before that fatal moment arrived, then God's plan would be thwarted.

So Satan hoped the betrayal by a friend would weaken His resolve.

He hoped that a trial filled with lies would crush Him.

He hoped a torturous beating would make Him collapse.

He hoped people mocking Jesus would compel Him to come off the cross and show them all who He really was.

Ah, but it had been so much easier to get Adam to sin.

In Eden, Adam ate the fruit of knowledge after a suggestion; in Gethsemane, Jesus drank the cup of suffering after a beating.

In Eden, Adam thought he was choosing life, wisdom, and glory; in Gethsemane, Jesus knew He was choosing death, shame, and humiliation.

In Eden, Adam invited death in, thinking it was life; in Gethsemane Jesus threw death out, in order to give us life.

In Eden, Adam innocently believed the lie; in Gethsemane, Jesus boldly embraced the truth.

And that is why Jesus was able to patiently endure the unjust lashings and suffer the agonizing nails without cursing or giving in to the temptation to call on an army of angels to rescue Him. It had been in the Garden where the path to victory began, and the arduous journey to the most loving act ever done by any man was set in motion.

# DESTINY

"Just as we have borne the image of the man of dust, we shall also bear the image of the man of heaven."

I Corinthians 15:49

There are two foundational truths that should give us peace when we come face-to-face with death: God is our creator, and Jesus rose from the dead. The first truth leads us to understand the second truth, and the second truth confirms the first truth. They are reciprocal in nature and together they form the foundation for understanding all things life: joy and sorrow.

In the first and second movements of this book, I sought to establish with evidence that God is our Creator. We can be confident that He is and the detractors shouldn't sway us. The evidence points to a creator whether some people want us to see the evidence for what it means or not, and no amount of intimidation or cajoling should cause us to lose confidence in that reality. Faith believes in the unseen God who has confirmed His existence by all that He has made, and He made everything the way He said He did. There is no reason to doubt.

But even if you still have doubts, the second truth should erase all misgivings: Jesus rose from the dead, and because the resurrection did occur, that means that the Bible's depiction of world history (and the world's future) is also accurate.

The two gardens were actual places where two men made two choices which radically altered the history of the world. But more than that, they radically affected our individual lives. We either live under the condemnation of Adam's sin, or we live under the protective forgiveness of Christ's righteousness. We are condemned, or we are forgiven. We are in darkness, or in the light. We are going to be held accountable for our disobedience, or we are going to be rewarded for Christ's obedience. When I come to Christ, I exchange my *inability* to obey with His ability to obey.

God created us to be in charge of His world and to thrive in a sinless relationship with Him. But after we abandoned Him, He never abandoned us. When Jesus rose again from the grave He cured our sin, conquered death, and restored our relationship with Him so that we could live forever, which is what He really wanted all along.

He designed us to be immortal.

Immortal: always living, never dying. Perfect. Not as we are, now, but rather in some sort of super hero-type body that will be able to do cool things like the resurrected Jesus did. His body is the showcase model we are looking forward to getting. No more aging, no more disease, no more weakness or starvation or frailty or fear. It will be amazing and well worth the wait.

That is the promise we have from Him, and the New Heavens and the New Earth will be worthy of all our dreams.

It is our guaranteed destiny.


## While We're Dead

But, until then, what happens to us while we wait for God to work everything out? What happens to our spirit after our body dies? If the atheists are right and nothing happens, then we're good to go so why bother ourselves about it? But if there is something more, what is it like and how will it affect me? It's a little scary. It's the "unknown;" it's the place of which dreams are made.

Mankind has been discussing the afterlife for millennia and, as far as I can tell, there is no consensus (not that a consensus will determine what's really true; a majority opinion can still be wrong). However, there are some commonalities that movies and TV shows like to focus on—the final season of *Lost* being one of the more recent and more popular presentations—but there are also major differences of opinion that cannot be ignored.

Is there a heaven? Is there a hell? Does purgatory exist? Does Satan torture us in a medieval dungeon armed with fire, a trident, and kids playing banjos? Is there just darkness and nothingness? Is our self-awareness eternal or are we annihilated? Do we have to journey through an underworld, or do we just get to go to heaven eventually because God loves us so much? Do we disappear into a light and become one with the universal consciousness? The options appear to be limitless and it seems like every variation has been explored by someone at sometime, somewhere.

To narrow the field, though, I would like to rebuild the concept as portrayed by the Old and New Testament writers. I have referred to what they teach already, but I think it is necessary to go into a little more detail because I have found in my own life that I have had some misunderstandings about the afterlife, and maybe you have, too.

For example, one of my earliest impressions about the afterlife was that we would become angels after we die. I think I got this idea from a painting I had seen, but I have come across only one Bible verse that could even remotely be confused with teaching it: Matthew 22:30, "At the resurrection people will neither marry nor be given in marriage; they will be like the angels in heaven." Yes, we will be like the angels in one of their characteristics, but we certainly won't become angels. The Bible clearly teaches that humans are different than angels, and that angels are a closed group with certain responsibilities, such as being God's messengers. Humans do not take on those responsibilities after we die. Sorry, Clarence.

But, then, what does happen to us after we die? Do damned souls burn in hell and blessed souls go through the pearly gates? Do some linger in a land of shadows, unable to move on but equally unable to come back? Or is there a third possibility known as purgatory? Or does something else happen altogether?

The following chart is a basic outline, but I think it captures the essence of what the Bible teaches. After we die we temporarily exist in one of two "waiting rooms." These are not to be understood as purgatory, but rather as places where our souls will wait for our impending judgment. Unbelievers will occupy a place—a prison—called *Sheol*, or *Hades*, and be separated from God's presence. Believers will occupy a place within *Sheol* called Abraham's Bosom, or *Paradise*, and be in God's presence. Both of these locations are temporary, and in both places our spirits will await the final judgment, or sentencing, when the decisive trial will occur called the Great White Throne Judgment. After that, we will either be cast into the Lake of Fire, called the resurrection of damnation (the second death), or we will be sent to dwell in the new heavens and new earth, called the resurrection of life.

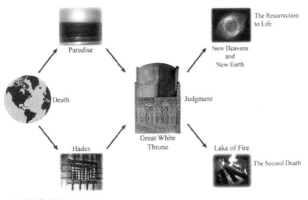

Paradise

The Resurrection
to Life

New Heavens
and
New Earth

Death

Judgment

Hades

Great White
Throne

Lake of Fire

The Second Death

www.vectortemplates.com
"Ravenna Maximian chair" Licensed under Public Domain via Wikimedia Commons - http://commons.wikimedia.org/wiki/
File:Ravenna_Maximian_chair.jpg#mediaviewer/File:Ravenna_Maximian_chair.jpg

**Overview of Life and Death**

# The Resurrection

We have already discussed the importance of the
historical reality of the resurrection of Jesus, but now we
need to understand what the resurrection is, and what we
have actually been promised will happen to us.

First of all, the resurrection does not refer to a purely
spiritual existence that we will enter into right after we die.
We do not get our resurrection bodies *immediately*. The
resurrection is a future event when our dead bodies are
transformed and made into brand new bodies—spiritual
bodies as Paul calls them in 1 Corinthians 15:42-44.

In this way, just as Christ rose physically from the dead,
so will we. It's God's promise to us, and just as His body
and His spirit were reunited into a brand new physical—yet
spiritual—form, so will ours be. Jesus still looked like
Jesus, but He could also do some other pretty amazing
things that He didn't do before.

For example, He appeared in rooms that were locked, and He made a conscious effort to prove to the disciples that He was flesh and blood and that He could eat (Luke 24:36-43; John 21:12-14). He also ascended into heaven, bodily (Luke 24:50, 51), and He will return someday, bodily, to right every wrong.

In 1 Corinthians 15:35-49, Paul explains to some skeptics who mock the resurrection, that our new body will be completely different than our current body. Paul compares our current body to a grain of wheat that, after being planted in the ground (death), will come up in a completely new form (resurrection). We won't lose our identity, but we will be different, and our new body will be imperishable, magnificent, powerful, and spiritual.

But more than that, the apostle John explains that after the resurrection we will be as Jesus is in character—in a condition of complete purity:

> Beloved, now we are children of God; and it has
> not yet been revealed what we shall be, but we
> know that when He is revealed, we shall be like
> Him, for we shall see Him as He is. And everyone
> who has this hope in Him purifies himself, just as
> He is pure. (I John 3:2, 3)

Indeed, we should be looking forward to this future, bodily resurrection every day because such knowledge helps us to live as God wants us to in the midst of all our challenges. The resurrection is our reward, the end result of our faith, the very purpose for which we believe:

> More than that, I count all things to be loss in
> view of the surpassing value of knowing Christ
> Jesus my Lord, ...that I may know Him and the
> power of His resurrection and the fellowship of
> His sufferings, being conformed to His death; in
> order that I may attain to the resurrection from the
> dead. (Phil. 3:8-11)

> But when you give a reception, invite the poor,
> the crippled, the lame, the blind, and you will be
> blessed, since they do not have the means to repay
> you; for you will be repaid at the resurrection of
> the righteous. (Luke 14:13-14)

The resurrection is our reward, and it will allow us to be in the presence of the Lord for eternity. What a glorious future is in store for us!

As a side note, some Christians have been taught that if their body is cremated, they may not get to join in the resurrection. For them, I would like to point out the following verse:

> And the sea gave up the dead which were in it;
> and death and hell [Hades] delivered up the dead
> which were in them: and they were judged every
> man according to their works. (Rev. 20:13)

Forgive me for being a little graphic, but if a body has been buried at sea, it will be dissipated by the corrosive power of the sea, and it will enter the diet of many fish. This is why I believe that cremation has no effect on our eternal destiny. If it did, what about all those martyrs who were burned at the stake? Did they lose their reward? God is not limited in his ability to find us. Our molecules exist whether our body has returned to dust, ashes, or bait. The bottom line is that if He can resurrect those who have been buried at sea, He can resurrect those who have been cremated.

We have been promised that we will get brand new bodies that will never die. Death will have been repealed, eradicated, knocked out, annihilated, and replaced with an eternal existence. That is an amazing truth!

---

*The resurrection is our reward, the end result of our faith, the very purpose for which we believe.*

So, the importance of the resurrection becomes clear: it confirms God's activity from creation to cremation, and it promises the reward of a new, physical (albeit very different) body which will be fused with our eternal spirit, which has been patiently waiting for that recombination.

But where have our souls been waiting in the mean time?

# Hades

You have perhaps heard the name before: *Hades*. It's the name of the Greek god who is in charge of the underworld, brought to the big screen with flaming hair by the Disney film *Hercules*.

And yet the term is also used in the New Testament eleven times, and the Hebrew equivalent, *Sheol*, is used in the Old Testament sixty-three times. Does that mean that the New Testament writers and Greek mythology were in alignment? Not at all. A simple investigation into the beliefs of both will illuminate their differences.

## *The Greek concept of Hades*

Hades, to the Greeks, is one of the Olympian gods, brother to Zeus and Poseidon, chosen to be the overlord of the underworld by lots. This underworld is also known as *Hades*, and it is the repository of souls from which there will never be an escape:

> "...give me now thy hand, whereon to weep; For never more, when laid upon the pyre, Shall I return from Hades;" (The Iliad, book XXIII).

It is a place of darkness, gloom, and forgetfulness, surrounded by five rivers. It is not completely different from the Hebrew concept of the underworld, but the differences they have are significant.

## *The Hebrew Concept of Hades*

The Bible portrays *Hades* as a prison cell of temporary status. It is a place of darkness. A pit. The grave.

> Job 3:17-19 "There [Sheol] the wicked cease from troubling; and there the weary be at rest. There the prisoners rest together; they hear not the voice of the oppressor. The small and great are there; and the servant is free from his master."

> Ps. 28:1 "Unto thee will I cry, O LORD my rock; be not silent to me: lest, if thou be silent to me, I become like them that go down into the pit [Sheol]."

> Ps. 142:7 "Bring my soul out of prison [a poetic reference to Sheol, but without using the Hebrew word itself] that I may praise thy name: the righteous shall compass me about; for thou shalt deal bountifully with me."

> 1Sam. 6: "The LORD killeth, and maketh alive: he bringeth down to the grave [Sheol], and *bringeth up*" [emphasis added]. (Note that there is the idea of being released. Existing there is a temporary condition.)

> Is. 24:21, 22 "And it shall come to pass in that day, that the LORD shall punish the host of the high ones that are on high, and the kings of the earth upon the earth. And they shall be gathered together, as prisoners are gathered in the pit (Sheol) and shall be shut up in the prison [Sheol], and after many days *shall they be visited*"

[emphasis added]. (This was fulfilled after Christ died: 1 Peter 3:19)

Is. 42:7 "To open the blind eyes, *to bring out* [emphasis added] the prisoners from the prison, and them that sit in darkness out of the prison house [Sheol]."

Matt.16:18 "And I tell you, you are Peter, and on this rock I will build my church, and the gates of hell [Hades] *shall not* [emphasis added] prevail against it."

So, as you can read for yourself, the biblical *Hades* is a holding cell; a prison; a spiritual Alcatraz. In addition, the terms *Hades* and *Sheol* are interchangeable. They refer to the same place. In Acts 2:27, Peter quotes David as saying "For you will not abandon my soul to *Hades*, or let your Holy One see corruption." The passage he is quoting is from Psalm 16:10, which says, "For you will not abandon my soul to *Sheol*, or let your holy one see corruption." So, as you can see, the terms are equivalent.

It is easy to get confused, though, when studying this topic. *Sheol* and *Hades* are frequently translated into English as "hell," which is fine, except that there is another Greek word, *Gehenna*, which is also translated into "hell" and *Gehenna* and *Hades* are two different places.

*Gehenna* was the trash dump of Jerusalem (where the dead bodies of criminals would also be thrown) and its fires burned perpetually. It was a rancid, horrible, terrifying place, and that is why it became a perfect illustration for God's final judgment in the Lake of Fire.

And so with this understanding in mind, when Jesus teaches in Matthew 5:22 "whoever says, 'You fool!' will be liable to the hell of fire [*Gehenna*]," He is referring to the final judgment in the lake of fire. In Matthew 10:28, Jesus says, "And do not fear those who kill the body but cannot kill the soul. Rather fear him who can destroy both soul and body in hell [*Gehenna*]," He is referring to the second death, when the bodies and souls of those who have not sought forgiveness from Christ will be cast into the lake of fire and burned up for all eternity. There will be no resurrection to life for those cast into the lake of fire.

And so, as you can see, *Gehenna* and *Hades* are not interchangeable terms like *Hades* and *Sheol* are, and yet "hell" is the English word used for all three. Confusing. [8]

## *Who's in Charge of Hades?*

After comparing and contrasting the Greek and Hebrew concepts of *Hades*, one can now see that Satan is not in charge of *Hades*. That is an erroneous idea that has infiltrated Christian thought from Greek mythology. In fact, the Bible never once claims Satan oversees souls in *Hades*. It doesn't even imply such a notion. *Hades* is a prison, not a god.

However, if Satan isn't the lord of the underworld, who is? The Bible makes it very clear that God is the one who oversees *Hades*. As R.C. Sproul teaches, God saves us from His own wrath, and God is the one who holds the keys to the gates of *Hades* (Rev. 1:18). Satan and his minions aren't down below torturing souls with punishments in line with our earthly offenses; God is the one who imprisons souls until the final judgment. He casts them there and He's the one who keeps them there, guarded by angels.

But, if that is true, where is Satan and what is he up to? According to Scripture, Satan is roaming the earth seeking whom he may devour (Job 1:6, 7; 1 Peter 5:8). He isn't the king of hell, or anywhere for that matter: he's just a wandering predator trying to destroy everything God has made, and trying to take as many people into the lake of fire

---

[8] For your own study, the Strong's numbers are: *Sheol* (h7585), *Hades* (g086) and *Gehenna* (g1067).

with him as he can on that final Day of Judgment. He's rather a pathetic figure if you get right down to it.

## *Hades is a prison, not a god.*

And to cement this biblical concept of *Hades*, I would like to quote Josephus. He was a Jewish historian who wrote a measured and thoughtful history of the Jewish people for Roman and Greek consumption in the first century A.D. In one of his many writings, he summarizes what the Jewish understanding of the afterlife was at the time of Christ. The essay is called, "A Discourse to the Greeks Concerning *Hades*," and it reveals that *Hades* was not some vague or undeveloped idea as some commentators try to imply; it was clear and well developed.

> Hades is a place in the world not regularly
> finished; a subterraneous region, wherein the light
> of this world does not shine.... This region is
> allotted as a place of custody for souls....
>
> In this region there is a certain place set apart, as a
> lake of unquenchable fire, where into we suppose
> no one hath hitherto been cast; but it is prepared
> for a day aforedetermined by God, in which one
> righteous sentence shall deservedly be passed
> upon all men...while the just shall obtain an
> incorruptible and never-fading kingdom. (Kindle
> Locations 28075-28076)

The Word of God is also abundantly clear that our souls will be held in *Sheol* until the final judgment and then be cast into the lake of fire.

> And I saw the dead, small and great, standing
> before God, and books were opened. And another
> book was opened, which is the Book of Life. And

the dead were judged according to their works, by the things which were written in the books. The sea gave up the dead who were in it, and Death and Hades delivered up the dead who were in them. And they were judged, each one according to his works. Then Death and Hades were cast into the lake of fire. This is the second death. And anyone not found written in the Book of Life was cast into the lake of fire. (Revelation 20:12-15)

How much clearer can Scripture be?

(As an aside, there is another place called Tartarus, aka the Bottomless Pit, which is mentioned in Revelation and which Peter refers to as the prison where the deceptive spirits at the time of Noah are being held (II Peter 2:4). At the end of days, in Revelation 9 when the fifth angel sounds his trumpet, this same bottomless pit is unlocked and the demons are released. I only mention this because Tartarus is a reference to a different prison than *Sheol/Hades*, one that holds particularly evil fallen angels.)


# Paradise

Ah, paradise. The very term evokes images of white beaches and turquoise waters. It's beautiful, relaxing, a place to be enjoyed and where the term "struggle" is never to be used. The Greek word, *paradeisos*, refers to a park, or an Eden—a well-tended orchard where all of our needs are met. It resonates with our hearts and is a very marketable idea, as many resorts would testify.

But, on a more theological note, it is a reference to a place in which the souls of the blessed will reside in the presence of God while they are dead. It is a temporary residence (as *Sheol* is) where as soon as the righteous die they enter into God's presence and await the final judgment—the final culmination of all things—and the reward of immortality. It is also called "The Bosom of Abraham."

As Jesus said to the thief on the cross, "Truly, I say to you, today you will be with me in Paradise" (Luke 23:43). He promised that the thief would join Him in paradise and be at peace. The other thief, by implication, would be descending into *Hades*—not something to look forward to.

In a similar vein, Paul intensely looked forward to being in the presence of the Lord: "I desire to depart and be with Christ, which is better by far" (Phil. 1:23). But Paul may have been more enthusiastic than most people because he had had a special insight into Paradise already. In 2 Corinthians 12:2, Paul humbly testifies that he had been caught up into paradise and had heard unspeakable words, which it is not lawful for a man to utter. He also referred to it as "the third heaven," which refers to the highest heaven where God dwells, and which is represented in the layout of the temple. The inside of the temple was divided into three partitions. There was the outer court, and then there was the Holy Place where two divisions were laid out, making a total of three. The first division was where the priests could enter, and the second division was called the Holy of Holies where the presence of God dwelt, a representation of the third heaven. As the author of Hebrews explains, "They [the priests] serve at a sanctuary that is a copy and shadow of what is in heaven" (Hebrews 8:5).

In this way, then, the presence of God and paradise are equated in Scripture. We will be with the Lord, but our bodies will be asleep in the grave. Our spirits will be alive and well, waiting for the culmination of all things; waiting to be reunited with our bodies.

It would be helpful to read Josephus again in order to get a clearer picture of how Jews in the first century conceived of the afterworld. According to Josephus, *Hades* includes paradise but they are distinct places. There is the prison section and there is the blessed section, but sometimes *Hades* generically refers to them both:

> [The righteous who have died] are now indeed confined in Hades, but not in the same place wherein the unjust are confined. For there is one descent into this region, at whose gate we believe there stands an archangel with an host…the just are guided to the right hand, and are led with hymns, sung by the angels appointed over that place…[where]there is no place of toil, no burning heat, no piercing cold, nor are any briers there; but the countenance of the just…always smiles them, while they wait for that rest and eternal new life in heaven, which is to succeed this region. This place we call The Bosom of Abraham. (Kindle Location 28088)

Josephus' description is consistent with Christ's depiction in Luke 16:19-31. Here, Jesus teaches that "between us (in The Bosom of Abraham) and you (in *Hades*) a great chasm has been fixed, in order that those who would pass from here to you may not be able, and none may cross from there to us."

Some believe that Paradise and *Hades* are two different places, and in one sense they are. Blessed souls are resting in the bosom of Abraham, and cursed souls are in a prison cell and no one can pass between the two. However, to the Hebrew mind death is a realm, i.e. a place to which we all will enter, and *Hades* and Paradise are sub-sets within that realm. The Bible refers to the dead as dwelling in the land of darkness, i.e. the grave, but it also divides the dead into the lost and the blessed; the unjust and the just. We die and we are either cast into a prison where we fearfully await judgment, or we are led into paradise, where we eagerly await our final reward.

Paradise, therefore, like *Sheol*, is temporary, but only in the sense that we are hanging out there until the resurrection. An important text to demonstrate this is found in Revelation, where the prayers of the martyred saints are crying out for vengeance: "When will you make everything right?" and God responds with, "Soon. Be patient" (Rev. 6:9-11). The souls of the martyrs—even though they are in the throne room of God Himself—are longing for justice and the righting of every wrong done to them. That means that they are looking forward to something far greater than their current, blessed condition.

All the believing dead are waiting for the same thing. My grandma Fay, my wife Tierre, and my best friend Pete: they are with the Lord. They are awaiting the final resolution of all things, until the time that all the saints will at last get the reward that we have been promised: the resurrection unto the New Heavens and New Earth. At that point, the Lord will reign on earth and He will rule us, and we will have our resurrected bodies, living forever in a perfected existence that will be beyond anything that we can currently imagine.

So, brethren, we have a great reward awaiting us, and it is called the resurrection of life. It is a future event in which all of those who have been written in the Lamb's Book of Life will participate, and in which we will get to *at the same time*. Therefore, in this life be humble, be bold, be true, and be convinced: our death will only be a temporary condition, a momentary pause in the grand scheme of God's magnificent plan. And then, after the resurrection, we will never have to face death again.

That is the truth that should give us peace when we come face-to-face with death: we are going to live forever. Death *is* temporary. Life *is* unending. Our bodies and souls will be reunited and death is just a momentary pause on our way to everlasting life. This is the glorious prize that we seek at the end of all our struggles:

> But the day of the Lord will come like a thief. The
> heavens will disappear with a roar; the elements

will be destroyed by fire, and the earth and everything done in it will be laid bare.

Since everything will be destroyed in this way, what kind of people ought you to be? You ought to live holy and godly lives as you look forward to the day of God and speed its coming. That day will bring about the destruction of the heavens by fire, and the elements will melt in the heat. But in keeping with his promise we are looking forward to a new heaven and a new earth, where righteousness dwells. (II Peter 3:10-13)

Think of it, we will be with Christ in the New Heavens and Earth, face-to-face with Him in His presence perfectly able to relate without the corrupting influence of sin, and we will have a resurrected body. We won't be dead anymore. Our bodies and spirits will no longer be separate, but united. We will be alive forevermore. Amen!

---

*Our death will only be a temporary condition, a momentary pause in the grand scheme of God's magnificent plan.*

## SECTION TWELVE

# DEATH, WHERE IS THY STING?

"Can you believe in the miracle coming?
Can you believe it will take you away?"

John Michael Talbot, "The Advent Suite"

L ife is sometimes discordant and sometimes harmonious. Sometimes it seems downright cruel and ruthless, and other times it seems effortless and poetic. Sometimes people kick you when you're down, and other times people will move heaven and earth to help you in your time of greatest need. In one corner of a coffee shop there can be a men's Bible study, and in another corner two gangster's can be plotting the demise of their rivals. How do we deal with such dichotomies? I know it may ring a little untrue when I say "life is a symphony," but when I do, I in no way mean to imply that life is always pleasant. I know that it can be knee-breaking, uppercut to the jaw brutal, but symphonies can also capture the raw despair and rage of life, too. Symphonies are a good analogy because they utilize all the emotions associated with life's vicissitudes, good and bad.

Also, just as we can never isolate every note that is played in a symphony, neither can we fully understand how all the events in our lives fit together. Sometimes we just have to sit back and feel the music and listen to the unfolding drama.

From my experience, life seems to unfold in stages—in movements—and each one has its own tone or lesson. I'm in awe of how God is orchestrating my life and in spite of all the challenges I have faced, I have come to totally trust the Lord of Life. Sometimes life seems like some dissonant rock opera instead of a symphony, but I have come to accept that all the apparent madness has a purpose and has a meaning. It's humbling because even though I want to understand, only God fully comprehends how all things work together for our good and His glory. We have to trust that even the bad things which happen to us will not thwart the good He has determined for us.

We are experiencing the music. We soar with the violins, and weep with the subtle bassoons. We delight in the trilling accents of the flute, and feel pride in the triumphant trumpets. We feel fear, anger, hatred, jealousy, and bitterness. We feel elation, joy, love, and forgiveness. We ponder destiny and free will, and we commiserate with each other over grief and pain.

> *We have to trust that even the bad things which happen to us will not thwart the good He has determined for us.*

And if we allow our hearts to remember Eden—our beginning—we may even begin to see the history of creation, the fall, and man's quest for immortality. These are all movements within the symphony: the mystery of death. The mystery of love, loss, suffering, and redemption.

As I sit and contemplate the human will and divine grace (albeit imperfectly), and relish the mercies of God and weep at His judgments, I have come to an inevitable conclusion—I can't put all the pieces together. My mind and heart are incapable of a god-like view of all things. The spinning, whirling mechanisms of His interactions with mankind defy my ability to summarize or synthesize, and just as soon as I think I have said the right phrase that puts it all into perspective, I find there is a next thought which defies my understanding:

God loves me, but He will judge me.
God chose me, but He requires me to choose Him.

If I abide in Him, He will abide in me—
If I walk away, He won't walk away from me.

Death comes to us all, but He has promised us eternal life—
He alone is immortal, and I am as the flowers of the field.

My will is my own to give freely to whom I will—
But no matter how much I want to follow God, my flesh is too weak.

My sins are my own, and so are my good deeds—
My sins are too many, and my good deeds not enough.

Mankind is the pinnacle of God's creation,
But we are so easily deceived.

I am helpless, but responsible;
Dependent, but independent;
Wise, but foolish—and God's foolishness makes me wise.

I should be content with simplicity—
But I should also strive for the elaborate wonder of perfection.

If I think I'm perfect, I'm not—
If I'm not perfect I won't get to heaven.

His grace is sufficient, but I fail every day.
His mysteries are endless, but God has told us all we
need to know.

So here, in this place of mystery, I am humbled and I
have to acknowledge that the wisdom of Solomon has
already been here:

He has made everything beautiful in its time.
Also, he has put eternity into man's heart, yet *so
that he cannot find out* [emphasis added] what
God has done from the beginning to the end.
(Eccl. 3:11)

From this I must conclude that God implanted in us a
desire for eternity—a mind capable of wanting to explore
the meaning of the stars—but that far from bringing clarity,
it only spawns these enigmas we wrestle with so that we
won't find out what God is doing. And humbled, I must
admit, I can't. He's God, not me.

But, just as I resign myself to this conclusion—that my
longing to understand only leads me to the realization that I
can never understand—my daughter wakes up, comes
downstairs, and wants to snuggle with me. Then all the
mysteries of God become crystal clear. It isn't so hard to
understand after all: He wants me to live, which is far
different than merely being alive. I don't have to figure it all
out in order to enjoy life.

He wants us all to experience life forever, but the
wonder of life is not found in the possibility that we might
be able to comprehend everything as God does. We need to
be okay with the mystery.

So, close your eyes and listen to the finale of the song.
Can you hear it? It is the song of redemption. Of

forgiveness. Of mercy and of joy. Can you feel the crescendo happening? Let your pain do its work: look forward to the day of justice and to the day of redemption. Let your anger be directed at evil, not God. He is good and He is orchestrating the eradication of suffering and death. No more will death rip our loved ones from our grasp. No more will evil reign and abuse take place. No more will we have to construct elaborate philosophies in order to explain its existence and figure out ways to put up with it. Death will have been obliterated.

## *We need to be okay with the mystery*

"But," you may ask, "how does that help me, now? I have friends and loved ones dying all around me. Evil has hurt me, and pain saturates my heart. What am I supposed to do about my heartache? How am I to deal with the devastating grief? The crushing sadness? The overwhelming, gut-wrenching sorrow?"

When such questions are asked by a mother who is crying at the edge of her child's grave, who has a solution? When a man finds out he has terminal cancer, who can say anything to numb the pain? When abuse is in your past or your present, who can help you cope? When a parent, a child, or your dreams die, who can give you hope? Friends can hug you. They can weep with you. They can empathize with your grief and anger. But a solution? The only solution I have ever found satisfactory is Jesus Christ and completely immersing myself in His presence. It is the most important thing to just be with Him and learn from Him. Put down the distractions, read His word, and listen. He is the comfort you need. He wants you to wrestle with the big ideas. Converse with Him, debate Him, question Him. Never be afraid to ask.

That is what helps us to mature in our relationships with each other and with God. The worse relationships are the result of one side not being allowed to speak. He wants you to talk with Him. He wants to be there for you and He can handle your hardest questions. Yell at Him! He won't be offended. In fact, He will understand completely:

> Seeing then that we have a great High Priest who has passed through the heavens, Jesus the Son of God, let us hold fast *our* confession. For we do not have a High Priest who cannot sympathize with our weaknesses, but was in all *points* tempted as *we are, yet* without sin. Let us therefore come boldly to the throne of grace, that we may obtain mercy and find grace to help in time of need. (Hebrews 4:14-16)

Tell Him your frustrations, fears, anxieties, and disappointments. Tell Him your hopes and dreams. Ask Him about creation and destiny. Tell Him what you need. Get on your face, repent of your sins, and cry out to Him for help. He's listening and He's weeping with you.

Jesus Himself is the solution to all our sorrow, even during our darkest moments. He alone is the Grand Composer who has written the symphony upholding all things.

He directs the trumpet blast of justice, and He is mercy.

He conducts the melody of immortality.

He leads the rising crescendo of voices throughout time which testify to Christ's victory over death. He has risen. He has risen, indeed.

# Our Trials

Take a look at the next picture, and ask yourself, what do you see? A river. A few rocks. The exposed roots of a pretty tough tree. Some snow. Maybe you see beauty. That's what I see, and that's why I love coming to this particular place.

**St. Vrain River**

But as I was sitting there looking at this scene, I had an odd feeling that I was missing something important, and so I persisted in asking myself over-and-over: "What do I see?"

And then I saw it. I saw the devastation. I saw the broiling waters of fierce agitation which had violently carried some of these boulders here. I began to see the rising mountains and the collapsing walls of stone. I saw the heat and forces that would have been necessary to melt and pulverize this land into the random, balanced beauty I was now enjoying. I could feel the raging brutality and I could hear the clanging dissonance of the riotous turmoil and upheaval.

And then I saw the peace. I saw the lingering snow and listened to the gentle sounds of the creek. I felt the warming light of the sun and basked in the promise of new life, soon.

Here I was, looking at this peaceful scene that I had visited for years, but only now did I see the disaster behind it all. It was beautiful in spite of the fact that it had been devastated. I was able to see beyond the darkness and I saw life in all of its terrifying glory.

When God said "all things work together for good", He didn't mean all things would be always good along the way. Nor did He mean that we should pretend the bad things were actually good things. He meant that we will have to look at the devastating moments in life as something He will use for our good and His glory.

He meant that someday everything will be alright, but maybe not today.

The scene, therefore, became something reflecting life itself:

I saw the tribulations working out.

I saw Tierre becoming someone who wasn't frail.

I saw my grandmother and parents young again.

I saw Peter healed.

I saw the boulders of wrath and the corrosive effects of difficulty transformed into their future beauty.

I saw evil being judged at last.

I saw that no thing, no matter how terrible, is able to thwart God's purposes.

I saw that I am not only His: I am forever His. Even all of my wounds.

> And we know that all things work together for
> good to them that love God, to them who are the
> called according to His purpose. (Romans 8:28)

And yet, as confident as I am about this truth of Scripture, I still struggle in this life. I still sin. I still doubt. I still suffer. I still continually want to justify my bad attitudes. I still fall prey to lies, and, to top it all off, I still want to wander. I get absorbed in my daily frustrations, consumed in my busy-ness, and engrossed in my immediate needs. That is sad to me—and to God.

But why does this happen?

It is because I have forgotten death has been conquered.

I need to remember.

I need to live in spite of the presence of death.

I need to live instead of giving in to despair.

In Christ there is an eternity of tomorrows.

Everything that is wrong with this world today is because mankind has wandered from our intended design. The human race has been infected with a spiritual virus, and one-by-one more people are getting infected every day and the infection results in the same thing: we forget our essential humanity and we become beasts ready to consume everyone around us for the selfish, instinctive hunger that controls our lives. We attack, betray, and consume each other and decimate our resources for one instinctive goal: to fulfill our own desires. God wants to change that, and God will deal with those who perpetuate that.

Listen to the words of Paul:

> But mark this: There will be terrible times in the
> last days. People will be lovers of themselves,
> lovers of money, boastful, proud, abusive,
> disobedient to their parents, ungrateful, unholy,
> without love, unforgiving, slanderous, without
> self-control, brutal, not lovers of the good,
> treacherous, rash, conceited, lovers of pleasure
> rather than lovers of God—having a form of
> godliness but denying its power. Have nothing to
> do with such people. (II Timothy 3:1-5)

The infection has taken root and the only inoculation that I know of is Jesus Christ. But even those who love Jesus can be tempted, so that is why Hebrews says:

> Therefore, brothers and sisters, since we have confidence to enter the Most Holy Place by the blood of Jesus, by a new and living way opened for us through the curtain, that is, his body, and since we have a great priest over the house of God, let us draw near to God with a sincere heart and with the full assurance that faith brings, having our hearts sprinkled to cleanse us from a guilty conscience and having our bodies washed with pure water. Let us hold unswervingly to the hope we profess, for he who promised is faithful. And let us consider how we may spur one another on toward love and good deeds, not giving up meeting together, as some are in the habit of doing, but encouraging one another—and all the more as you see the Day approaching. (Hebrews 10:19-25)

Our faith should result in us becoming more human—more like Jesus Christ in His compassion, love, truth, and humility. We should be people who are growing closer to the image of God. We should want our essential humanity—that which we lost—to be restored to us. We should want a restoration of all that is good. We should want the "refusion" of our spirits to our bodies after the final judgment.

So, in one sense, we are not supposed to get over our grief. This world isn't right. There's something fundamentally wrong with it and grief is the natural response to the horrible things we experience. This answer, though, is not a solution, but rather an encouragement to turn to the One who does understand all the trials in our life. Turn to the One who will solve it all. The storms will come, we just need to be on the same boat as the Master of the storms.

Death, pain and suffering cause grief because there are things going on which we should grieve about. So let grief play its role: let it wake you up to the promises of God. Let grief help you see what the Gospel of Jesus Christ really means! Don't be ashamed of your grief or think there is something wrong with you. Grief is a sign of a healthy soul. It means you care that things aren't right.

Allow godly sorrow to play its role and accept that it's okay to hate death. Then ask the most important question of all: "How do we overcome death? How do we crush its head and put a Hulk fist through its face?"

The answer can only be Jesus Christ.

*The storms will come, we just need to be on the same boat as the Master of the storms.*

If salvation were just psychological health, then maybe Dr. Phil would be all I need. Or, if salvation were just spiritual feelings, then maybe the Dalai Lama could contribute. Or, if salvation were intellectual stimulation, Aristotle could give me that spark. Salvation, though, is being rescued from death itself. Only Jesus can do that.

God accomplished something beyond our human ability when He resurrected Jesus, so why would we turn our backs on it? Why would we reject such an offer? Really. Why?

Perhaps we want to do it ourselves by developing a ritual, making a law, forming a society, mixing a concoction, unveiling a secret code, or going on a quest. How are we doing with that? The very thing we want more than anything is also the very thing that we can't achieve on our own. We can choose to do good things, but we can't choose to be perfect. Christ was perfect for us, and His resurrection is evidence that those who have trusted Him for salvation will rise from the dead someday, too. Do you trust Him? Have you surrendered your efforts to improve yourself? Have you accepted His offer to forgive you? Pain and suffering in this world will be over. Evil will be judged, *and there will be no more death.*

Christ came to conquer death.

Life is awaiting us beyond the darkness.

Believe!

---

*And this is eternal life, that they may know You, the only true God, and Jesus Christ whom You have sent. (John 17:3)*

# The Lazarus Creed

There is a God;

He created this universe for us to enjoy;

We have sinned and have shattered the image of God in us;

We keep trying to regain our lost glory by our own efforts;

Only God can restore to us what we were intended to become;

God became a man, Jesus Christ, and was punished for our sins;

He never sinned, and He was resurrected in order to prove that God will do the same for us when we entrust ourselves to His Son;

He gives us His Spirit to give us hope and to help us endure in the Faith;

He gives us each other to help us along the difficult path we are on;

He will return to finally make all things right;

If we die before He returns, we will either dwell with Him while we await our glorious new bodies, or we will dwell in darkness, mourning over our impending judgment;

He will punish sin—He will forgive sin.

He has spoken clearly to all of humanity through the prophets and His Son, and He has proven His word time and time again.

Praise God that "the last enemy to be destroyed is death" (1 Corinthians 15:26).

Praise God that "death and Hades [will be] thrown into the lake of fire" (Rev. 20:14).

Praise God that death will not be able to hold us in its clutches, and that we can look beyond the grave to an everlasting life with God on a new earth under a new heavens.

He is the resurrection and the life!

---

*"We hope to meet thee in heaven."*

**Tomb of Squire Stoten Whitman and his wife**

# End of the Fourth Movement

# God Alone

Compelled by Heaven's sorrow,
He, grievous, Deep-felt
Our separation from Himself,
And clothed His glory
   —God Alone—
In mortal flesh.

Friendless, Unknown,
He walked
Along with us, beside,
To heal our weary weights,
To soothe our heaving desperate groans
   and sighs.

And more sorrow upon sorrow
He embraced,
   as us,
To crown us all through His mercy,
With His glory
   Divine.

Though veiled by man's flesh therein,
His heavenly mien,
Still shone within,
And was seen by eyes
Awakened
   to see.

And though God by God forsook,

'twas to unite us together again
   with Him,
Restored by God to His wondrous presence,
Embraced
   forever.

*CODA*

# REMEMBER

I remember a day once so very long ago in which I woke up entranced by beams of light pushing through the wood-slated blinds of my window. I did not have to roll over to look for them, because my eyes merely opened and I was seeing them. Slowly my awareness grew of what I gazed at, and it was more than light. Awake, but not fully, the sunlight enlightened my soul with possibilities I had never thought of before. I envisioned beaches of pure white sand, and waters warm with shades of greens and blues, wavering with the unending shifting colors, vibrant, so alive with grace and being. And in this light, disease melted away like varnish on silver, and living became pure.

The sensation of beauty overwhelmed me and I lay there paralyzed by it upon my bed, wrapped in its comfort.

Then suddenly I gasped as though I had not been breathing, and I felt as Adam must have felt when God first breathed life into him. I saw the world through new eyes.

And at that moment I saw things as I had never seen them before, but, sadly, they have dimmed and only the memory lingers. Today, darker visions—the death of friends, the suffering of children—compete with these beautiful ones, but I want to sustain that first dream. I want to remember Eden. I will try, but that dream must sustain itself—indeed it must—because it is a reality beyond what we know even if we have forgotten.

We have been given a treasure house of grace, and in the end everything is going to be made right.

Remember.

# IRRECONCILABLE DIFFERENCES?

My entire Christian life I have heard that Genesis 1 and 2 are very different accounts about the same event—Creation—and that, taken separately, they are completely incompatible with each other. Genesis 1 is a nice story, and Genesis 2 is a nice story, but they cannot be blended into a single narrative and, thus, they cannot be considered historical accounts of God's act of creation.

However, I have come to strongly disagree with that viewpoint and I hope to prove that it is an unsupportable assumption to think that they were not meant to work together to create a comprehensive picture of God's act of creation. To isolate them is to weaken them; to combine them is to strengthen them, and I believe they say exactly what they were intended to say *together*. Far from their purported differences being irreconcilable, they are complementary perspectives of creation and they tell a singular story.

## Differences and Similarities

Modern textual criticism has noted some very distinct structural and stylistic differences between Genesis 1 and 2, and much of what they note is valid. Yet, as with anything, the conclusion one draws from facts is itself precarious and could indeed be merely an assumption masquerading as a conclusion. In order to investigate their compatibility more closely, let's analyze the text.

If one looks closely at the following chart, the criticism that these two accounts don't match up is not very strong. The chart exposes that, in fact, the events pretty much stay in the same order—minus any mention of the heavens in the second account—and only one major event seems out of place: Adam is created on day three instead of day six. Granted this is a major difference, but there is a literary explanation which I hope will clear up the apparent problem.

| Account 1: Genesis 1 - 2:4a | Account 2: Genesis 2:4b - 25 |
|---|---|
| **Chaos** | |
| **1. Light** | — |
| **2. Heavens** | — |
| **3. Creates Land and Seas. Plants.** | **Land and Seas; Adam formed Eden created; Description of Eden** |
| **4. Celestial Bodies** | — |
| **5. Air & Sea Creatures** | **Days 5 & 6 combined** |
| **6. Beasts of the Fields. Man and Woman completed** | **Beasts/Birds created Woman formed; mankind completed** |

**Two Accounts of Creation?**

## *The Architectural Perspective: Genesis 1:1 — 2:4a*

I have labeled this range of verses as The Architectural Perspective because it presents a very god-like, outside, lofty, exalted perspective of creation which only the Designer Himself could possibly know and have revealed. Genesis starts out with the phrase: "In the beginning God created the heavens and the earth," and then it ends in 2:4a with, "These are the generations of the heavens and of the earth when they were created...." These are nice bookend phrases, and they clearly demarcate the boundaries of the architectural perspective. In addition, we find a multitude of repeated phrases throughout this chapter, as the following chart illustrates.

| Genesis 1:1 — 2:4a Parallel Phrases | |
|---|---|
| Then God/And God/God + "Action Verb" | Multiple times |
| "heavens and earth" | 1:1; 2:1 |
| "So the evening and the morning were. . ." | 1:5, 8, 13, 19, 23, 31 |
| "and it was so" | 1:7, 9, 22, 15, 24, 30 |
| "and God saw that it was good" | 1:4, 10, 12, 18, 21, 25, 31 (very good) |
| "According to its kind" | 1:11, 12(2x), 21(2x), 24(2x), 25(3x) |

**Repeated Phrases**

Also note that there is a repeated literary pattern in the text of how God created on each day:

1) God intends what He is to create;
2) God declares its name and purpose;
3) It comes into being (it is created);
4) He inspects it;
5) He declares it good (i.e. it functions as planned).

All of these phrases and patterns repeat throughout Genesis 1 with few variations, leaving one with the impression that the overall structure is repetitious for a reason. Formally, this style of writing is called Parataxis, which means "a strict adherence to the coordination of repeated grammatical elements" (Webster's II), and Moses uses this style to amplify the content. To put it another way, the content is enhanced by the style. Moses writes in a poetic yet precise, architectural style to better convey the idea that God is the Great Architect of creation. He shows us with the content and with the style that God is the one who carefully planned and methodically implemented all aspects of His design; that God is the one who organized all of creation according to a logical plan, placing mankind— male and female, unique of all His creation—as its overseers. The style Moses uses, therefore, communicates as much about God as the content does.

## *The Artistic Perspective: Genesis 2:4b — 25*

However, The Artistic Perspective starts in 2:4b, and it presents a much more down-to-earth, human perspective of creation. Here we see God "molding" Adam from the earth like an artist, not as an architect. Also, when Moses uses the introductory phrase, "…in the day that the LORD God made the earth and the heavens…" he is using a transitional formula that he continues to use throughout the book of Genesis:

> 5:1 "This is the book of the generations of Adam."
>
> 6:9 "These are the generations of Noah."
>
> 10:1 "These are the generations of the sons of Noah, Shem, Ham, and Japheth."
>
> 11:10 "These are the generations of Shem."
>
> 11:27 "Now these are the generations of Terah."
>
> See also 25:12; 25:19; 36:1; 36:9; and 37:2.

The introductory nature of this phrase becomes apparent and its intentional placement at the beginning of each chapter points to a single, unifying author who was compiling the history of his people: Moses. Moses is the author of Genesis in the sense that he arranged and edited the oral and written traditions of his people guided by the inspiration of God. These repeated phrases indicate that he organized Genesis with an obvious historical purpose. The structural and stylistic changes from Genesis 1 to Genesis 2 do not indicate a haphazard record, but a carefully planned one.

But, in Genesis 2:4b-25, Moses begins using an entirely different style of writing called Hypotaxis, which means an "elaborate syntactical subordination" (Alter 7). This involves the use of clauses that are dependent on each other with connectives. In other words, Moses now uses complex sentence structures (not the simple, concise, formulaic ones in Genesis 1) in order to produce a much more natural, human, flowing style of writing.

For comparison, in Genesis 1:11 Moses writes in a technical style:

> "And God said, 'Let the earth sprout vegetation,
> plants yielding seed, and fruit trees bearing fruit in
> which is their seed, each according to its kind, on
> the earth.' And it was so."

But in Genesis 2:8-9 Moses writes in a narrative style:

> "And the Lord God planted a garden in Eden, in
> the east, and there he put the man whom he had
> formed. And out of the ground the Lord God
> made to spring up every tree that is pleasant to the
> sight and good for food."

See the difference? The first perspective is very matter-of-fact and technical, and the second includes such notions as "pleasant" and "good."

The stylistic shift is also carefully demarcated in the arrangement of words. Moses says in 1:1 and 2:4a,

> In the beginning, God created **the heavens and
> the earth**... These are the generations of **the
> heavens and the earth** when they were
> created....

However, in Genesis 2:4b he says "the **earth** and the **heavens**,"

> ...in the day that the Lord God made **the earth
> and the heavens**, when no bush of the field was

yet in the land and no small plant of the field had
yet sprung up....

Moses reverses the placements of "earth" and "heaven"
and *that is not an accident*. The literary value of this reverse
formulation is that it alerts us to a shift in focus. Moses is
drawing our attention to the earth, i.e. to the events that are
happening on it during the week of creation. This explains
why there is no mention of any celestial objects in chapter
2. He isn't writing a second account but, rather, *an
elaboration of the first account* from a more human
perspective. He will now focus on the creation of Adam and
Eve during the week of creation instead of on how God
ordered creation overall, and his style of writing changes
accordingly. It's brilliant, not disconnected.

## *Day*

All through Genesis 1, Moses makes it extraordinarily
clear that when he says "day," he means a standard day and
night cycle. He uses an ordinal number combined with the
phrase "evening and morning," thus leaving no doubt as to
his intended meaning. Anytime one finds this combination,
it always refers to a standard day.

However, in 2:4 he uses only the word "day" without
any of those other qualifiers. He just says "day." This is
important because "day" can also mean an indefinitely long
period of time. It could mean eons or ages, or an era, or
refer to a specific event that takes place over an unspecified,
or specified, length of time. Why would Moses switch his
usage?

For example, when the prophets refer to the "Day" of
the Lord, they do not mean a standard day and night cycle,
they mean a time period in which a certain sequence of
events will take place, namely the judging of the world in
righteousness. No one would interpret "day" to mean a 24

hour period, and it's difficult to know exactly how long the "Day of the Lord" will take.

In another example, some have implied that when Peter says, "...with the Lord one *day* is as a thousand years, and a thousand years as one *day*," we should infer that "one day" can be also be "a thousand years." If that were true, then when Moses says "evening and morning, the first day," he was leaving it open to being a thousand years, or whatever. With God it would seem like a day, but for us it may have been a thousand years, or millions.

The problem with that interpretation, though, is that one cannot extrapolate that idea from Moses' writings at all. The idea that Moses' "evening and morning, the first day," formula could mean a thousand years is not inherent in the text. In other words, when reading Genesis 1, the idea that a day means anything other than a day cannot be derived from the text. That is an idea which comes from elsewhere.

Furthermore, Peter is not saying a literal thousand years is equal to a literal day. Time is still time. A day is still a day and a thousand years is still a thousand years. Peter's point is that *from God's perspective* of time God is being patient with us. What may seem like a long time to us—a thousand years—is actually no time at all to God. Peter is warning us against looking at God and saying, "Why don't you get moving? What's the hold up? Why don't you judge the world for its sins already? Why don't you give us the new heavens and the new earth *now*?" Peter is saying that God has His timetable and He will accomplish His will in His own time, but that is *not* how Moses uses "day" in Genesis 1.

And yet, in Genesis 2:4, Moses does use "day" without the same qualifiers that he uses in Genesis 1. Could Moses be implying that Genesis 1, after all, was symbolic? That the creation week could have been an indefinitely long period of time? This would open the door for the idea that the universe could be very old and that the week of creation wasn't a literal week. That is possible, except for one very important thing: Moses includes a qualifier along with the word "day." It isn't "evening and morning" combined with an ordinal number as in chapter 1, but rather it is a phrase: "...in the day *that the Lord God made the earth and the heavens....*" Here, "day" equals the timeframe when God made the earth and the heavens. How do we know how long that is? Moses, in chapter 1, had just defined that "day" as one literal week.

Hence, the importance of Genesis 1. We couldn't leave it out of the Bible and have a proper understanding of how God created us. This interpretation is supported by the fact that Moses continues his narrative by letting the reader know exactly *when* during the week of creation he is beginning this second account from: "no shrub of the field being yet on the earth." If we look back at Genesis 1, this description would place the forthcoming events in the middle of the third day, just after the earth and water have been gathered into their distinctive attributes and just before the plants have actually sprouted.

The point is, when "day" is defined we don't have the liberty of redefining it. Moses clearly meant to teach us in Genesis 1 that God assembled the universe in one week. He didn't do it instantaneously as Aquinas implies, nor did He do it gradually over bazillions of years. He made all the fundamental components and then assembled those building blocks rapidly and purposefully. When he uses "day" in Genesis 2:4, he is referring to the creation week, not an actual day.

## *God's Name*

One of the most noted changes Moses makes from perspective one to perspective two, is his use of God's name. In Genesis 1 he only referred to Him as "God" (Elohim), but in Genesis 2 he calls Him "Jehovah God"

(Jehovah Elohim), or, as it is generally translated, "Lord God." Most commentators agree that it shifts the reader's focus from God as the lofty, divine designer, to a personable God who is our caring creator. Throughout this account, Moses uses many anthropomorphic images to describe God: God has a name (Jehovah); God fashions man as a thoughtful craftsman would, and places him in a garden which He specifically designs for his pleasure; God speaks with Adam directly; He cares for Adam's well-being: He wants to make a sustainer suitable for him; He acts as a surgeon; and later in chapter 3 God is seen "walking about in the garden in the evening breeze." All of these references to God are meant to personalize the magnificent maker we admire in chapter one.

## Going Back in Time

It is critical at this point to move away from the first two chapters of Genesis and to look at a literary method Moses uses throughout the entire book of Genesis. It is a story-telling method where he continues a story line until its completion, and then he returns to take-up a previous story line.

For example, after Cain slays Abel in Genesis 4, God puts a mark on him to keep others from slaying him, which presumes that everyone knew his crime. The question is always asked, "But where did all the people come from since Adam and Eve hadn't had any other children yet?" That question is easily answered if one is aware of Moses' narrative structure. Notice that the entire history of Cain's family is recounted in chapter 4—obviously covering hundreds of years—and then Moses goes back in time at the end of chapter 4 to the story of Adam and Eve. He says at the end of chapter 4 that they had more children (4:25 — 5:3, 4). Read it with this narrative structure in mind and you'll see it clearly: Adam and Eve's other children grew up, spread out, populated the earth, and built cities, which is then who Cain encounters. To put it succinctly: the reason everyone knew about Cain's crime is because he was family.

Other examples of this technique are when Esau's descendants are recorded before Jacob's descendants (Genesis 36). Also, Isaac's death is recorded in 35:28, but if you keep track of how old he is, of how old Jacob is when he dies, and how old Joseph is when he is taken into captivity, you will see that Isaac is still alive when Joseph is in captivity in Egypt. Isaac's death is simply recorded where it is because it fits with the flow of the narrative better than it would later. This literary method doesn't destroy the historicity of the account; it shows a pattern that Moses uses throughout Genesis. The technique reveals a unified design, constructed by a single author who is tying together the oral and written chronicles of his nation's history.

Now, let's go back to Genesis 2:5 (see, I use this method, too), where Moses clearly takes us back in time to the middle of the third day in 1:9-11. Nothing is growing yet, but there is the earth that is watered by a mist. It is clearly an incomplete planet, primitive and not fully developed. But as Genesis 1 explains, it didn't stay in this condition for very long. The issue that throws everyone off is that at this point Adam is formed from the dust of the ground during the third day of creation, not on the sixth. So, was Adam formed before or after the beasts of the field and the birds of the air?

The answer is within the literary technique. Far from contradicting Genesis 1, the events recorded in Genesis 2 are a clarification—or elaboration—of what *exactly* transpired in Genesis 1. Adam was created on day three, not Eve. He was then placed in Eden, and over the next two days God created the animals to see if he would identify any suitable mates. When none of them qualified, God performed divine surgery and formed woman from man, thus completing creation and proclaiming it very good.

The following chart summarizes how the order of events would look if we were to tell them in a single narrative.

| | |
|---|---|
| *1* | *The earth is formless and void; God creates light and separates the light from the darkness. He brings order to the chaos.* |
| *2* | *God makes the heavens, i.e. the fabric of the cosmos.* |
| *3* | *God gathers the sea and raises the land; the earth is watered by a mist;* **God forms Adam***; the plants are created; Eden is formed; man is placed in Eden.* |
| *4* | *God creates the sun, stars and moon to keep track of time, even though time (the light and dark cycle) was formed on day 1 when light and darkness were separated.* |
| *5* | *God decides it isn't good for man to be alone so He creates the sea animals, the air animals, and then...* |
| *6* | *God forms the beasts of the field; Adam names them, but none are suitable companions; God puts Adam to sleep and forms Eve through divine surgery. Man and woman are now created and creation is complete; they are the pinnacle of creation and in charge of it all and commanded to populate the earth and take care of it.* |
| *7* | *God rests.* |

To help understand the idea that both Adam and Eve were not created on day six (and why that interpretation doesn't contradict Genesis 1), one must see that we are dealing with nuances in language. Genesis 1:27 (KJV) says "God created *man* in his own image, in the image of God he created *him: male and female* he created *them*." Why does the translator switch from the singular "man" and "him" to the plural "them" when the verse is obviously talking about *both* Adam and Eve all the way through?

The translator's challenge is that the Hebrew language allows the pronoun "him" to contain the idea of plurality. We call them collective nouns, such as "class" or "herd." Therefore, Genesis 1:27 could be translated: "So God created humanity in his own image, in the image of God he created them: male and female he created us." It comes clear then that man and woman *together* is the image of God, not just Adam, nor just Eve.

Why this is important is that when we take both Genesis 1 and 2 as two perspectives of the same event, it reveals that God's image was <u>completed</u> on day six *only after* God had created woman. Adam was created on day three, Eve was created on day six, and that is when the image of God was completed. Isn't that a magnificent truth? Not until they both existed did God call them the image of God, and who now—together—become the pinnacle of creation. And we only see that when we compile Genesis 1 and 2 into a single, unified narrative, each one supporting the other and each one distinct from the other. It's beautiful!

## *Adam was created on day three, Eve was created on day six, and that is when the image of God was completed.*

Some have argued that Adam was the image of God even before Eve was created, but it shouldn't be forgotten that it was God who pointed out to Adam that he wasn't complete without a partner. *God* said Adam needed a sustainer. He was flawed and it was God who created Eve to correct that deficiency. It wasn't until then that He proclaimed all of creation to be "very good," and not until then. It isn't only man who is in God's image, nor only woman: *God's image is both together*. This idea does not contradict the order of their creation and the roles He set for man and woman. I feel it is too much to try and have a full discussion about that here, so suffice it say that Genesis teaches that man and woman *together* are the "very good" complete and supreme caretakers of planet earth.

But here's the elegant outcome of this interpretation: just as Genesis 1 and 2 are different perspectives of the same event and together they say more than they ever could individually, even so is the mystery of male and female. Genesis 1 and 2 present a complete portrait of creation; Man and woman *together* present a complete portrait of God. The two shall become one is contained in the very structure of the narrative itself!

I can't explain why Moses' literary structure hasn't been taken seriously before, but I believe it reveals a skillfully constructed account of creation. I think it is worthy enough to be taken seriously and not off-handedly dismissed.

In conclusion, I believe Moses chose an appropriate style to communicate the appropriate truths he wanted to focus on at the appropriate time in the chronicle of the history of the nation of Israel. His style enhances the meaning, and together (style and meaning) they say something neither one could say on their own. He uses a succinct, elegant narrative structure, and in two chapters, under divine inspiration, adequately, sufficiently, and efficiently communicates to humanity all the important truths we need to know in order to understand our Maker and His purpose for us.

# DEVELOPMENT B

## ADAM'S RIB

Some food for thought: Did God really take a rib and transform it into a woman? Sounds rather fantastical. But if God did take a rib from Adam, how did He transform it into a woman? The original Hebrew word itself might give us a clue. By the way, I really want to dispel the idea some Christians have that men and women have an unequal number of ribs. Just so you know, men and women have 24 ribs. Pretty easy to confirm that. It would be the equivalent of saying that if you had a surgery to remove your arm, then your children would be born without an arm. Adam's surgery did not leave a heritable trait.

However, modern genetics may actually come to the Bible's rescue, here, because "Rib" is not the only possible meaning of the original Hebrew word.

The original Hebrew word is *Tsela*, which means:

side, rib, beam
rib (of hill, ridge, etc.)
rib, plank, board (of cedar or fir)
leaves (of door) Half.
Side, half, (of ark)
side-chambers or cells (of temple structure)

*Tsela* contains the concept of an entire side, essentially half, of a structure and a *chamber* within that structure. A cell.

Fascinating.

So then, "rib" is only one potential meaning, and with the advent of genetics and our understanding of DNA, the other nuances of the Hebrew word open up to us. Even though Moses didn't have the faintest clue about DNA, God did. The word, being divinely inspired, does not contradict the discovery of DNA, and when we combine the ancient revelation with the modern revelation, we get a clearer picture of what God did when He created Eve.

Here's a possible interpretation: the following picture is of a normal set of chromosomes. Note that there are 22 evenly paired chromosomes plus the sex chromosomes. The XY means male, and the XX means female.

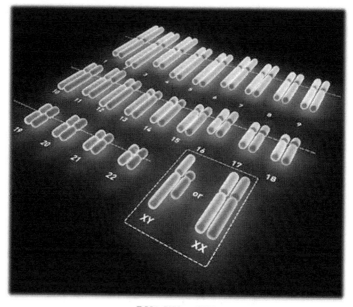

**DNA XX or XY**

Now, apply this to Genesis and we can see that the word *Tsela* fits perfectly: God created Adam first, then took out one of Adam's ribs, extracted the DNA from a cell, added information to half of the twenty-third chromosome, and made woman.

This would explain why women have more genetic material than men, and this would also explain one of the greatest mysteries of mankind: why guys can't understand women!

Take this as you will, but I like the idea more and more as I think about it. However, it's more of an intriguing aside that I believe has merit, than an orthodox doctrine that I am willing to be martyred for.

# FULL TRANSCRIPT OF PETER'S TESTIMONY

*Video*

AMANDA. It's Friday, August 12th [2011] and we were just wanting to document what God is doing in our lives right now.

PETER. ...and the progress of the cancer that is in my body. My arm has been in a sling for probably the last two weeks.

AMANDA. And in a great deal of pain.

PETER. A great deal of pain. I would have to lift my arm up just to do something like this [he lifts his right arm with his left arm, only bending at the elbow]. And yet

God through His provision is just.... He's healing me. Slowly. Not fast. Slowly. So I can do this [He raises both arms above his head in praise].

AMANDA. [She laugh/cries].

PETER. Just give Him glory for what He's doing in my life, and how He's changing my heart. To focus on Him. To Him be the glory, not anything else. [Peter is waving both arms above his head back and forth, pain free]. Whether He takes my life or He keeps it, it's all for His glory. And I just praise Him that I can do this. And I just look forward to seeing what He's going to continue to do. But again, whether that's on earth or in heaven, to Him be the glory. Amen.

AMANDA. And we were saying that if He were to heal you for one more day, we're thankful. Thankful for one more day. One more day with our kids. One more day with each other.

PETER. It's all a blessing. It's better than anything life can give. Amanda and I have had such an awesome evening.

We've just been here at the house, dancing, praying, listening to music, just praising our Lord Jesus for all that He's done in our lives. And how He takes schmucks like us who make stupid decisions and choices in life, and just turns them…. He uses those to bring us to our knees so that we can see every trial is actually a blessing. And only when you go through that trial, can you understand that it is a blessing. And the world will never understand that. You have to go through it to experience it, so that you can even understand what this means. I'm not a guy just waving my arms, I'm a guy that's praising the Lord because He's doing great things. And He's going to continue to do great things. He wants to do it in all of our lives. But we have to submit. And sometimes we submit willingly, and sometimes we don't, but it's all coming from a heart where He wants to bring us into connection with Him so that we can enjoy His presence. So I'm nothing more, than I'm just happy to be a guy who has stage 4 cancer—they don't even know what kind of cancer it is—and I can wave my arm, and I wasn't even able to wave it two days ago. Even this morning. God's so good, and we're just enjoying the Lord right now. I just praise God that He's divine. He's bigger than this world.

AMANDA. And this is not all that we have to look forward to.

PETER. No, this isn't all we have.

AMANDA. This is nothing.

PETER. You know, I'm a 35 year old guy just enjoying my bride. You know we don't know what the future's going to hold, but God is so good. And I'm excited just this moment. Not about the future, not about a minute ago, but just right now. Because God is in the moment and He wants us to enjoy this moment. And I've been made weak so that He is strong, and I pray, "God, more of You, less of me." And in order for that to happen He has to drain me, and He has to bring me low in order for you [us] to become more of Him. He must always have supremacy.

He doesn't share His glory with anyone. He shares it with no one. He's God and God alone. And I praise Him for that. Cause I fought against that for years. There's times I questioned Him. And I questioned, God, why do You allow things to happen? It just seems so illogical. But you know what? I don't have everything up here [points to his head]. And it's when you're brought low, and Christ is brought up, that things start to come into clarity, and that you start to understand that there's so much more than what I can see, what the mind can comprehend. He's God. Not me. He's God. And so again, I just… I'm a guy waving my arms, got cancer; don't know what's going to happen. But I've had a…I've had a wonderful time with the Lord. I'm not saying this is a permanent healing, but for this second right now I'm praising the Lord. And that's all that matters. That's all that matters.

# Bibliography

Arking, Robert. "Extending Human Longevity." *The Fountain of Youth: Cultural, Scientific, and Ethical Perspectives on a Biomedical Goal.* New York. Oxford University Press, Inc. 2004.

Arrison, Sonia. "Done with Death." Technewsworld, Dec. 10, 2004.

Aristotle. *Physics*. iBooks. https://itunes.apple.com/WebObjects/MZStore.woa/wa/viewBook?id=378247201

Barzilay, Joshua I. M.D. , et. al. *The Water We Drink: Water Quality and Its Effects on Health.* New Brunswick, New Jersey, and London: Rutgers University Press, 1999.

Batmanghelidj, Foredoom M.D. Global Health Solutions, Inc. http://www.watercure.com/

Bonhoeffer, Dietrich (2012-03-20). *Ethics*. Touchstone. Kindle Edition.

Chesterton, G. K. *Orthodoxy*, 1994-05-01. Public Domain Books. Kindle Edition.

Cobb, Sharon E. http://www.geocities.ws/sharonecobb/death.htm#Death%20Metaphors

Conrad, Joseph. *The Heart of Darkness*. iBook. https://itun.es/us/HH4Kx.l

Cryonics Institute, 2002. http://www.cryonics.org/

Darwin, Charles (2011-03-06). . . . ILLUSTRATED . . .*On The Origin Of Species*, by Charles Darwin - NEW Illustrated Classics. 2011 Edition (FULLY OPTIMIZED FOR KINDLE). Novellum Ebook Works. Kindle Edition.

Delumeau, Jean. *History of Paradise: The Garden of Eden in Myth and Tradition*. Translated by Matthew O'Connell. Continuum, New York, 1995.

D'Holbach. *The System of Nature, Vol. 1*. Project Gutenberg [EBook #8909], 2005.

*Buddhist Stories from the Dhammapada Commentary, Part II*. Translated from Pali by E. W. Burlingame. Selected and revised by Bhikkhu Khantipalo, 2006.

Emoto, Dr. Masaru. http://www.hado-energy.com/hado_water.php

Epicurus. "Letter to Menoeceus." Epicurus and Epicurean Philosophy website, hosted by Vincent Cook. http://www.epicurus.net/en/menoeceus.html

Free Dictionary. http://www.freedictionary.com

Flavius, Vegetuis Renatus. *The Military Institutions of the Romans*. Text written in 390 A.D. John Clarke trans. from the Latin. British translation published in 1767. Etext version by Mads Brevik, 2001.

Greer, John Michael. *Monsters: An Investigators Guide to Magical Beasts*. St. Paul, Minnesota: 2002. Llewellyn Publications.

Hall, Stephen S. *Merchants of Immortality: Chasing the Dream of Human Life Extension*. Boston, New York: 2003. Houghton Mifflin Company.

Hitler, Adolf (2012-11-30). *Mein Kampf* (Kindle Locations 6780-6781). Kindle Edition.

How Stuff Works. "How Much Water is There on Earth?"
    http://science.howstuffworks.com/environmental/earth/
    geophysics/question157.htm

Immortality Institute. "The Scientific Conquest of Death:
    Essays on Infinite Lifespans." http://imminst.org

Kirkwood, Tom. *Time of Our Lives: The Science of Human
    Aging.* Oxford: Oxford University Press, 1999.

Langer, Walter C. "A Psychological Analysis of Adolph
    Hitler: His Life and Legend." Office of Strategic
    Services. Washington D.C.: 1991 — 2005.
    http://www.nizkor.org/hweb/people/h/hitler-adolf/oss-
    papers/text/oss-profile-05-05.html

Lindsay, Jay. "Inventor sets his sights on immortality."
    Review of *Fantastic Voyage: Live long enough to live
    forever,* by Ray Kurzweil. MSNBC, AP, Feb. 12, 2005.
    http://www.msnbc.msn.com/id/6959575/

Milton, John. *Paradise Lost & Paradise Regained,* ed.
    Christopher Ricks (New York: Penguin Books USA
    Inc., 1968).

Nature 441, 610-613 (1 June 2006) |
    doi:10.1038/nature04668; Received 7 July 2005;
    Accepted 21 February 2006

Nietzsche, Friedrich Wilhelm (2011-03-30). *The Antichrist.*
    Kindle Edition.

Nietzsche, Friedrich Wilhelm (2011-11-27). *Human, All
    Too Human.* Kindle Edition.

Oedekerk, Steve. *Patch Adams.* Directed by Tom Shadyac.
    Universal Pictures, 1998.

ÓhÓgáin, Dáithí. *The Lore of Ireland: An Encyclopedia of
    Myth, Legend and Romance.* Woodbridge: The Boydell
    Press, 2006.

Pas F. Julian. *Historical Dictionary of Taoism.* Lanham, M.D. & London: The Scarecrow Press, Inc. 1998.

Pearson, Ian. "2050 — and immortality is within our grasp." The Observer UK, May 22, 2005. http://observer.guardian.co.uk/uk_news/story/0,6903,148963 5,00.html

*Peter's Testimony (Video).*
*http://www.youtube.com/watch?v=RLsCp4bMSco&feature=y outube_gdata_playe*

Poe, Edgar Allen. *Complete Tales and Poems.* Random House, New York. Vintage Books Edition, 1975.

Post, Stephen G. & Robert H. Bitstock, eds. *The Fountain of Youth: Cultural, Scientific, and Ethical Perspectives on a Biomedical Goal.* New York: Oxford University Press, Inc. 2004.

Shaputis, June. Funny Stones to Tickle Your Funny Bones. 1980. http://www.webpanda.com/ponder/epitaphs.htm.

Shelley, Mary. *Frankenstein.* New York: Barnes & Noble Classics, 2003.

Starr, Cecile & Taggart, Ralph. *Biology: The Unity and Diversity of Life, Sixth Edition.* Belmont, CA: Wadsworth Publishing Company, 1992.

*The Evil of Tezcatlipoca.* The Odyssey World Trek for Service and Education, 1998. http://www.worldtrek.org/odyssey/mexico/mexstories.h tml#evil

Tolkien, J.R.R. *The Two Towers.* 50th Anniversary Edition. Boston, New York: Houghton Mifflin Company, 2004.

Twain, Mark. *What is Man? And Other Essays.* Project Gutenberg, Release Date: June, 1993 [Etext #70] Last Updated: February 14, 2013.

Villarreal, Phil. "Pirates: Third Times no Charm." Arizona
Daily Star, May 24, 2007.
http://www.azstarnet.com/sn/aznightbuzz/184398

*Vishnu Purina.* Translated by Horace Hayman Wilson.
1840. http://www.sacred-texts.com/hin//vp/index.htm

# *Notes*

## _Notes_

# _Notes_

Made in the USA
Middletown, DE
28 March 2018